THE REMINISCENCES OF
Captain Slade D. Cutter
U.S. Navy (Retired)

INTERVIEWED BY
Paul Stillwell

Volume I

U.S. Naval Institute • Annapolis, Maryland

Copyright © 1985

Preface

When the top submarine skippers of World War II are considered, Slade Cutter's name is invariably on the list. He wound up tied for second in number of confirmed Japanese vessels sunk. Richard O'Kane was tops with 24; Cutter and Dudley "Mush" Morton sank 19 apiece. In this memoir Cutter explains that he was both lucky and good. He was trained expertly in the *Pompano* by Lieutenant Commander Lew Parks, and that training was invaluable when Cutter got command of his own boat, the *Seahorse*. In addition to discussing the many sinkings for which his boat accounted, Cutter provides the flavor of World War II submarine life---the relationships among officers and enlisted men, how time was spent relaxing between patrols, and the ways in which men coped with the possibility of sudden death.

This is much more than just a story of submarine command in World War II. It deals with an entire career, including one that contained a good deal of involvement in sports. Cutter was an all-America football player as a midshipman at the Naval Academy, ran the all-Navy sports program right after World War II, and still later served as director of athletics for the Naval Academy in the late 1950s.

Cutter talks about his experiences in large ships as well---as an ensign in the battleship *Idaho* right after graduation in the mid-1930s, as executive officer of the submarine tender *Sperry* in 1949 and 1950, and as commanding officer of the fleet oiler

Neosho and command ship Northampton in the late 1950s and early 1960s. Among his postwar submarine tours were command of the USS Requin, of Submarine Division 32, and of Submarine Squadron Six. He also served on the staff of Commander Submarine Force Atlantic Fleet in the mid-1950s when the first nuclear submarine, USS Nautilus, was proving her worth.

While ashore, Captain Cutter had duty as Director of Special Services in the Bureau of Naval Personnel, as Director of Public Information in the Navy's Office of Information, as chief of staff to Commander Striking Fleet Atlantic, as Commander Naval Training Center, Great Lakes, Illinois, and as Director of the Navy Memorial Museum in Washington.

Captain Cutter's oral recollections are remarkable for the degree of candor and introspection he brought to their telling. With the transformation of the tape recordings into a printed transcript, Cutter's life becomes literally an open book. He has thus made a considerable contribution to our understanding of what went into the making of a highly successful submarine commander and how that individual adjusted to a postwar Navy in which both submarines and their missions changed dramatically. Slade Cutter has swept through life with great enthusiasm, and we are fortunate that he has brought that same enthusiasm to this project. He has gone through the transcript and made corrections in considerable detail to make it as complete and accurate as possible. After he had been through the transcript of the initial three interviews, he willingly consented to a fourth to make the story even more complete and then painstakingly corrected that transcript as well. His efforts have been ably augmented by Mrs. Deborah Reid, who did the transcription, and Ms. Susan Sweeney, who compiled the detailed index of the contents.

                                                                            Paul Stillwell
                                                                            Director of Oral History
                                                                            U.S. Naval Institute
                                                                            November 1985

Captain Slade D. Cutter
United States Navy (Retired)

Slade Deville Cutter was born in Oswego, Illinois, on November 1, 1911, son of W.C. and Esther (Sundeen) Cutter. He attended Severn School, Severna Park, Maryland, prior to his appointment to the U.S. Naval Academy, Annapolis, Maryland, from the Twelfth District of his native state in 1931. As a midshipman he was an outstanding athlete, winning his letters in football and boxing for four years. He also qualified as an expert rifleman, and, as a three-striper, received a commendatory letter from the Superintendent of the Academy for contributing to the development of naval spirit and loyalty within the regiment. Graduated and commissioned ensign on June 6, 1935, he subsequently advanced in rank, attaining that of captain, to date from July 1, 1954.

Following graduation from the Naval Academy in 1935, he joined the USS Idaho (BB-42) and served in that battleship until June 1937. After six months' duty in the department of physical training at the Naval Academy, he reported for submarine training at the Submarine Base, New London, Connecticut. Upon completing the course in June 1938, he served briefly in the USS S-30, and in August of the same year was again ordered to the Naval Academy for duty in the department of physical training. In December 1938 he was assigned to the USS Pompano (SS-181) and was aboard that submarine when the United States entered World War II, December 7, 1941. For outstanding services while attached to the USS Pompano, he was awarded the Silver Star Medal, the Bronze Star Medal with Combat "V," and a Gold Star in lieu of the Second Silver Star Medal. The citations follow in part:

Silver Star Medal: "For conspicuous gallantry and intrepidity in action as Assistant Approach Officer of a submarine during three successive war patrols. With outstanding skill and courage, (he) carried out his duties during aggressive attacks against the enemy which resulted in the sinking of a large amount of hostile shipping. His excellent judgment, resourcefulness, and bravery in action contributed materially to the success of the ship . . ."

Bronze Star Medal: "For meritorious service in connection with operations against the enemy on the USS POMPANO during the first war patrol of that vessel in the Marshall Islands area from 18 December 1941 to 31 January 1942. As Executive Officer, Navigator, and Assistant Approach Officer, his excellent judgment and thorough knowledge of attack problems as well as his skillful navigation of his ship assisted his Commanding Officer considerably in conducting successful attacks which resulted in the sinking of one YAWATA-class vessel of 16,500 tons and conducting a reconnaissance of enemy installations which contributed materially to the success of a raid on 31 January 1942 by air and surface forces . . ."

Gold Star in lieu of the Second Silver Star Medal: "For conspicuous gallantry and intrepidity in action as Executive Officer, Navigator, and Assistant Approach Officer of the USS POMPANO during her second war patrol in the East China Sea from 20 April to 18 June 1942. His excellent judgment and thorough knowledge of attack problems as well as his skillful navigation of the ship assisted his Commanding Officer considerably in conducting successful attacks which resulted in the sinking of 16,485 tons of enemy shipping . . ."

Detached from the Pompano in November 1942, he returned to the United States for duty fitting out the USS Seahorse (SS-304) at the Navy Yard, Mare Island, California. He became executive officer of that submarine upon her commissioning, March 31, 1943, and assumed command on September 30, 1943. For his services while in command of the Seahorse he was awarded the Navy Cross and Gold Stars in lieu of the Second, Third, and Fourth Navy Cross. He is also entitled to the Ribbon for, and a facsimile of the Presidential Unit Citation awarded the Seahorse. The citations follow in part:

Navy Cross: "For extraordinary heroism as Commanding Officer of the USS SEAHORSE during the Second War Patrol of that vessel in enemy Japanese-controlled waters. Alert and aggressive as he navigated dangerous seas in search of Japanese shipping, Commander Cutter conducted bold attacks against the enemy and, maintaining a high standard of efficiency throughout this important patrol, succeeded in sinking nine vessels totalling 48,000 tons, and in damaging another ship of 4,800 tons . . . [He] inspired confidence and maximum effort among the officers and men of his command, inflicting heavy losses upon the enemy and bringing his ship back to port undamaged despite intensive hostile countermeasures . . ."

Gold Star in lieu of the Second Navy Cross: ". . . as Commanding Officer of the USS SEAHORSE during a war patrol of that vessel in enemy-controlled waters. In spite of the thorough enemy aircraft patrols and intensive methods in which the Japanese conducted their anti-submarine measures, he aggressively attacked and successfully delivered damaging torpedo attacks against heavily escorted enemy convoys . . . [sinking] five enemy ships totalling over 30,000 tons. On one occasion it was necessary to pursue an enemy convoy over a period of eighty hours and only by exceptional determination and skill was he able to penetrate escort screen and sink two freighters . . . [evading] severe enemy counter-attacks to bring his ship back to port undamaged . . ."

Gold Star in lieu of the Third Navy Cross: ". . . As Commanding Officer of the USS SEAHORSE, during a War Patrol of that Vessel in enemy Japanese-controlled waters of the Pacific, from March 28 to April 27, 1944 . . . [He] launched repeated torpedo attacks to sink four hostile ships totalling over 25,000 tons and to damage an enemy submarine of over 600 tons. Although subjected to severe depth charging and aerial bombing, he skillfully evaded the enemy and brought his ship safe to port . . ."

Gold Star in lieu of the Fourth Navy Cross: "For extraordinary heroism as Commanding Officer of the USS SEAHORSE, during the Fifth War Patrol of that vessel in enemy Japanese-controlled waters, from June 3 to July 19, 1944. Penetrating heavy and unusually alert escort screens, Commander Cutter pressed home well planned and executed torpedo attacks to sink six enemy ships totalling 37,000 tons and damaged an additional ship of 4,000 tons. Undaunted by severe enemy anti-submarine measures, he directed his vessel and succeeded in bringing her safe to port . . ."

Presidential Unit Citation: "For outstanding performance in combat and distinguished service during war patrols against enemy Japanese surface forces in the Pacific War Area. Employing highly aggressive tactics, the USS SEAHORSE struck boldly at the enemy at every quarter and inflicted extensive damage on Japanese combatant units and heavily escorted convoys. By the extreme accuracy of her intensive torpedo fire through brief periods of concentrated attack she sank an exceptionally large amount of enemy shipping and damaged other vessels. Her notable achievements attest the SEAHORSE's constant vigilance and readiness for combat and reflect the heroic fighting spirit of her officers and men."

Relieved of command of the Seahorse in August 1944, he then served on the staff of Commander Submarines, U.S. Atlantic Fleet. Following an assignment in charge of fitting out the USS Requin (SS-481), he assumed command of that submarine upon her commissioning on April 28, 1945. (When the Requin was launched, January 1, 1945, she was sponsored by Captain Cutter's wife.) He continued to command that submarine until October 28, 1946, when he reported as officer in charge of physical fitness and athletics, Special Services Division Welfare Activities in the Bureau of Naval Personnel, Navy Department, Washington, D.C. He remained there until February 1949, when he joined the USS Sperry (AS-12) as executive officer.

Detached from the Sperry in July 1950, he was in command of Submarine Division 32 until February 1951 when he became Director of Special Services in the Bureau of Naval Personnel. In July 1952 he transferred to the Office of Public Information, Navy

Department, where for two years he served as Director of Public Information Division. His next duty was on the staff of Commander Submarine Force, Atlantic Fleet, and, under orders of March 1, 1956 he became Commander Submarine Squadron Six.

He reported in July 1957 as head of the department of physical education and director of athletics, U.S. Naval Academy, and two years later was ordered to sea as commanding officer of the USS Neosho (AO-143), transferring in October 1960 to command of the USS Northampton (CLC-1). In August 1961 he was assigned as chief of staff to Commander Striking Fleet, Atlantic and in June 1963 was designated Commander Naval Training Center, Great Lakes, Illinois. He was ordered detached in July 1964 for duty as Director of the Naval Historical Display Center, Washington, D.C. In July 1965 he was retired from active duty upon completion of 30 years of service.

In addition to the Navy Cross with three Gold Stars, the Silver Star Medal with Gold Star, Bronze Star Medal with Combat "V," Presidential Unit Citation Ribbon, Captain Cutter has the American Defense Service Medal, Fleet Clasp; American Campaign Medal; Asiatic-Pacific Campaign Medal with two silver stars (ten engagements); World War II Victory Medal; and the National Defense Service Medal.

Captain Cutter and his first wife, the former Frances Leffler of Baltimore, Maryland, had two chidren, Anne W. (born March 6, 1938) and Slade, Jr., (born August 7, 1947). After the death of his first wife, he married Ruth McCracken Buek in 1982.

Authorization

The U.S. Naval Institute is hereby authorized to make available to individuals, libraries, and other repositories of its choosing the transcripts of four oral history interviews concerning the life and career of the undersigned. The four interviews were conducted on 30 November, 1 December 1982, 27 July 1983, and 17 June 1985, in collaboration with Paul Stillwell for the U.S. Naval Institute.

The undersigned does hereby release and assign to the U.S. Naval Institute all right, title, restriction, and interest in the four interviews. The copyright in both the oral and transcribed versions shall be the sole property of the U.S. Naval Institute. The tape recordings of the interviews are and will remain the property of the U.S. Naval Institute.

Signed and sealed this ninth day of October 1985.

Slade D. Cutter
Captain, U.S. Navy (Retired)

Interview Number 1 with Captain Slade D. Cutter, U.S. Navy (Retired)

Place: At the home of Captain K.G. Schacht, Annapolis, Maryland

Date: Tuesday, 30 November 1982

Subject: Biography

Interviewer: Paul Stillwell

Q: Captain, could you begin your story, please, by telling when and where you were born and something about your family background?

Captain Cutter: I was born in Chicago, Illinois, on the 1st of November 1911, and my father was a farmer; he graduated from the University of Illinois. My mother was at the University of Illinois, and that's where they met. Dad graduated in the class of 1910. He was president of his class at Illinois, and he had to be a farmer because his mother wanted to get off the farm. They sent him to school there in agriculture, and he graduated in three years at the university and came back and took over the farm. My grandmother, who was a Methodist minister's daughter, got into the club work that she liked, and she was very happy in it.

So I went to school. I was five years old, and there wasn't anybody in the first grade, so they put me in the second grade. When I got to the fifth grade, there wasn't anybody in the fifth grade, so they put me in the sixth grade. So I missed fractions.

Cutter #1 - 2

And I have always blamed that for my problem with mathematics before I got to the Naval Academy.

When I was 11 years old, I graduated from the eighth grade, and they wouldn't take me into high school. So I went for another year to a junior high school in Aurora, Illinois, and then I went into high school. I was a very indifferent student but got very much interested in music. I was getting pretty big then; kids on the farm are pretty strong, you know. They get a lot of exercise and hard work, so they wanted me to go out for football. But my father wouldn't let me do it, so I got into the band and in the orchestra. I played the flute, and in my senior year I won the national interscholastic flute solo championship, and I was thinking of going into music as a career. But there wasn't much in it at the time. I was taking from Arthur Kitt, who was the first flautist in the Chicago Symphony Orchestra, and I took from him for about a year. I realized that I really didn't have the talent. The mechanics of it I did, fast play and all that, but I didn't have the sense of rhythm---the 3/2 time and 9/8 time and the different things you get in symphonic music scores. I didn't have it, so I decided that I was not for that. Then I went to work with the All-Steel Equip Company which makes lockers; I was timekeeper there. Then one day on the farm---it was a Sunday---a LaSalle automobile drove in, and it was Mrs. Loomis, whose husband was a division commander out in the

Philippines, division commander of a destroyer division.* She had brought her two sons back, because one of them had gotten undulant fever, and they said he had to get out of the Philippines. His name was Sam, Junior. She came out there just cold turkey, because the doctor had said the boy should get out in the fresh air and all that sort of stuff you get on a farm, so she brought him out there. She had gone with my father in high school a good many years before and wanted to know if Sam could come out to the farm. So he did, and we became very close friends. When I graduated from high school, he went to Severn School to prepare for the Naval Academy. He didn't make it after the first year, and Mrs. Loomis, for some reason known only to her, thought that I was a good influence on him. So she thought that if I went to Severn the next year that her son Sam would study more and get in the Naval Academy.

I didn't have an appointment and had no political connections except the one barber in Oswego, Illinois. He was Kendall County chairman of the Republican Party and very active in politics. He heard of my problem and volunteered to help. He said he would go to Congressman Buckbee in Rockford and see if he could get an appointment.** On a Sunday we drove over there, and he told the

---
*In the mid-1920s, Commander Sam C. Loomis, USN, served simultaneously as commanding officer of the destroyer Tracy (DD-214) and as Commander Destroyer Division 38, Asiatic Fleet. He then served as Captain of the Yard, Naval Station, Cavite, in the Philippines before his return to the United States.

**Representative John T. Buckbee, Republican, of Rockford, Illinois.

story that nobody from Kendall County had ever been appointed to the Naval Academy or to West Point, and he thought that the county should be given an appointment. The congressman, Mr. Buckbee, agreed to give me a tentative appointment--it wasn't definite--to see how this boy makes out. So I went to Severn School, which is nine miles up the Severn River from Annapolis. I didn't have any money to go there. It was during the days of the Depression, and a friend of my father's, named Dudley Edwards, lived in Chicago. He was in the construction business there. He came out one day, and he had $600. I'll never forget it--six one-hundred-dollar bills--and he loaned me those. I gave him a note. I was then 18 years old, and my father said, "I'll sign it, Dud."

And Dud say, "No, I will take Slade's signature."

So, anyway, I went to Severn. Mrs. Loomis was on friendly terms with Roland M. Teel, headmaster at Severn, and arranged for me to wait on tables to help pay my tuition. So that's how I got to Severn. Well, here I was, weighing 200 pounds, and they had a football team. The school had only 135 students, I guess, and they had a 125-pound team, 135-pound team, a junior varsity team, and a varsity team. Then they had those who were not physically able to engage in football, and they were playing soccer or just running around. So I was relegated to that outfit, because my father said, "You cannot play football, because it will interfere with your academics."

Well, Paul Brown was right out of Miami University of Ohio, 22 years old, 135 pounds—I'll never forget—a very intense guy.* He came there as an assistant coach; really, he was head coach. I mean, he took over. The school was academic, and athletics were just secondary. As things developed during the year, they just happened to have about 12 real good kids in there, good football players, and we won the state championship, due almost entirely to Paul Brown. I started playing football for the first time at Severn School. I liked it. I made all-state in Maryland that year. A big farm boy, you know; it was no problem.**

So then I went to the Naval Academy. I passed the examination, and Mr. Buckbee gave me the appointment. When I entered Annapolis, I had never had solid geometry, which is one of the requirements at the Academy, so we had to take that during

---

*Paul Brown, who was born 9 July 1908, was a 1930 graduate of Miami University, Oxford, Ohio. His job at Severn Prep, starting in the fall of 1930, was his first as a coach. He later gained fame as a coach at Massillon, Ohio, High School; Ohio State University; Great Lakes Naval Training Center; and two professional football teams, the Cleveland Browns and Cincinnati Bengals.

**Brown's autobiography, written in collaboration with Jack Clary, is PB: The Paul Brown Story (New York: Atheneum, 1975). On page 40, the noted coach recalls the following: "Out of the eighteen games we played at Severn during my two years, we won sixteen and tied one, and some of the players went on to become stars at Navy. One was Dick Pratt, one of my favorite young men, a quarterback who later became an admiral. Another was Slade Cutter, whom I still see for an occasional round of golf, a bubbling exuberant young man who ... became a great end and kicker for the midshipmen.... When Slade came to us from Elmhurst College in Illinois, he was supposed to have preferred playing the flute to playing football, but we made him a tackle and, on some goal line plays, even our fullback because he was so strong."

plebe summer with other plebes who had not been exposed to it. My academic preparation wasn't too good. You go to a prep school like that, and they jam the stuff into you. It was a great school, and they did a good job, but my basic academic background wasn't good. Anyway, I completed the course--also you had to have trigonometry, so I took trigonometry, too. Then plebe year started, and I felt very fortunate being at the Naval Academy, and that was the beginning of four really wonderful years. I enjoyed it very, very much.

Spike Webb was the boxing coach, and somehow or other he got me interested in boxing, so I went out for boxing.* Football and boxing kept me busy and kept me out of trouble, and it was a very happy four years.

Q: Going back to your parents, how was it that you were born in Chicago when they were living on a farm?

Captain Cutter: I don't know. I mean, my mother and my father, as I say, were students at the University of Illinois. Dad graduated and married Mother, and they came back to Oswego, Illinois, and I was born in Chicago on the 1st of November in 1911.

---

*Hamilton W. ("Spike") Webb was involved in Naval Academy athletics from 1919 to 1954, including service for more than 20 years as varsity boxing coach. For more on his history, see Jack Sweetman, The U.S. Naval Academy: An Illustrated History (Annapolis: Naval Institute Press, 1979), pages 181-182.

Cutter #1 - 7

Q: What were the names of your parents?

Captain Cutter: He was Watts C. Cutter, and my mother's name was Esther Sundeen. She came from Moline, Illinois, and her parents were both immigrants from Sweden, wonderful people. Her father, Frederick Sundeen, was a very successful businessman there in Illinois. Moline, in those days, had a large Swedish population.

Q: Was there any company at all there?

Captain Cutter: No, first he had a department store, in which he became very successful. At an age under 50 he retired, spent a year in Sweden. He took his wife over, and they had three daughters, and they were all in college. Then he came back, 40-some years old, with nothing to do. He got bored and went into the wholesale produce business, and there he lost his shirt. Things were bad, and he lost a lot of money, but he was able to keep his lovely home, and he always kept his spirits up and provided for his family. He died at the age of 83 years old, and he was really a great guy.

Q: How did you come by the name Slade?

Captain Cutter: My great-grandfather, Henry Cutter, came from Arlington, Massachusetts, and went out to California in the gold

Cutter #1 - 8

rush in 1849. They took a ship to Panama, walked across the isthmus there, boarded another sailing vessel, and went out into the Pacific heading for San Francisco. They got becalmed in the Gulf of Tehuantepec. The horses died, and they threw them over the side. And the water got rancid, and everything else happened. He was with a cousin, and the cousin died. They got to Acapulco, finally. They buried the cousin there, and then they walked overland from Acapulco, Mexico, all the way to San Francisco.

Q: That's a long trek.

Captain Cutter: Yes, it was. Then he went to Sutter's Creek. I was there in 1973 or 1974 with my wife to look up the history of the place, which is very interesting. He was justice of the peace there. He picked up a little gold, I guess. Anyway, he walked back across the country to Illinois and in the Fox River Valley he saw this very fertile land. He had enough money to buy a farm, and that's where I was reared. He had four sons and a daughter. The boys were named Scott, Watts, Slade, and Cyrus—all named after friends of his back in Massachusetts, and two of them were last names—Watts and Slade. I run into it quite often now; it is always a last name. Not only did he name his boys after these friends of his, he told them what they would do. One would be a doctor, one a pharmacist, one a veterinarian, and one would be a farmer. And my grandfather, Watts D. Cutter, was the farmer. The daughter was in the first graduating class from Wellesley, back in Massachusetts. It was a very interesting thing, and that's how I got the name Slade.

Q: Is there a story that goes with your middle name?

Captain Cutter: Deville—that's one I had quite a bit of trouble with as a kid growing up, because, of course, they called me "Devil." It was one of his friend's middle names; it's a French name, I think. My grandfather's name was Watts Deville. My mother liked an uncle of my father—who was a brother of my grandfather—very much, because he was so good to her and so on. And that's how I got the name of Slade, and the Deville was from my grandfather.

Q: Did you have brothers and sisters?

Captain Cutter: Yes, I had two brothers and a sister, and they are all living. One is Watts C., Jr., and the other is named after my mother's father, and my sister is named after my mother. She lives in Portland, Oregon. One brother, Fred, lives in Thousand Oaks, California, and the other, Watts, lives in New Orleans.

Cutter #1 - 10

Q: How did they fit chronologically? Where were you among them?

Captain Cutter: I was the oldest. Mother had three boys, 15 months apart, on the farm, and I'll tell you, her work was cut out for her. We got in all sorts of problems.

Q: What are some of your memories of growing up on the farm?

Captain Cutter: You worked. You worked hard. When I was 12 years old, I went out in the fields and did a man's work as soon as school was out. One of the recollections of school when I was a little bit younger than that--my grandmother (I was the favorite, I was the first-born grandchild, so I was the apple of her eye, I guess). I spent a lot of weekends with them. I spent this one weekend, and they drove me home in the Model T Ford, and my brothers were in real serious trouble. My mother had collected 12 dozen eggs for a neighbor to put in an incubator to hatch. My two brothers, who had gotten these eggs, went out into the yard and had thrown all of them away. And to this day, that barn--up in the rafters inside--has these egg yolks and egg shells still sticking to it. It really does. Of course, they were going to get a spanking, and my father was there to give them the spanking, and I said, "Grandma, take me back." Because every time any one of us got a spanking, we all did, because we were always into things. So I just assumed I was going to get a

Cutter #1 - 11

spanking, too. But I didn't.

It was a pretty hard life during the Depression, but it was a good life.

Q: That was a time when it was difficult to sell things that you produced on the farm, wasn't it?

Captain Cutter: Well, you could sell them, but I remember oats at 10 cents a bushel, corn at 25 cents a bushel. Today corn is something like $2.50 a bushel. I don't know what wheat was; we didn't grow much of that. Things were pretty rough, but we were able to keep our farm, which many people couldn't. The Northwestern Life Insurance Company got a lot of them in our area, but Dad was able to hang onto it. He was a good farmer, and he was frugal and a good manager. And we survived, so today I can have this motor home and stuff that I got from my father.

Q: Was it unusual for a college graduate to be running a farm back then?

Captain Cutter: Yes, it was, but, as I said, it was a pact between him and his mother. He went to the University of Illinois to get a degree, and then he would come home and take care of the farm. That was the deal, and he kept the deal. He was never happy. The poor man, when he was 39 years old, got

Cutter #1 - 12

cancer in his eye—this is why I couldn't play in athletics, because, according to medical people, it was from an athletic injury he got in his eye. He lost the sight in it for quite a little while, but his sight came back. Years later, he had a cancer in the eye, a malignancy, and he had the eye removed; he was 39 years old. He lived until he was 47. It went away for five or six years but came back, cancer of the pancreas. He died from it. He never saw me play a game of football until the Army-Navy game in 1934, and this was only four months before he died. He came back for the game. We beat Army, and I kicked the field goal that beat Army. Of course, that made him very happy.

Q: He had relented then in his opposition to football?

Captain Cutter: He went along with it after Severn School. He was a very reasonable person and didn't interfere, but he just felt, going through high school and stuff, that he didn't want to happen to me what had happened to him; that was all.

Q: I think that's a normal reaction on the part of a parent.

Captain Cutter: I wouldn't want a son of mine to play football until he got into high school. This thing of kids playing in the eighth grade and so on, I don't believe in at all. Because their muscles are not strong enough, and the tendons aren't tough enough. You see a lot of kids get seriously hurt—see, I never really played football—I was 18 years old before I played. As a result, I was pretty well matured physically, and I never had any serious injuries.

Q: You were probably unusually big for your age all through school, weren't you?

Captain Cutter: In those days, yes. Today, you know, I wouldn't be big enough to make a B squad tackle with these football teams. They're so big and so strong—weight lifting and all that stuff. But in those days, it was a little different.

Q: Football and other sports were much more of a form of recreation than the system they have become in schools now; it's almost semipro.

Captain Cutter: Well, we took it pretty seriously at the Academy. We had a good football team, and everybody went both ways, which I kind of wish they did today.* I think it makes it more interesting.

Q: Specialization has hit sports, no question about it.

---

*"Both ways" refers to the practice in those years of individuals playing both offense and defense. At present there are separate platoons for offense and defense.

Cutter #1 - 14

Captain Cutter: Yes, yes, yes.

Q: Why did you start school so early, when you were only five years old?

Captain Cutter: I was five. There were no rules. It was a little country school. The most we ever had was 17 students total in eight grades. The teacher graduated from high school and had two years in what they called a normal school.* I was always a real good speller and was good in English. They had these spelling bees, and we were all sitting there watching it, so I would ask to get in them when I was really quite young. That was one thing I was interested in and excelled in--the spelling--because of this environment there.

Q: Perhaps it helped you just being in with an older group of children.

Captain Cutter: Oh, yes.

Q: What was the quality of the teaching from these normal school products?

---

*Normal schools were intended primarily for training elementary school teachers. One such at Normal, Illinois, has since evolved into Illinois State University.

Cutter #1 - 15

Captain Cutter: Pretty bad. Pretty bad. Their heart was in the right place, and they tried. They had a disciplinary problem. These farm kids came in there, and we were more interested in recess than we were in the classroom. They had a tough time. They were good people.

Q: It sounds as if you really stumbled onto a naval career almost by accident.

Captain Cutter: It sure was. If Mrs. Loomis's son hadn't gotten undulant fever in the Philippines, and her family hadn't sent her back to her mother who still lived in Aurora, Illinois, and if the mother hadn't previously dated my father, it never would have happened. Hell, I didn't know where Annapolis was. They were talking about Annapolis; I thought it was in Indiana—Indianapolis. I had no idea where—the biggest body of water I had ever seen was Lake Michigan, and that was only a couple of times. I had been to the Mississippi, because my grandparents lived in Moline. That's all I had ever seen.

Q: Did you follow college and professional sports teams before you came to Maryland—as a school student? Were you a sports fan?

Captain Cutter: Oh, sure. I think all kids are. My whole

interest was the University of Illinois, because that's where my father was from and he used to take me down there to the football games. He did do that, we went down to his fraternity house and stuff. I was supposed to go to Illinois, but then we didn't have any money.

Q: Well, that was the Red Grange era, so you had a good team to root for.*

Captain Cutter: You bet. I'll never forget, we went down for one game and Michigan beat Illinois, 3-0, and Red Grange—I guess that was his last year—but I remember thinking even then, I didn't know anything about football. But I remember that fellow, when they punted—he was a safety man—and he would wait back from the ball, and he would catch the ball on a dead run. He wouldn't stand to get under the ball and then catch it. He would stay back of it so he could catch it full bore with no fair catch business at all. He was a great football player.

Q: It sounds as if your father was a lot more willing to let you make your own choice on a career than his parents had been.

---

*Harold ("Red") Grange, a halfback, was one of the best known players in college football history. Right after finishing his career at the University of Illinois in 1925, he turned professional with the Chicago Bears and helped popularize the fledgling National Football League.

Captain Cutter: Yes, he never--he was 100% behind my going to the Naval Academy. I got some wonderful letters from him, and he did everything he could. He didn't have any money; that's the thing. So this friend came through with the $600 that got me through Severn School. During Christmas, I was the only student at Severn School who didn't go home. Later on, I was headmaster of a boys' school in Arizona, and I'll tell you---if any of our students stayed there over Christmas, I don't know what we would have done. You've got to feed them; you've got to have somebody to supervise them; and they did it at Severn School. I had to stay. I couldn't go back to Illinois. But then, after I had passed my exams to get into the Naval Academy and had been accepted at Annapolis, I didn't have any money to go home, so I hitchhiked. And I'll tell you right now, boy, I'm lucky to be here.

I had a couple of dollars and spent the night in a YMCA in Youngstown, Ohio. The next morning I got out on the road, and this fellow stopped and picked me up, and he was going all the way to Joliet, which was only about 25 miles from my home. We were driving on U.S. 30 through Ohio, which was a brick highway in those days, two ways, and we were going up a little rise. He was passing a car, which he shouldn't have done, on the rise. And coming up the other way was a Cord. Remember that front-wheel-drive Cord automobile? You're too young to remember that.

Cutter #1 - 18

Q: I've heard of them. I don't remember them.

Captain Cutter: They were very fast and very low. They'd go well today. They were very sporty. And this guy—hell, we were going 60 miles an hour, and I'll never forget. I was looking at my watch and was timing us with my second hand. We were going a mile in 60 seconds or 55 seconds. And he was passing this car, and all of a sudden this other car was there. So instead of—I don't know what would have happened, but he went off the road to the left into the ditch. And the other guy—normally, you would expect him to go that way, but the other fellow did the right thing. He stayed on his side of the road, and we just went across him in front of him into the ditch. It didn't hurt the car at all, but it was in soft mud up to the hubs. There was a farmer across the street—we were really lucky. He was hauling something with his team of horses and a wagon of hay. He unhitched and brought the whiffletree over and had a rope or chain or something and hooked it on and pulled us out, and on we went. We got back to Illinois safely, but that's about as close as I ever came to getting knocked off, really.

Q: Worse than being in submarines?

Captain Cutter: It really was, yes.

Cutter #1 - 19

Q: Had you heard much about the Navy when you were living in Illinois?

Captain Cutter: No. I'll never forget the 1926 Army-Navy football game, I was pulling for Army. Navy tied them, and I was very unhappy, because Army was leading in that game towards the end.

Q: That was the game where Navy won the national championship.

Captain Cutter: That's right, yes.

Q: Did you go to the game?

Captain Cutter: No, it was in Soldier Field in Chicago, and I was about 50 miles away. No, I didn't go.

Q: Again, probably a matter of money then.

Captain Cutter: I wasn't that interested. If it had been Illinois playing Chicago, I would have been interested in going.

Q: Did you have a real desire to get away from the farm and into something else?

Cutter #1 - 20

Captain Cutter: Very much, very much. And my mother was the motivating factor there. She would never let any of us be farmers. Not that she would prevent us from doing it, but she kept harping on it: "You've got to do better than that; you can't be here." So none of us ever settled on the farm.

Q: It sounds then as if you had that sort of impetus from both parents.

Captain Cutter: Oh, yes, I would have done something else. I don't know what it would have been. Dad didn't want us to follow in his footsteps. Of course, as I say, he died pretty young. In the summertime of my senior year at high school, I went to work at the All Steel Equip Company in Aurora and got a little bit of indoctrination into industry. In those days, it was open shop in Aurora, and anybody that tried to organize the plant got fired. And if you got fired, you couldn't get another job anywhere in the Aurora area. Because there was what was called the Fox River Valley Association, which my father worked for. After he had this cancer problem, he couldn't work on the farm anymore. So he got this job, through a friend, with the Fox River Valley Manufacturers' Association. He got paid $150.00 a month, which wasn't bad. It helped. I was timekeeper at All Steel Equip Company, and I knew about the Fox River Valley Manufacturers' Association. Nobody was supposed to know about it, because the people who tried to get union organizing there would get blackballed. The names were sent in to the central place where my father worked. They had cards on every single employee, and they would be blackballed and they couldn't get a job in any other major concern there in the area. I never told anybody that I had anything to do with the Fox River Valley Manufacturers' Association. They weren't supposed to know about it. So I worked there for one summer, and then the next summer I came back--that was before I went to Severn--and the first summer I was there I got 25 cents an hour, and I did a good job. I was very conscientious, worked hard, kept the records real good. The next summer I went back, and they paid me 26 cents an hour. You know, that is really something, isn't it? So I became kind of pro-union, and I still am sympathetic to the problem of the workers of our country. Of course, it works both ways. If they get the upper hand, they will grind--like Chrysler--grind the company in the dirt, and, likewise, the industry will give them a bad time. I will never forget, for instance, we had a fellow-- Harry Hardwick was his name. He had six children, didn't have any teeth; I guess he was 45 years old. They had a paint shop and these pieces of all-steel equipment--we made lockers--the doors, the sides, and the backs were all in sheets before they got assembled. They would bring them on a conveyor belt, go down into this tank of paint, come up, and then go into the baking oven. The tank was about 10 feet deep, 5 feet long, and maybe 2

Cutter #1 - 22

feet wide. After a while, the paint would get skins in it, and they had to strain it and clean the tank out. I saw this several times. They would pump the paint out, and they would lower Harry down there on the hoist which they used. He would pass out. They would haul him up, take him outside, and lean him up against the building until he came to, and then put him down again.

Q: What did he do down in the tank?

Captain Cutter: Clean it out with rags. I didn't know then what caused him to pass out. It was carbon monoxide, of course, and what it did to his liver and his kidneys—isn't that terrible? That is what they did to people in those days. You go up, as I have done, to Newport, Rhode Island, and see those homes on the waterfront up there, where the Morgans and the Vanderbilts and whoever they were—they all came out of the blood of the immigrants that they put into the coal mines and railways. I'm not what you would call a liberal exactly, but I am sympathetic to those people who suffered that way in the time when they were terribly exploited. I saw it in this factory that I was in.

Q: Chicago was notorious for that in the meat packing industry.

Captain Cutter: Oh, hell yes, very bad.

Cutter #1 - 23

Q: Did you children have to take up the slack on the farm then when your father did come down with cancer?

Captain Cutter: Yes. Well, in those days we had 250 acres, which was a big farm, and no one man could farm it. You had to have somebody living there. We had a hired man who lived there the year round. I think we paid him $40.00 a month or something and gave him a house and garden and a cow and that sort of thing. He could take care of things on his own pretty well. Then, when my father got sick, we would hire people by the day. You could hire them for $1.50-$2.00 a day. By this time, I was gone; I was at the Naval Academy and got out of it, but my two brothers weren't. It was pretty tough on them; they had to do a lot of the work.

Q: Did you farm with a team of horses or mules?

Captain Cutter: Yes, we had all horses, no mules, and we had a Fordson tractor, which was quite innovative in those days. Now that farm---the fellow who lives on there now, farms that farm plus some other farms in the area, plus 1,800 acres at the Illinois State Penitentiary at Joliet, which is 25 miles away. He and his wife operate the tractors and he hires one person, but my goodness, there are not more than three of them and doing all that with the equipment they have today. But they are paying

Cutter #1 - 24

$125,000 for each piece of the equipment that he is using. Every time I go out there, I stop in to see them; we are good friends. Golly, the old days of the farming industry have changed a great deal. They're making 125 to 150 bushels of corn per acre; the production has gone up a lot. They get more money, but they have to spend so much for their equipment. Farmers have my sympathy. They are still not getting what they should for the investment they have. We sold that farm of ours for a little over $500,000, and these farmers today who have 250 acres--they're worth more than $500,000. If they could just sell the farm and put it in money market funds, they would do a heck of a lot better than they are working their tails off.

Q: That is an unfortunate connection between effort and reward. It certainly takes away the incentive.

Captain Cutter: Yes.

Q: How much did you keep up with events of the wider world such as elections, the Lindbergh flight, and things of that sort?*

Captain Cutter: Oh, yes, I was interested in things like that. We had a radio, and we certainly listened to that a lot. You

---

*Charles A. Lindbergh made the first solo flight across the Atlantic in 1927.

Cutter #1 - 25

see, my father was a college graduate, and Mother had completed one year at the University of Illinois; they were very interested in current events. I certainly never felt deprived in any way. I had a very loving family, and I have no regrets and wouldn't want anything different, as a matter of fact.

Q: Were they able to help you with your schoolwork, since you didn't have the greatest of teachers?

Captain Cutter: No, they didn't really. It's a good question---I don't know why, but academics were not of primary importance. They were very much interested in music. I took piano lessons till I convinced myself that I would never be a pianist. And then I took over the flute, which I loved, and I would practice that by the hour. They were behind me all the way in that. Because, my goodness, I was paying $5.00 a lesson for a half hour in Chicago, and I had to go into Chicago on a Sunday morning for my lessons. Five dollars---boy, that's like $25.00 or $50.00 or something today---a lot of money. But I was giving lessons, so actually I paid for my own. I got a dollar a lesson, and I had enough pupils to pay for my own music lessons.

Q: Where do you think your parents' interest in music stemmed from?

Captain Cutter: They were just interested in us. My father was interested in music; he was a good singer and was in a barbershop quartet. They used to practice in our home, and he had a real good voice. He was interested in music, but they didn't play any instrument. Mother played a little piano but not much. They just wanted to help us; that's what it was.

Q: I am surprised to hear you say that you won a national championship and still you didn't think you had the appropriate talent to go on.

Captain Cutter: Oh, well, technique is everything; the faster you can play, the better. If you can triple tongue and things like that, which I could---that's the criteria for that---I played the "Carnival of Venice." That's a trumpet solo, a famous trumpet solo with all the variations. The flute doesn't go below middle C, so it had to be changed. And I had taken music appreciation and a little bit of composition, so I rewrote the thing. I did it with black India ink and did a real good job. I wrote it as I played it. I had a marvelous accompanist in high school. She was a real sweet gal, but she wasn't the sexy type that 16-year-old boys are looking for, so I really missed the boat there, because she was a lovely person. Anyway, she was just my accompanist.

First there was a city championship, then the district

championship, then the state championship, then the national. And the national was in Joliet, Illinois, in 1928. We went over there for that, and I had this thing that I had written out myself and also for my accompanist and a fellow by the name of Goodman. There were two touring bands in those days--one was Sousa, and the other was Goodman--that went around the country. Goodman was the judge of the flute solo that day. I handed him my piece, and we won. That night, they had the presentation, or late in the afternoon, for the winners, and the winners had to play. I played, and my accompanist was magnificent; she really won the championship. The other people were good. It was just separating the wheat from the chaff, and she was just really marvelous. John Philip Sousa was there judging the bands; the bands also played.* After the thing was over, he asked to see my accompanist, and they took her up there to him. He wanted to compliment her. Wasn't that something? John Philip Sousa.

Q: You had a brush with the Navy even before you came East.

Captain Cutter: I didn't know he was in the Navy then. I didn't know who he was. Then, that summer, I got an offer to go on one of his several farewell tours. I was offered a position in his

---

*Sousa (1854-1932) was a noted bandmaster and composer. He was dubbed "The March King" for such compositions as "Stars and Stripes Forever." During the course of his career, he led, at different times, both the Marine Corps and the Navy bands.

Cutter #1 - 28

band on a farewell tour, but instead of that I went to the Sherwood School of Music for the summer and got arranging and composition and so on, but by this time I began to realize that I didn't have it. You've got to have everything. If you want to be a top musician, you've got to have rhythm. I had the ear, and I had the technique, but I didn't have the rhythm.

Q: That was a sort of painful self-assessment at that point, I would think.

Captain Cutter: Yes, in a way, but it didn't bother me. I just said, "I can't do it. I've got to do something else." When you are 17 years old, you don't worry too much about those things.

Q: How were you looked upon by your peers? Was that considered to be a sissy type of thing to do?

Captain Cutter: Not at all, not back there. You see, everybody in the band had to take private lessons. Everybody in the junior high band had to take private lessons. Well, I couldn't afford private lessons. But what we would do would be to get one teacher, and maybe four or five of us would take lessons at the same time. I remember mine were 25 cents apiece for a half hour, and there were four or five of us there. The band was magnificent. Today, in Philadelphia, I just heard the Christmas parade they had there, and they had some high school bands that they brought from New Hampshire and so forth—just horrible. The instruments weren't tuned. My ears—I could hardly stand it, and you see that in a lot of college bands today. They don't tune up, and they are just not good musicians. Their concert bands are good. I'm talking about the marching bands they have out there—just horrible.

Q: Were you in a marching band yourself?

Captain Cutter: Oh, sure. I was playing the piccolo, and I was the biggest guy in the band, and the piccolo is the smallest instrument. And that was something I just didn't want to do, so I said, "Hell, I'm not going out there and play that piccolo, Mr. Rosenbarger," who was the bandmaster, so he put me on the bass drum. So I played the bass drum.

Q: That seems a little incongruous—a flute player and an All-American football player, combined in one.

Captain Cutter: Yes. Well, it has been interesting.

Q: You probably have some more recollections about Paul Brown since he has become perhaps the top football coach in professional football history.

Cutter #1 - 30

Captain Cutter: Paul Brown came there, 22 years old, and he was tough. Today they do more than they used to, but it was a big transition from high school football to college ball, because they hit so much harder in college. The high school kids weren't taught to hit like that. He did. He was always fair, always clean, never took advantage of any of the rules or anything like that, just a real fine man. As I said, he was only 22 years old but he made a great impression on all of us, and I have kept in touch with him over the years. Paul Brown is really a wonderful person. He was a great coach, and he took over from this head coach who was, I guess, 40 years old. Looking back on it, Paul Brown undermined him without Hoover knowing it.* He took charge without Hoover realizing that Brown really was the thing. On weekends we would go scouting other teams, which the school never did. And he would take as many as he could get. We had this old Packard touring car, and he would put about six of his players in there. And we would go scout the team we were going to play the next week or two weeks from then. I learned a lot of football from him in a short time. Of course, he made his mark later on, but he showed then that he had the ability to handle people and motivate them.

---

*Brown offers an explanation in his autobiography. He says that William Hoover, who was in charge of Severn School's sports program when Brown arrived, was suffering from the early effects of cancer, and for that reason, Brown took over some of his duties.

Cutter #1 - 31

Q: He was widely regarded for his innovative tactics. Did you see that back then also?

Captain Cutter: Oh, sure. Oh, yes, he had to be innovative. I played guard on offense, and then whenever we needed a couple of yards he put me in as a fullback. I was the biggest guy on the team, and I would lumber in there and try to pick up a couple of yards. I played defensive halfback--that was unusual in those days. You played one position, and you stayed in it. He moved us around. I was fast, so I played defensive halfback. On offense I played guard. We pulled; we used the old double wing, you know, and I would pull out on offense. He was a hell of a guy.

Q: How did you get into boxing at the Naval Academy?

Captain Cutter: That was Spike Webb. This roommate of mine, Sam Loomis, the one I told you about whose mother got me in.* I don't know why or how he got to know Spike, but he did and, when I was a candidate, we were walking down the grounds of the Naval Academy, and we came upon Spike Webb walking there, and he gave me a left hook in the belly--Spike did. I didn't know him; I had never seen him before, and I thought, "What the hell's

---

*Midshipman Sam C. Loomis, Jr., USN, who was graduated in the Naval Academy's class of 1935 and eventually retired as a captain.

going on?" Sam had been talking, because I had been boxing a little bit up at Severn. We had a math teacher by the name of Wilmot T. Debell up there who had been an amateur boxer, and he got me interested in boxing. So I guess Sam had told Spike, so Spike hit me in the stomach, and that started my association with Spike. When I got down there, the Olympic team was in training for the 1932 Olympics. This was 1931, and they were there for a year. Among them was a fellow by the name of Crinkley, who had been the heavyweight intercollegiate champion at the Naval Academy.* So I was his sparring partner. Well, I got a deviated septum from sparring with him. Of course, it was good training, but he was experienced, and he was a big man, but I stuck in there. So I got interested in boxing, and I went through plebe year and wasn't defeated. Then I guess it was my senior year when Crinkley came back to PG school and I had no sparring partners. There wasn't anybody who could work out, so Spike Webb asked Duke Crinkley to come over and be my sparring partner.

Q: To return the favor.

Captain Cutter: Oh, was I looking for him. Boy, was I after him. And he wouldn't do it, which was wise on his part. I could have taken him easy, but anyway . . .

---
*Ensign Francis D. Crinkley, USN.

Cutter #1 - 33

Q: How good a boxer were you?

Captain Cutter: How good? I was pretty good, modestly speaking.

Q: What was your record?

Captain Cutter: I wasn't defeated, and I was offered $50,000, which was a lot of money then, when I graduated, from a guy by the name of Bill Brennan in Philadelphia, who was manager of one of the white hopes. It wasn't Schmeling--Joe Louis was then the heavyweight champ--and he offered me $50,000 to turn pro.* My father said, "No, you owe it to the Navy to stay in the Navy," and all that. It was a good thing, because I would never have beaten Joe Louis the best day of my life. He was too quick, and speed is everything in boxing. It was just as well.

Q: Max Baer and Primo Carnera were some of the champions back then.**

Captain Cutter: They weren't too tough, but Louis was.

Q: Would you put yourself on a par with those two?

---
*Max Schmeling was the heavyweight champion from 1930 to 1932 and Joe Louis from 1937 to 1949.
**Primo Carnera was heavyweight boxing champion in 1933-1934 and Max Baer in 1934-1935.

Cutter #1 - 34

Captain Cutter: Yes, sure. Spike thought so, and he encouraged me to do it. I saw Louis, and I was pretty objective about it; he was just too good. Why not be honest? I was good in my league, but he is out of my league. Oh, yes.

Q: So you didn't regret that decision at all?

Captain Cutter: No, I went into the Navy and was very happy there.

Q: From an academic standpoint, do you think that the Severn School experience was the difference in your being able to succeed at the Naval Academy?

Captain Cutter: I couldn't have gotten in without that. There's no way. As a matter of fact, in November, the first part of November—now school started as I recall the 30th of September—it was quite late. I hadn't gotten over 1.5 in any algebra exam, so one night I went up to see this Wilmot T. Debell, the guy who was a boxer, the one who had gotten me interested in boxing. He became a real good friend of mine, but at this time he didn't know me at all. I went up and asked for help in this algebra, and he said, "Mr. Cutter, you don't know how to do fractions." Mind you, 18 years old and didn't know how to do fractions.

And I said, "That's right." I didn't.

"Well, we'll have to do something about that."

So in a matter of no time at all--I guess that night, really--he told me how to add and subtract fractions. Of course, multiplying and dividing fractions was no problem, but adding and multiplying you had to get a common denominator and get the numerator lined up so that you could add them. I didn't know how to do it. Here I was 18 years old--think of that. How lacking I was in the basic elements of mathematics. Geometry was real easy, because that's really not mathematics. It's sort of a logic thing, and I had never had that before either before I went to Severn. I had never had ancient history. I had never had physics. And algebra, forget it, because I couldn't do fractions, but I blundered through, because, you know, they just pass you. It was really quite a handicap, but he helped me. At least I went into the Naval Academy knowing how to do fractions. You had to get 2.5 in everything, and I got 2.6 in algebra--just barely made it. In the rest of the subjects, I did all right.

Q: How soon were you able to pay off the note for going to Severn School?

Captain Cutter: I've got that note at home with me right now, and I paid that off about the second year after I graduated from the Academy. I had to pay 6% on the note of $600.00. I had to pay $36.00 a year, and I paid the interest every year. My father

Cutter #1 - 36

paid the interest while I was in the Naval Academy. When I graduated, I picked it up, and I paid it off in 1937. In the meantime, I had gotten married and from my $143.00 a month, I was paying $18.80 for insurance, $30.00 mess bill, $40.00 for rent.

Q: It didn't leave too much.

Captain Cutter: No, but it was enough, you know.

Q: Didn't they have the requirement then that it was two years after graduation before you could get married?

Captain Cutter: That's right. That's right, but I didn't wait. I didn't do that; I got married before. You see, if you waited the two years, you got $225.00 a month. But I had gone with this girl since I was in Severn, all through the Naval Academy, the only date I had. Her mother died, and her father was very sick. He had had a stroke and so on, and so they came out to the West Coast. She was at loose ends. They were staying out there, she and her father. We decided to get married, and I resigned from the Navy.

Q: What year was that?

Captain Cutter: 1936. And in just one paragraph, I resigned,

Cutter #1 - 37

because I could not be married and be an ensign. And that was the only reason I gave. It came back denied; they wouldn't accept it.* In the meantime, my father-in-law was a very good friend of Senator Millard Tydings.** They were classmates together in grade school and high school in Havre de Grace, Maryland. He got in touch with Tydings to push this thing through the Secretary of the Navy. The Navy would not accept the resignation, so I went ahead and got married. I got a lot of criticism for that, bucking the system and being arrogant and so on, but those are the facts. I was honest. I told them I was going to get married; therefore, I resigned. They said, "You can't resign," so I got married. I didn't put in for marital allowance or anything like that and didn't flaunt it in any way.

I will never forget, during the war, any time you came in from a good patrol you would go up and see Admiral Nimitz.*** Admiral Lockwood would send you up at noon hour.**** Admiral Nimitz's son, Chester, Jr., was in submarines, too. Admiral Nimitz was a submariner; he was commander of the submarine base at New London at one time. So I would go up there, and jeez, he was a wonderful man. This one time, I got up there and was

---

*The denial came from the Bureau of Navigation, which was the predecessor of the Bureau of Naval Personnel.
 **U.S. Senator Millard E. Tydings (Democrat--Maryland).
 ***Admiral Chester W. Nimitz, USN, Commander in Chief Pacific Fleet from 1941 to 1945. As a captain, Nimitz had served as Assistant Chief of the Bureau of Navigation from 1935 to 1938.
 ****Vice Admiral Charles A. Lockwood, Jr., USN, Commander Submarines Pacific Fleet, 1943-1945.

Cutter #1 - 38

talking to him, and he said, "You know, Cutter, when I was in the Bureau of Navigation, a senator sent a thing over to us. He had gotten a letter from a mother of an officer who wanted to marry, and she said it was common knowledge that Slade Cutter was married."

So Admiral Nimitz wrote back to the senator and said, "If you can provide the proof of that, he will be dismissed."

And he said, "We never heard from it again. That's how close you came. I knew you were married. I had heard it, but we didn't have the proof, so we didn't do anything about it."

Q: Why wouldn't they accept your resignation?

Captain Cutter: Well, the war was coming along, I think. Several of them were accepted up to that time, but just about that time, the decision was made not to accept any resignations. Shortly after, they rescinded that ridiculous thing. What the hell? I was 25 years old, and I had gone with this girl for seven years. It was ridiculous.

Q: You were older than most of your classmates.

Captain Cutter: Yes, I was—one of the oldest.

Q: Did you come pretty close to the age deadline for entering?

Captain Cutter: No, not too close, but I was older. In those days, there was a lot of competition to get into the Academy, so everybody got in as soon as they could. I was 19 when I entered, and the deadline was 21.* I was 19 years and six months before I entered, but I am one of the oldest members of my class. There are very few older than I am.

Q: Where had you met the girl that you eventually married?

Captain Cutter: During that time at Severn when I didn't go home for Christmas, I went to a party. I was going with a girl. And she was something; she later became a Powers model; she was some gal. And she was invited to this party in Round Bay, so she took me along. I was invited, too, because I was her date. We got there, and there was a guy by the name of Burt Davis, who was second classman at the Naval Academy: intercollegiate middleweight boxing champ, first-string football player, a handsome guy, and a four-striper.** You know, he was a catch that night, but what's this gal going to do with a candidate whose clothes were kind of seedy and all this sort of stuff? So, very early in the evening, it didn't take very long for them to

---
*At that time, a candidate for admission had to be under 21 years of age as of 1 April on the year of entering the Naval Academy. Thus, there would have been a possibility for Cutter to have been admitted even one year later than he was, for he was 20 years old as of 1 April 1932.
**Midshipman Joseph Burton Davis, USN, who was graduated from the Naval Academy in the class of 1932.

make connections. They would go outside. They went out twice during the night, and I knew what for. So I commenced looking around for somebody else, you know, and my future wife was there, unattached. She had been invited to the party as a friend and classmate of the hostess and did not have a date.*

Q: What was her name?

Captain Cutter: Her name was Frances Leffler, and she was an only child and a lovely gal. So that's where it all started with her.

Q: As far as the academic routine at the Naval Academy, how did you endure plebe summer?

Captain Cutter: I enjoyed it. I loved it. I loved everything about the Naval Academy.

Q: Most people don't enjoy plebe summer.

Captain Cutter: I guess not. We did; I think our group did. It was a little different then. This was during the Depression, and everybody was so doggone happy to be there, you know. I don't

---

*The hostess and future Mrs. Cutter attended Country Day School, a private school in Baltimore.

remember anybody griping about it, and the upperclassmen were fair. We had a lot of hazing and stuff like that, but it was all done in good spirit. My goodness, I thought it was great.

Q: You perhaps were luckier than most, because some ran into the real sadists who were not fair about it.

Captain Cutter: Well, not many, because their peers would take care of them. I don't know of any of that that went on; I really don't. I got my butt beat. You could say that the guy who beat my ass was a sadist, but I don't think so. The one who was the worst, I'll never forget—God, he was awful. He was about my age almost. He was 20 years old as a senior, a smart rascal, and he gave me an awful time—harassment, and he beat my butt and all this sort of stuff. Well, night came along—do they still have that at the Academy—Hundredth Night, where they reverse roles and the plebes become upperclassmen?

Q: I think so.

Captain Cutter: Well, I went to work on that guy, and, "By God, I'm going to pay him back for all I got and build up a little velvet." I beat his butt unmercifully, and do you know what he did when I got done? He "spooned" on me.* A great guy. We

---
*"Spooning" was the practice of an upperclassman befriending a plebe. The friendship was created by a handshake.

Cutter #1 - 42

shook hands, and we were friends forever.

Q: What was his name?

Captain Cutter: John Francis Jacobs.* He was a Jewish fellow but just a hell of a nice guy. I never knew what happened to him. I never followed him after he left the Academy. He was younger than I was and smart as a whip.

Q: Along about that time, according to Admiral Loughlin's oral history, it was announced that only half of the class of 1933 would graduate.** Did this have an influence on your studying?

Captain Cutter: No. We didn't worry about it. It wasn't close enough to graduation. Then right after '33 graduated, in '34 it did not happen, and it didn't happen to us either. That wasn't a problem.

Q: Did you have any particular pressure to do well academically there?

---

*Midshipman John F. Jacobs, Jr., USN, class of 1932, born 26 December 1911.
**Rear Admiral C. Elliott Loughlin, USN(Ret.), class of 1933 at the Naval Academy. Loughlin's oral history is in the Naval Institute collection. Loughlin was a submarine skipper in World War II and was Cutter's immediate predecessor as director of athletics at the Naval Academy in the late 1950s.

Cutter #1 - 43

Captain Cutter: No.

Q: Were there any subjects that gave you more trouble than others?

Captain Cutter: Well, I wasn't good in math. I was never unsat, though, except my last semester. I suffered a broken eardrum in boxing, and it became infected. Before it was cleared up, my father died, and I had to go home for the funeral. The ear got worse during the ten days I was home, and when I came back to the Academy they put me in the hospital to get this ear infection squared away. There was a rule there that if you missed so many days, you could take a delayed exam; you didn't have to take the regular exam. I didn't lose that many days, so I had to take the regular exam in electrical engineering and in English. Well, I hadn't studied and, boy, did I flunk--bad. I came out of the hospital and the next day I took the exams. Then I got to work, and I'll never forget--I got a 3.6 in my electrical engineering the next time and three-something in the English exam. I thought, "Why in hell haven't I done this before? This is really kind of easy if you give it a little time." But I was rooming with a very, very brilliant guy named Wooster Taylor--what a guy he was.* His father was secretary to the Governor of California.

---
*Midshipman David Wooster Taylor, Jr., USN, who stood 34th of 442 graduates in the Naval Academy's class of 1935. Cutter stood 344th in the class.

He was also a by-liner with the San Francisco Chronicle, and I wished I could have met him. But Wooster was brilliant; he starred with no effort at all. He had gone to the University of California for two years before he came here, and anybody who spent the whole night studying was absolutely a dullard. So all he wanted to do was play cribbage. He would go through the lessons with me. He would brief me, but I didn't study them. He told me what I should know about it, but that isn't the way to learn, you know. You don't go into depth. He cost me a lot of numbers at the Academy, he really did. God, he was a great guy. I got through the Academy, and he probably helped me in that respect. But, poor Wooster, he later became an aviator, and he was killed during the war.* In those days, the academics were really very simple. They were really simple compared with what these kids are taking today at Annapolis. My goodness.

Q: So you didn't feel particularly challenged by them?

Captain Cutter: No, you really weren't. Something else, you didn't feel educated. We got a degree in electrical engineering that was a farce. I learned more in submarine school than I did at the Naval Academy about engineering. But what difference does that make? I'll never forget Admiral Holloway saying, "The

---
*Taylor was a lieutenant commander at the time he was killed in a plane crash at Quonset, Rhode Island, on 16 May 1944.

Cutter #1 - 45

mission of the Naval Academy is to preserve the traditions of the naval service."*

If you want to get an education, why don't you go to one of the Ivy [League] schools or Cal Tech or MIT? Naval Academy can't do any better than that; I think today they do just about as well, from what I have heard. But you need the customs and traditions of the naval service—very, very important, as I found out during the war.

Q: Wasn't the education really pretty much rote as opposed to stimulating?

Captain Cutter: It was; it was rote. You didn't have to think. You just had to memorize. Little things that you were interested in—for instance, the torpedo—we had to diagram it, draw a diagram of a torpedo, very complicated thing. That I got very interested in, very good. I always got 4.0 on that one, because I liked torpedoes. A good thing, because later on I got very familiar with them, you know. It met our needs at the time. It prepared our people for war, and this was what we were headed for. I hope they are preparing them for war today, and I hope to God we don't get into it. But, just in case, I hope that they are instilling in these people a devotion to duty and answering

---

*Rear Admiral James L. Holloway, Jr., USN, was Superintendent of the Naval Academy from 1947 to 1950.

the call.

Q: What about foreign languages? Did you study them?

Captain Cutter: That was a farce; that was terrible. We had a Spanish teacher who was a naval officer; he couldn't speak Spanish any more than I could. I'll never forget—the only thing I ever learned from him was, "No tengo tobacco, no tengo papel, no tengo dinero, Goddamnit to hell."

That's all I ever learned from him. We only had him for two months. I think we changed every two months and got a new prof. He didn't know anything about Spanish, and, of course, we didn't learn anything either. That was funny, but you picked up enough so that you could go to Spain and get along. They would all laugh at you, but you could make yourself known.

Q: There have been some people trying to draw a correlation between success in contact sports at the Naval Academy and success in the submarine force during the war. Do you agree with that sort of connection?

Captain Cutter: I don't know whether engaging in contact sports does it, but I think the person who is attracted to the contact sports is the kind of person who will be attracted to submarine duty. I think that is pretty accurate, because the good submariners that I knew—I mean the real good ones—were pretty rough guys.

Q: Two qualities that were very helpful were aggressiveness and fearlessness, and these might go along with the contact sports.

Captain Cutter: Yes, in other words, you stick your head in a buzz saw and hope for the best. Yes.

Q: With aviators, there was also a connection made but more than on pure athletic ability, as opposed to which sports.

Captain Cutter: I think it may be—I don't know about your fighter pilot; I think he's got to be a heck of an aggressive guy, and I think our very best aviators would be in that same category—the ones that I knew. Buzz Borries, Lou Bauer, Stan Ruehlow, Killer Kane, Jim Reedy—they were all pretty aggressive people, not worried too much about what's going to happen to them.* I mean, you take football. Today I look at these football players and think they are nuts. When I look back, 50 years ago I thought it was great. They will look back on it 30 years from now and wonder, "Why in the world did I do

---

*Fred Borries, Jr., who was a Naval Academy classmate of Cutter and a star in football, basketball, and baseball; Louis H. Bauer, class of 1935; Stanley E. Ruehlow, class of 1935; William R. Kane, class of 1933; James A. Reedy, class of 1933.

it?" Same way during the war; during the war, anybody who reached age 35 in submarines was taken out of command; 35 was too old, because then you begin to get some sense. If you have no sense, you do all those things, you know.

Q: So you have perhaps a diminished sense of self-preservation when you're younger.

Captain Cutter: That's right. I'll never forget a Marine who was a general during the war. And he was in command of the Marine detachment of the battleship Idaho--Johnny Beckett, a wonderful guy, All-America from the University of Oregon in his day.* On the Idaho we had 800 men on the battleship in those days; we had a Marine detachment of 40. I was coaching the football team. Six of my starters out of the 11 were Marines, and out of 800 and some the sailors provided the other four, because I was one of them. And I said, "How come these guys are so good?" They all had at least two years high school, which was a lot in those days. They had to be 5 feet, 9 inches tall, and they were really sharp.

"Well," I said, "how come the Marine Corps can do this when we've got people in the Navy that don't measure up?" You know, the average.

---

*Captain John W. Beckett, USMC, who was with Cutter in the USS Idaho (BB-42) during the mid-1930s.

"Well," he said, "we put a fancy uniform on them and we don't want anybody over 25 years of age, so we don't try to make them career minded. Enough of them will want to make it a career, and they'll never get married. The Marine Corps is their life; they'll stay in the Marine Corps and become the master sergeants. We get enough of those people to keep the Corps going, and these other fellows get out. Because a fellow over 25 is no good as a combat guy in the trenches, because he's got too much sense."

Well, that's kind of exaggerating a bit, but this point was pretty good. As you get older, you get more cautious. You consider the consequences; you don't feel like those guys who stormed the beaches at Normandy---God knows how they got them to do it, knowing that a lot of them were going to get killed. But they say, "It won't be me; it will be the other guy." So in they go.

Q: I think that's a general philosophy of life, whether you are driving a car or flying an airplane. You presume it's the other guy.

Captain Cutter: Yes, but when you get my age you are a lot more careful driving.

Q: Wasn't it unusual for you, as an officer, to play on one of the ship's athletic teams?

Captain Cutter: Not in those days. Every team had one officer, and only one officer could play at a time. They all had to have an officer playing on there, and generally the officer was the coach. And it was a pretty good football team. Some of these fellows were playing fleet football for 10-12 years, and they were good football players. We had a lot of fine competition and built up the _esprit de corps_ of those ships. Each ship had its song, and I remember the battleship _Idaho_, when I was aboard, our colors were orange and black. And the sailors would dye their hats orange. They wouldn't wear them through town, but when they would get to the game, they would put on their orange hats, just like a bunch of college kids or high school kids. It was good, it was real good for the _esprit de corps_.

Q: I read that you drew a comparison between training and coaching the _Idaho_ football team and later on with the submarine crew. What are the comparisons?

Captain Cutter: Well, football is getting into the details. The best football teams are those who pay attention to the details—blocking and tackling and timing and running the plays with precision and running the pass patterns properly, and their defense, and all that. It is a team effort; if one guy falls down the whole team suffers. Well, submarines—that is exactly what happens in a submarine. For instance, in a diving situation, the engineman has to shut off the engines at the diving alarm. The man on the hydraulic manifold in the control room closes the outboard induction valve by hydraulic power. When the engine room personnel hear the outboard valve close, they close the inboard inductions. The guys in the maneuvering room have to shift to the batteries for propulsion. The fellow in the control room opens the vents, and then he closes the vents after the submarine is submerged. All these things have to happen independently. Nobody is supervising them; nobody can be there. The officers have their own responsibilities. All these things have to be done and you have to count on the people doing them in the proper sequence. It's teamwork.*

Q: Ability to execute as trained.

Captain Cutter: As trained. For instance, when we would be on the deck, the deck in action, with men up there. You've got four lookouts, two officers of the deck; the captain will always be up there---a lot of people on the deck. We would sound the diving alarm, and we would be under in 50 seconds, and everybody would be below. Now that takes teamwork. When they go down the hatch, they don't just go down the ladder; they jump down, and the guy who jumps first better get the hell out of the way,

---

*This comparison by Cutter is in Clay Blair, Jr., *Silent Victory: The U.S. Submarine War Against Japan* (Philadelphia: J.B. Lippincott Company, 1975), page 518.

because another guy is coming down on top of him. It takes an awful lot of teamwork, a lot of training. Likewise, your torpedo fire control party—my goodness, it is just constant training. When we would start out on patrol, we would train all the way out—dummy exercises, you know. A paper thing—we would make up fire control problems and then throw them into our torpedo data computer, and the people would have to do what they would do when we got to the patrol area. When we hit the area, I passed the word over the loud speaker system, "From now on, any battle stations will be the real thing," and a cheer would go up; they were so tired of the training. They were real happy to have no more drills and know that they could settle down and know that the next time it would be for keeps, for real. That's where football helped. Now boxing wouldn't help you very much in that, but football did, very much.

Q: I think another parallel is that success breeds success. As you gain the victories in sports or in submarining, that gives you the confidence to become better for the next time.

Captain Cutter: Yes, it does. In the end, you get too confident. Our submarines—statistically, our skippers were lost and, of course, the poor boats were lost, too, on the first patrol or the fifth. On the first patrol, skippers lacked experience, but when you made your fifth patrol, you became careless; you had lost respect for the enemy. I think you are really a little neurotic. It's an awful strain.

Q: What about fatigue as a factor at that point?

Captain Cutter: Oh, yes, my goodness. You can't sleep. I lived on benzedrine; that's what I lived on. The doctors gave it to us. I mean the skippers could have benzedrine, which is a bad thing to take. I guess today it would be looked on as an amphetamine or something, but it did make you think quicker, kept you awake. There was one experience with a convoy; I was in the conning tower 82 hours and 33 minutes except for when I went down to the toilet--never changed clothes. I was in pajamas when I was called to the conning tower, and I was in pajamas when it was all over 82 hours later.* God, they must have smelled. It was a long, hard thing, and you just stick with it, but it leaves a mark on you. You get along on coffee and benzedrine. After this thing was over--we sank our last ship just at daylight--it wasn't quite daylight when we sank him. And, boy, I was exhausted. So I went down--we dove--and the crew was wiped out; they were exhausted too. This was off Truk somewhere. We dove and went down to 200 feet and leveled off, and everybody was secured

---

*This action began at 1719 on 28 January 1944, when the *Seahorse* picked up a contact in the Palau Islands, and ended at 0352 on 1 February 1944 when the submarine fired at and sank the last target. The submarine then headed for Pearl Harbor.

Cutter #1 - 54

except the bare watch just to keep the submarine going. I went into the wardroom, and a guy by the name of Frank Royal Fisher, after World War II became vice president of Arco up in Anchorage. He later was in charge of the environmental part of the Alaska pipeline, a very responsible position. He was just a lieutenant (j.g.) then from Colorado School of Mines. And he was sitting in there and said, "How about a game of acey-deucy, Captain?"

I started to play, but I couldn't think about acey-deucy. And the pharmacist's mate came in and wanted to know how I felt, and I said, "I don't feel very good. I can't relax and cannot sleep."

So he went back and got medicinal whiskey. He brought a pint of Old Crow whiskey up, and I drank it.

Q: The whole pint?

Captain Cutter: A pint, and it didn't do me a bit of good. I didn't get the least bit sleepy. I couldn't go to sleep, see, so then he gave me Nembutal or whatever--a sleeping pill. I guess he gave me a couple of those things. I don't remember what it was, but, anyway, he got scared and he said, "Captain, no more of this, try to go to sleep."

So I went into my cabin, laid down, and about an hour and a half later, I woke up with a terrible, terrible headache. I was lucky, really. I couldn't sit down. I walked back and forth,

Cutter #1 - 55

back and forth in the narrow passageway from the control room to the forward torpedo room, back and forth, back and forth, and I was just beside myself. Then it wasn't long after that, that night or something we got a dispatch ordering us to Wake Island. I had only been in the patrol area five days, and we had our torpedoes expended. We were to go to Wake Island to lifeguard for the Liberators, which was the B-24, C version. They were flying over to bomb Wake from Midway. They would come over about midnight every night, and, by golly, they came over, and we were there to pick up any people who were shot down, but none of them were shot down. We were there for about a week—nothing to do. It was just terrible. Finally, we were released and headed back to Pearl. I went on and made another patrol after that. Oh, yes, I was still in pretty good shape, but it takes a lot out of you.

Q: Did you feel any after-effects from that sort of experience in your health?

Captain Cutter: Gosh, I don't think so.

We got in from my fourth run and Rear Admiral Babe Brown—a wonderful guy; he was a good friend of mine.* He was graduate manager in the athletic department for football when I was playing there, so I knew him then. He was an admiral and was

---
*Rear Admiral John H. Brown, USN.

training officer, so when I came in to Pearl after my last run he said, "I think you need a little leave." I hadn't been home for 13 months and he said, "I think you'd better go home and see Frannie."

And I said, "That seems a good idea to me." So he sent me back there, with no intentions of ever having me come back, but he didn't tell me that.

Q: And let Weary Wilkins take over?*

Captain Cutter: Yes. He said, "Let Weary Wilkins take the boat, and then you come back and you can take it over." He had no intentions of this. Because they sent a PCO out, Harry Greer, and Greer took command after Wilkins left.**

Q: He saved you from that fifth patrol.

Captain Cutter: Yes, and I might not have come back, because you get very careless. You don't give a damn; you get so cocky you think you're---you just lose perspective and don't give the enemy any credit. That's foolish.

Q: It reaches a point of overconfidence.

---
*Commander Charles W. Wilkins, USN.
**Commander Harry H. Greer, Jr., USN. PCO--prospective commanding officer.

Cutter #1 - 57

Captain Cutter: That's right. You are overconfident and sort of, you don't care. I can remember originally, when I first got command I was very cautious really. We went in, but one time off Saipan in our first patrol my radar operator said, "There's a destroyer alongside the target."

Well, there was another ship beyond that, so I bypassed that ship and went over to the next column. But that wasn't a destroyer alongside, it was what they call side lobes. You get another loop alongside. It was not another ship; there was just that one ship there. Later on, I wouldn't have paid any attention to that, but then I was a little more cautious and had another opening, so I took after that one. As I told you in that letter I wrote, I saw the naval aviators performing in a very heroic manner, and I think they were kind of off their rockers to do what they did. Jeez, they were a brave bunch of men.

Q: What were the qualities you admired in Babe Brown?

Captain Cutter: Well, he was just really a marvelous judge of men. When he talked to you, he always talked to you as to an equal. You didn't feel that you were talking to God or an admiral. He was just a wonderful fellow. After the war, I played golf with him. He was commandant up there in Portsmouth, so we played golf. He had the Secretary of the Navy, and a guy by the name of Peter Fuller who was an excellent golfer. And the

Secretary of the Navy had won an open amateur golf championship in New Hampshire—John L. Sullivan, a topflight golfer.* He and Peter were playing, and Admiral Brown and I were going to play, and I didn't want to play. What happened, we were going over to Martha's Vineyard. The Naval Academy football team was over there practicing. Tom Hamilton was coach, and we were going to fly over there and watch them practice.**

It was socked in, and we couldn't go, so what are you going to do? The Secretary of the Navy was up there with his plane and stuff, so we'll play golf. I said, "Admiral, I haven't played golf. I never was any good and haven't played any golf since God knows when."

"Oh, yes, you can," and all that sort of stuff.

So we went out and played golf, and I got 135, I'll never forget, and they didn't count them all. It was terrible. The Babe was needling me the whole time, and I thought, "You son of a bitch, you're going to pay for this." So I went out to the Portsmouth Country Club, and I took some lessons. We were there for overhaul, and I had a lot of time. One day I called him up and wanted to know if he was playing golf any more?

"Yes, what's your handicap?"

---

*John L. Sullivan was Secretary of the Navy from September 1947 to May 1949.
**Captain Thomas J. Hamilton, USN, head football coach for the 1946 and 1947 seasons and director of athletics at the Naval Academy from 1946 to 1948. Hamilton had also been coach previously in the 1930s when Cutter was a midshipman and a player for the Naval Academy football team.

And I said, "Well, I play about like you do, Admiral. I'm playing pretty fair."

"Like hell you are." You know, that sort of stuff.

Anyway, we got a game going up. We went out and played, and I had a real good game. But I'll never forget on about the 17th hole--350 yard, par 4 or something. He got a drive off and I got a drive off and I was well ahead of him, so he took a seven-iron out to hit, and I said, "Admiral, I don't think you've got enough club." And he went to over-hit the damn thing, and he took a lot of turf and the ball just flipped out there a little ways.

He said, "I could throw this damn club farther than that," and he did. I laughed so hard, I hit mine over the green and into the shrubs and stuff, but anyway we got back. So I beat him pretty bad.

He had his driver, so he was providing transportation. We drove back to his house, where my car was, and I was going to drive on home.

"Come on in and have a drink."

So I went in and had a drink, and Kate, a wonderful gal, his wife, was upstairs. When he poured a drink, it was an honest-to-God drink, three to four ounces, so we had a couple of those things, and finally he said, "You son of a bitch, what have you been doing?"

And I said, "Admiral, you humiliated me, and I didn't like it." He could understand that. He was a great guy.

Q: I think he must have been particularly perceptive—you say he was good at evaluating people—to know when it was your time to leave from the patrol.

Captain Cutter: Oh, absolutely. He wanted me to get back and take a rest. You see, they felt at that time—for instance, I just heard when I was up there at the Seahorse reunion in Hartford, Connecticut, last August—that some of the boys who had come on the ship didn't want to go out, because they felt I had used up my luck. People didn't want to stick with somebody who had been at it too long.

Q: Well, you got off the Pompano in time.*

Captain Cutter: Yes, I did. Of course, that ship—her test depth was 252 feet, and they were the first of the fleet class; they were not good submarines. I don't think the enemy—maybe they hit a mine or something. I don't know. They had a good boat, good skipper, good exec, an overall good ship.

Q: You said you had had some contact with Brown back at the Naval Academy. What was the nature of that?

---

*Cutter was detached from the USS Pompano (SS-181) less than a year before she was lost with all hands.

Cutter #1 - 61

Captain Cutter: When I was a midshipman, he was graduate manager of football. That's where I knew him, because he was the officer representative for the football team—that's what it amounted to—so I saw a lot of him. I had a lot of respect for Admiral Brown; he was a very good man.

Q: What about your own football career at the Naval Academy? We haven't really gotten into that too much.

Captain Cutter: When I was a plebe, I played fullback, because I was pretty fast. Hell, I wasn't a fullback. I was too lumbering. I hadn't played enough. And I punted. I was a kicker, and I played fullback. So then, in my youngster year, I was center. You see, in those days you had a six-man line, a fullback in the center backed up the line, and he had two halfbacks and a safety man. In football there was no imagination in those days. So because I played fullback and backed up the line as plebe, they put me playing center and backing up the line as a sophomore. I played quite a bit, because the first stringer would get knocked out frequently—Butch Harbold.* He was a good football player. He was a boxer too, and later on they wouldn't let him box any more, because he was susceptible to concussion. So he would get knocked out and they would hold up fingers—how many fingers was it, and he didn't know—so then I

---
*Midshipman Robert P. Harbold, Jr., USN, class of 1934.

would go in. So I played quite a bit, although I wasn't much good. Then we had a fellow named Killer Kane who graduated.* He was a good football player--a tackle--so they moved me to tackle to take his place. I started playing tackle, and I didn't catch onto it until the season was well under way. It's just an entirely different ball game when you have never played defensive tackle before. I didn't distinguish myself at all, I don't think, but then the next year, my senior year, I came back, was older and had more confidence or something like that, and I did all right.

Q: Do you think the change in coaches had an effect?

Captain Cutter: No, because we had the same coach. Rip Miller was the head coach my first two years on the varsity, and he was a line coach my last year.** And the head coach was Tommy Hamilton and he never interfered with Rip, so Rip was my coach--same coach, and a tremendous guy.***

Q: Both of those were well known in the history of Navy football. What could you say about your recollections of them?

---

*Midshipman William R. Kane, USN, class of 1933, who became a top-notch naval aviator in World War II.
   **Edgar E. Miller, head football coach at the Naval Academy for the seasons of 1931, 1932, and 1933.
   ***Lieutenant (junior grade) Thomas J. Hamilton, USN, Naval Academy football coach for the seasons 1934, 1935, and 1936.

Captain Cutter: Well, there is only one Rip Miller—a marvelous human being—most of all, that. As a football coach, I don't know how good he was. I wasn't qualified to say, but he certainly taught me a lot as a lineman, because that's what he was. He was a tackle, and he was an All-American tackle.

Q: He was from Notre Dame.

Captain Cutter: Yes, he was in the class of '25, I think, at Notre Dame.

Q: Played under Rockne.*

Captain Cutter: Yes, with Harry Stuhldreher and Miller and Crowley and Layden. He was one of the seven mules.** A great guy. He is still going strong. I called him tonight.

Q: What about Hamilton as a coach?

Captain Cutter: Innovative and a wonderful leader, a very good

---
*Knute Rockne, the legendary football coach at Notre Dame from 1918 to 1930. His overall record during those seasons was 105-12-5.
**Notre Dame's famous backfield in the early 1920s was known as the "Four Horsemen:" Harry Stuhldreher, quarterback; Don Miller, right halfback; Jim Crowley, left halfback; Elmer Layden, fullback. The linemen who played in front of the "horsemen" were nicknamed the "Seven Mules."

coach in those days. Tom was an excellent coach; he had a staff that was, I guess, adequate. We were third in the nation that year behind Minnesota and Pittsburgh.

Q: That team turned around during your tenure there, from a losing team to a winning one.

Captain Cutter: Yes, well we did, and I think a lot of it was due to Tom. He changed our system and we went from the Notre Dame system, which we never should have used. Rip put that in, because he came from Notre Dame. So we went to Tom's, which was basically a single wing. He understood that and we were more adapted for it and then had Buzz Borries, who was probably the best back I ever saw.* He was absolutely fabulous, a tremendous football player. The rest were a bunch of little guys. I was the biggest by far. The next heaviest man weighed 185—think of that. Today I would be considered too small to make a freshman team as a tackle.

Q: What was your weight at that point?

Captain Cutter: 225, but still that is not very big today, not for a tackle.

---

*Midshipman Fred Borries, Jr., USN, an All-America football player.

Q: A couple of your submarine cohorts were on that team—Dusty Dornin and K.G. Schacht.*

Captain Cutter: That's right—Dusty Dornin and K.G. Schacht and Dave Zabriskie, who was a very good football player; he was lost in the Harder. No, it wasn't the Harder. I forgot which one. I saw him off on patrol, his last patrol.**

Q: Harder was Sam Dealey's boat.***

Captain Cutter: Yes, Sam Dealey's. Sam Dealey was a topflight skipper. He and I left Pearl Harbor together en route to our patrol areas. We went to Johnston Island and refueled. He was going to Truk, and I was going into the East China Sea. We trained together all the way until he broke off and headed for Truk. We worked day and night training. Boy, he was a taskmaster. And his crew was trained in teamwork, and so was mine. When I went back to the States from the Seahorse, I received orders to command the Requin. I had the new construction training school for four months, because the Requin was not yet ready. Our job was to take the men reporting in from

---

*Midshipman Robert E. Dornin, USN, and Midshipman Kenneth G. Schacht, USN.
**David Zabriskie, Jr., was lost as a lieutenant commander while in command of the USS Herring (SS-233), which was sunk 1 June 1944.
***Commander Samuel D. Dealey, USN, was in command of the USS Harder (SS-257) when she was lost on 24 August 1944.

the fleet and from submarine school, and assign them to the submarines. So whenever I got a *Seahorse* man coming in during that period, I put him on the *Requin*. There was a woman up there who was the secretary of the skipper of the school. Helen Tolman was her name. She was a good friend of my wife's and mine, too, so I said, "Helen, give me the names of the guys who graduated at the top in submarine class, enlisted men."

So she did, so I picked them for my ship. So I had a great crew. We went down to Panama for training and Johnny Johns was the training officer down there.* We were the 53rd submarine that he had trained in Panama, and he said it was by far the best submarine that he had seen come through there. We were ready to go. Then we got out in Pearl Harbor and were loaded and ready to go on patrol, and the war ended. I'll never forget--two kids came back. They called me about 2:00 o'clock in the morning when they got the word. I went back in the crew's mess and was having a cup of coffee with the guys and talking about the war being over and so on. I'll never forget--I didn't feel the relief I thought I would feel, because there was a nagging thing about the Russians. Isn't that strange? They were our allies, too, but somehow, for some reason, I just had this feeling about the Russians: "It isn't over; it isn't done." Anyway, these kids came back, and one of them--tears coming down his face.

---
*Captain John G. Johns, USN.

And I said, "For God's sake, what's the matter?"

He said, "I can't get a submarine combat pin." Isn't that something? He said, "It's been two and a half years since I enlisted to get into a submarine to make a war patrol, and now the war is over."

I said, "Boy, you are lucky. You are alive."

Q: Did you feel a sense of frustration at not getting another crack at the Japanese?

Captain Cutter: I didn't want it, frankly. I was happy to be out of it. There was nothing out there. Our mission was to go out and bombard with rockets. They had loaded our bow---they gave me two 8-inch guns; two 40-mm. guns; eight .50-caliber machine guns, and rocket launchers up on the bow for 5-inch shells. We were going into a place on the Island of Hokkaido which was an operating base for patrol boats and bombard it. Isn't that silly? Our submarines had little else to do; there was so little ship traffic.

Q: Ned Beach felt great frustration, because after all the time he had been Dornin's exec in the *Trigger*, he finally got his own command, and the war ended.

Captain Cutter: Ned was great, and I'll tell you, everybody that he served as exec did very, very well as skipper--that says something.* I'll tell you, having an exec--I just came from Cincinnati where this officer--he wasn't an exec--I told you about Parks in the Pompano. Well, we had a fellow by the name of Pleatman.** He came aboard the Pompano and Parks, God rest his soul, told him that he didn't want him aboard and he would have him off in a month, for two reasons--one, he was a reserve; two, he was a Jew.*** I couldn't believe that Lew Parks would say that, but Ralph Pleatman told me that he did two or three days ago, and I am sure he did. But Parks came to really love that guy, and when Parks died about six months ago, Pleatman went from Cincinnati to Arlington to attend his funeral.**** It was really very touching.

Out in the Pompano, Pleatman was very aggressive, and he was--I was the TDC operator. That was the guts of the fire control system, and he was my assistant. Well, he was sharp as a tack. He caught on to that thing; his mind was really something.

When I got command of the Seahorse, the skipper had recommended me for disqualification for submarines, and I had

---

*Lieutenant Commander Edward L. Beach, USN, was executive officer for Commander Robert E. Dornin, USN, in the USS Trigger (SS-237) and Commander George L. Street III, USN, in the USS Tirante (SS-420). Dornin was credited with ten sinkings during the war, and Street won the Medal of Honor.
**Lieutenant (junior grade) Ralph F. Pleatman, USNR.
***Lieutenant Commander Lewis S. Parks, USN, first commanding officer of the Pompano. Parks eventually became a rear admiral; he is referred to frequently during the course of this oral history.
****Admiral Parks died 26 April 1982.

written a letter to the Secretary of the Navy putting him on report for cowardice, which was—I shouldn't have done that. That wasn't his problem; it was something else. Anyway, that's the way I felt, because he put me under hack. I came back from patrol, and I was under hack, because he said I was nuts. All I did was say what Parks had done. Parks was tremendous as a submarine skipper. So we got into Midway, and were going to refit there, and the first piece of paper that came aboard was a dispatch ordering me—this Brown did this, Captain Brown, ordering me to relieve this fellow as skipper.*

Q: Don McGregor?**

Captain Cutter: Yes. I don't want to be hard on him, because he was not a coward. That's what a lot of people thought. It wasn't that at all. He was a very conservative person; he was too damn old to be a submarine skipper; that's all. He had been mixed up in sonar, and he believed that any time he ran into a sonar screen, they would pick you up, because he believed in the equipment. He wouldn't attack a screen with active sonar. We didn't run into any that didn't have active sonar, so we didn't

---

*Captain John H. Brown, USN.
**Lieutenant Donald McGregor, USN, was the first commanding officer of the Seahorse. He made one patrol in the boat, leaving Pearl Harbor on 3 August 1943 and winding up at Midway Island on 27 September. Cutter then took command, and she began her second war patrol on 20 October.

attack them. Thirty-three convoy contacts, and we didn't attack any of them--convoys. Well, when I got command, the crew who had heard him say that I was crazy and that the Pompano was a hooligan ship and that they didn't do the things that this crazy exec said they did and all this sort of stuff--he was under strain. Well, I had a morale problem, big, a big morale problem. So Admiral Lockwood came out to inspect Midway, and he had been my seamanship instructor when I was a midshipman. He was a commander then. He asked me to see him, and I caught up with him in the library. We were playing softball, and I came in all sweaty with just a pair of trunks on and tennis shoes. The admiral was in the library, "Slade, is there anything I can do for you?"

Well, Dave White, who was earlier skipper of the Plunger, had come through Midway in his new command, the Cero, about two or three days before, having left Pearl four days prior to that.* Dave said, "Ralph Pleatman is back on the relief crew with Savvy Huffman and is very unhappy. He wants to get the hell out of there."**

"Oh," I thought, "By God, he does. Well, I think he'd like to go to sea with me, because we were in the Pompano together."

---

*Commander David C. White, USN, who was first commanding officer when the USS Cero (SS-225) went into commission in July 1943 and began her first war patrol from Pearl Harbor in late September. White got to know Pleatman during the prewar period when the Pompano and Plunger were in the same submarine division.
**Commander Leon J. Huffman, USN, Commander Submarine Division 42.

So, just as if a bell had rung, I said to the admiral, "Yes, there is something. I would like to have Ralph Pleatman for one war patrol. He is on the relief crew of Savvy Huffman in Pearl."

The admiral turned to his aide and sent a dispatch. Well, about two days later at 6:30 in the morning the door of the Gooney Bird Hotel room, where I was, flew open. A briefcase hit me in the chest. "You son of a bitch."

It's my fourth officer reporting for duty. He had gotten orders between the time White left and the time he got the orders back there to go back to new construction and he had been married three months when they sent him back to submarine school. That was all he had been married, and he was anxious to get back to his bride.

I said, "What the hell's wrong?"

Then he told me what had happened.

I said, "Good God. Well, anyway, Ralph, here you are."

So I took him aboard; we had three Naval Academy graduates, one out of '39, one out of '37, and one out of '43, who was pretty junior.* But Pleatman came into the force in '41, just before the war. Well, we already had our assignment of officers, and the only place for him to sleep was in my cabin---upper bunk---so I put him in there. Right away, the other officers saw that

---

*Lieutenant E.C. Linden, USN (1939), Lieutenant Commander J.P. Currie, USN (1937), and Lieutenant (junior grade) W.A. Budding, Jr., USN (1943).

we were real good friends. And I made him TDC operator, displacing the guy from the class of '39 who had been TDC operator all during the war. It was kind of tough to do, but we were playing for keeps and I wanted a guy that I had worked with. So I put Pleatman in as torpedo data computer operator. Obviously, he was a very good friend of mine, but I didn't worry about it. We got out on patrol, and the first thing that we ran into were some fishing boats---trawlers. They had about 15 or 20 men aboard, pretty good size ships, and we were told to knock them off because they were supposed to be serving a dual thing---fishing and also outpost. This was after the Doolittle raid, so they had all these boats out there with radios, supposedly.* I didn't like the idea of attacking what I thought was an unarmed ship. Pleatman came down there with an operation order, and the first paragraph said, "You shall attack all enemy ships encountered with either gunfire or torpedoes." "You shall"--imperative.

And he said, "You've got to do it, Captain." Okay, so we did. We knocked one off that day. The next day we knocked off another one. And the third day another one, just before sunset. And there were no survivors.

It was just too much, and I said, "Goddamn it, I'm not going

---

*During the B-25 bombing attack against Tokyo in mid-April 1942 by Lieutenant Colonel James Doolittle and his Army Air Forces pilots, small Japanese patrol boats forced the planes to take off earlier than planned from the USS *Hornet* (CV-8) because of the possibility that they had radioed warnings to Japan.

Cutter #1 - 73

to do this any more."*

So then we moved into the area where we were firing torpedoes and it was sort of forgotten. When I got back from the patrol I ran into my very first skipper, whom I had for a very short time—Bob Rice—a wonderful guy, and I said, "What do you do, Bob, with these things?"**

He said, "I let them alone."

So I went up to see Admiral Lockwood, routine—every time we came in off patrol, we went up to see the boss. I said, "Admiral, I sank three of these things out there with gunfire. And, jeez, it was just murder. We went aboard one before we sank it, and there were 15- and 16-year-old kids aboard. So what should you do?"

He said, "Slade, let your conscience be your guide." Hell of an answer, isn't it?

"Well," I said, "I'm not going to attack any more."

Q: That's a modification, then, of the op order.

Captain Cutter: Yes, that's right—let your conscience be your

---

*This incident occurred in late October 1943, during Cutter's first patrol in the Seahorse after taking over command from Lieutenant Commander McGregor. It is discussed in Clay Blair's Silent Victory, pages 518-519.
**Commander Robert H. Rice, USN, who was skipper of the USS S-30 when Cutter served briefly in that boat right after submarine school.

Cutter #1 - 74

guide. So we never bothered any more. I never fired a gun again.

Anyway, we got out on patrol and Ralph Pleatman was marvelous. His attitude was always, "Fuck 'em, let's go."

He was something, so I said, "Look, Ralph, you can't say 'Fuck em' in front of the enlisted men like this."

So he said, "I can say 'fuke 'em', goddamn it."

So I said, "Okay, you can say 'fuke 'em.'"

So he would, "Fuke 'em, let's go."*

We came in from that patrol and this was the best patrol in the war up to that time; there were others that were better later but that was a good one. The quartermasters had made a pennant up, and it had "Fuke 'em" on it and they attached it to a raised periscope as we came into port. Well, Pleatman did a magnificent job. He just turned the crew around, you know, because he was just as aggressive as hell and he supported everything I wanted him to do---tremendous help. I saw him last week out in Cincinnati. He later became chairman of the board of the United Shoe Company, a multimillionaire; he would succeed at anything, you know. He was a Jew, you know, and he made Parks become no longer anti-Semitic, which was real good.

Q: How and why did you draw a distinction between the obvious

---

*Pleatman altered the pronunciation so that "fuke" rhymed with "spook."

killing of people with gunfire, as opposed to the obvious killing with torpedoes?

Captain Cutter: Well, when we sank a ship with torpedoes, we were sinking a target, and that hurt the enemy. And I don't think that sinking those fishing boats hurt the enemy. It was just hurting some people, the few fish that they were going to take in to feed some people that were already starving to death or that were hard up. But it wasn't hurting their war effort. I didn't think it would contribute anything to the war effort. If you sink a ship, you do, particularly in the traffic lanes going to Saipan and Southeast Asia down to New Guinea and the Philippines—that hurt.

Q: So you were opposed to the unnecessary taking of lives?

Captain Cutter: Yes, that's right. It's pretty tough. You see people in the water, and you want to pick them up but you can't. We did, however, generally pick up one for intelligence purposes. They were a menace, those people. They were fanatics, and you were always worried about them sabotaging in one way or another. Whenever we went in to attack when we had a Japanese aboard, we always handcuffed him to a bunk so that he couldn't do anything to mess us up. Submarines were very vulnerable to internal sabotage.

Q: Or even personal attacks against individuals on board if he had not been restrained?

Captain Cutter: I never worried about that.

Q: You thought that would have been suicidal for him?

Captain Cutter: Yes, I mean they had no weapons, and, my God, the ones I saw, they were little bitty fellows; they weren't very big. As a matter of fact, they all became very friendly. The crew sort of made pets out of them. You know, something to do, a novelty, talking sign language and stuff. We always brought one back, always got one.

Q: You were talking about Dealey. Do you think he got to the point of overconfidence?

Captain Cutter: Sam was—yes, I do; I really do. He was a very brave man, very good. He was good, an excellent approach officer. I found that out on our way out there with him, but when you start going after destroyers firing down-the-throat shots at 1,200 to 1,500 yards, you are going to get it.*

---

*A down-the-throat shot came when a submarine and destroyer were on the same course or reciprocal courses. The submarine fired torpedoes directly at the destroyer, the idea being that if the destroyer turned to either port or starboard, she would catch a torpedo broadside.

Q: A little too macho?

Captain Cutter: Yes, a little too much. It is much better to let them go and knock off a merchantman or a tanker or something that will hurt the enemy a lot more than losing that patrol boat. These weren't big destroyers; these were patrol boats. But Sam was that way. God, he was good and Mush Morton was another one.* So was Dick O'Kane.** And there were some others that were that way, but they weren't as proficient. They weren't as good approach officers. I won't name them, but I admire them very, very much, but they didn't do too well, because they weren't skillful.

Q: There is also the element of luck, which can't be controlled.

Captain Cutter: You can say that again. You betcha, you bet. Admiral Lockwood once said to me, "You know, Slade, I wouldn't be surprised to see you run into a target off Pearl Harbor."

I was lucky as hell running into ships. And that's another thing--a lot of guys just didn't have the opportunity. They didn't get the targets.

Tony Gallaher, who was one of the top skippers out of the

---
*Commander Dudley W. Morton, USN, who was skipper of the USS Wahoo (SS-238).
**Commander Richard H. O'Kane, USN, who won the Medal of Honor for his achievements as skipper of the USS Tang (SS-306).

class of '33--I went on war patrol with him.* We were in a wolf pack. I was in the area seven days, torpedoes gone and heading for home. Poor Tony stayed there for 30 days and asked for a week's extension, still had torpedoes. Nothing came through. Just purely luck.

Q: Well, we jumped forward from your Naval Academy football career--the '34 season had to be a highlight in your life, I would think.

Captain Cutter: Yes, it was. Of course, the Army game meant a lot to a lot of people. It did to me too, because my father was there; it was the only game he ever saw me play. We won it 3-0. We were all disappointed. On a dry day, we would have beaten Army four touchdowns. We had a real good football team, but it was muddy and we had that one chance. There really wasn't any pressure on me when I kicked the field goal, because I thought we were going to run up a score on them, but then we just never did. So finally that was the only score.**

Q: Could you describe that moment and the situation that led up

---

*Lieutenant Commander Antone R. Gallaher, USN, put the USS Bang (SS-385) in commission as her first skipper and took her on patrol in the Pacific. In five war patrols, he was credited with sinking eight ships with a combined tonnage of 20,181.
**The game was played 1 December 1934 at Philadelphia; Cutter's 20-yard field goal came in the first quarter.

to it?

Captain Cutter: Yes. We had really a great punter by the name of Bill Clark, a great kicker.* He won more games for us than anybody else, even more than Buzz [Borries] did, because he put the enemy in a bad hole so often. This particular time, he kicked one for the out of bounds, and Dusty Dornin was down under it and knocked it out on the one-yard line. And Army had to kick out, and when they kicked, I got my hand on the ball. I didn't block it, but stopped it quite a bit. It only got to about the 20-yard line and we got the ball, and, hell, I guess we ended up with the fourth and nine; we couldn't advance it. So Dick Pratt came back and said, "Cutter back to place kick."**

I thought he was out of his mind in the damn mud, and I said, "Time out."

The mud was really something. So we got down there. We built a little mound and patted it down. The water got out of it, so we had a little something to put the ball on. He put the ball down. Clark was also the holder--a placekick is 75% the holder, really. I am not saying that to downplay the importance of the kicker, but if the guy doesn't get the ball down right, I don't care who the placekicker is, he's not going to make it. It's got to be exactly where that point is, because the kicker

---
*Midshipman William C. Clark, USN, a classmate of Cutter's.
**Midshipman Richard R. Pratt, USN, class of 1936, eventually a rear admiral.

starts forward--you watch a pro game, they do it, too. Before the ball is down there, they are going forward to kick, and if the ball isn't there where they think it's going to be, it's going to be off one way or the other. He was very good at that, and the ball went over. Anyway, after the game was over, Tommy Hamilton and Rip Miller had been sitting there together, and we put in a fake placekick just for the Army game, and they were sure this was what it was.

Q: Who was sure?

Captain Cutter: The coaches, the Navy coaches. You see, they didn't send in plays in those days. You couldn't. So they were sure it was a fake placekick--the play they had been working on for the past two weeks. Then, when they saw I was going to kick it, they said, "The goddamned fool." [This is what they told me later they said.] "He's going to kick it!"

And then when it went over, "Great." And we were heroes.

This came from Rip. Rip can tell it a lot better than I can; he is a great storyteller. Anyway, it was Dick Pratt's decision, and the kick went over. Before the game, I had been practicing placekicks, and Dick Pratt would hold for me in practice before the game, because Clark was the punter and he was punting. I didn't make a damn one, not even from points after--the damn mud, you know--and I had on mud cleats, they are about that long. I went in between the warm-up period and the start of the game and I told the equipment manager, Red Rasmussen, "Jesus, take these things off and put on regular cleats on my right shoe." And they did, because, you know, you groove a kick like a golf swing, and my cleats were catching the dirt as I kicked. When they put the short ones on, so that I had long ones on the left foot and short ones on the right foot, I was able to kick it. Hell, it went way up into the stands. That damn thing would have gone from 40 yards out.

Q: I would think that having kicked that field goal, after Navy had been without beating Army so long, made you a real hero throughout the Navy.

Captain Cutter: I think it did--13 years and we hadn't won a game. But you know, later on, when I was in public information in the Navy Department, we had an incident happen, and Time magazine wrote up this article about me, and it said, "Captain Slade Cutter, who in 1934 kicked the field goal that defeated Army ..."*

This had to do with a professional thing, and this put me in

---

*The quote was in an article titled "Full Speed Astern," Time, 18 January 1954, page 20. The sentence read, in part, "A Parks aide and fellow submariner, Commander Slade Cutter, onetime Annapolis football hero (he kicked the field goal that beat Army 3-0 in 1934) was the direct source of the leak. . ." Cutter discusses the Time magazine incident in detail later in the oral history.

the category of a "jock"---you know, "this dumb fool." I ran into that a little bit. I never felt like any hero or anything like that. I wasn't. But it made a lot of people in the Navy happy, and we won the football game, and for 13 years the Navy hadn't won. You know, last year, I thought of that when I went to the Army-Navy football game. And in the last quarter, Army was playing their hearts out, and they were playing better than Navy was, and, you know, I was pulling for Army.*

Q: I'm surprised to hear you say that.

Captain Cutter: I'll tell you why. None of those cadets in the stands had seen Army win, and here their team was playing their hearts out against a much superior team. Navy had a lot better football team than Army last year, but breaks went against them, and they were worrying more about the dance after the game, I think, more than they were worrying about the game. This happens. And Army was hungry, and they outplayed them. It means a great deal, I think, which it doesn't in a lot of schools, but it does at the Academy. To go through four years without seeing your team win is pretty tough, but we avoided that my last year at the Academy, and that made me something of a hero, I guess. But I never thought much of it.

---

*The 1981 Army-Navy football game wound up a 3-3 tie.

Cutter #1 - 83

Q: I would think, then, as you proceeded out into the fleet that would give you a name recognition over most junior officers?

Captain Cutter: Oh, sure. Another thing I think gives you a name--recognition wherever you go, too, is your name. If you have an odd name--think of that, you know. Who forgets Slade Cutter? The name is different. I've run into that more than I have run into anything else, really. A lot of time I'll call, and I hear, "Is that really your name?"

And I say, "Yes, that's my name."

The only Slade I knew was a black, light heavyweight fighter from somewhere, whose last name was Slade--about ten years ago.

Q: What about the training cruises when you were a midshipman? What do you recall of those?

Captain Cutter: Well, they were, of course, very enjoyable. Not much to recall about them really. We made one trip to Galveston, Texas. That was during the Depression, and they didn't want to spend the oil, I guess, so they didn't send us over to Europe. But in '34 we went to Europe, to England, to Villefranche, and to Naples, Italy. It was a great cultural experience for us, and we certainly had a wonderful time and learned a lot. Rip Miller was with us on that cruise; we met the Pope, and Billy Clark held his right foot out for the Pope to bless--all this sort of stuff, kid stuff, but we had a great time.*

Q: Did religion play a fairly large part in your life at that point?

Captain Cutter: No. I was reared as a Methodist, you know, and anybody who was a Catholic--that was a dirty word--terrible, looking back on it. That's one thing--you got at the Naval Academy, and you just forget all about whether you are a Catholic, Jew, or Protestant; it doesn't make any difference. That's one great thing about the Academy that I suppose still holds there.

Q: I guess it stayed with Parks a little longer.

Captain Cutter: It did. Of course, you see, with Parks, his situation--I don't know where he got the anti-Semitic viewpoint. I was surprised to hear Ralph Pleatman say that. I never knew that Parks felt that way. I knew how he felt about reserves; he had no use for them. And the reason for it was it took Parks 11 years to make lieutenant commander from lieutenant. He made it in '39, was of the class of '25--he was 14 years out of the Naval Academy before he made lieutenant commander. And the reason for

---

*Clark wanted his foot blessed, of course, because he was the football punter, as mentioned earlier.

it was, after World War I, you had a lot of people that stayed in reserves, and in those days your promotion was not based on selection until you got to be commander; it was based on seniority. So, I don't care how good you were, you just had to wait until the guys ahead of you were phased out before you could be promoted. The younger Naval Academy officers deeply resented these people. I'll never forget, one time during a battleship short-range battle practice, I was observing in the <u>Mississippi</u>. I was from the <u>Idaho</u> and observing officer in a <u>Mississippi</u> turret. And their turret officer was a lieutenant, a senior lieutenant, ex-reserve, and, my God, they couldn't even get the shells out of the gun. I mean, they had so many safety precautions that they couldn't shoot—not within any time limits. It was just ridiculous, and the reason for it was, according to the senior members of our inspection party, if this guy didn't do anything, he wouldn't make a mistake. He didn't want to make any mistakes, so he just didn't do anything—that philosophy. Which is something that is kind of drilled into Naval Academy graduates, as a matter of fact, when you first get out. You pay a price for everything you do wrong as a midshipman, and then you read all the court-martial proceedings—we used to at least—in the Courts and Boards course we had there. And any time a ship went aground, the captain got a court-martial, and, of course, everybody in the watch that had anything to do with it got hurt. Careers were ruined on something for which you weren't responsible. Of course, they are responsible, because they are in charge of the training. So the Navy isn't wrong, but the system promotes a hesitancy to do something without proper authority; I think that's what it is. If you are out—during the war I ran into this a lot with Naval Academy graduates. When they first come out to the submarine force, before they found out how we felt about it, they would always say, "Captain to the bridge." They didn't want to make a decision until the captain got up there. Sometimes, you worried that there might not be enough time. They might just wait too long. Your reserve—you never had to worry about him; he would do something. It might be wrong, but he would do it, and they didn't make too many mistakes. Of course, they were very smart. They were all highly selected. They were all tops of their class, while the Naval Academy people, the Navy assumed that because they were graduates of the Naval Academy, they were superior people. I guess that's all right, but they were put into competition with people who were academically superior to them, people who weren't inhibited by this "making a mistake" syndrome. They would just go ahead and do it, and like Pleatman, would say, "Fuck 'em all, boys, let's go."

Q: Now you were exceptional then, being a Naval Academy graduate who didn't feel inhibited in this way.

Cutter #1 - 87

Captain Cutter: Well, that's because I had been out long enough, other than submarine. I'm talking about your fresh-caught graduate. Listen, my Naval Academy graduates after four war patrols were tremendous. It was only at the beginning, but this we had to live through. Every war patrol, I would know when I went out on patrol I had one chance in five of not coming back--- based upon statistics, and so you have a couple of people aboard that you can't trust, because all you know is they are going to send for you. You know they'll do that, but maybe an emergency arises that there is not that much time. So it bothered me. These reservists who were smart and weren't inhibited this way, they would go ahead and make a decision. As I say, most times, they were right. Like the one person I remember saying, "If you make a mistake, for God's sake, make a big one." Do something. There is something to that.

Q: On these cruises that you found broadening in the sense of traveling--this was really also your first taste of the Navy, wasn't it?

Captain Cutter: Oh, yes, my goodness. The biggest body of water I had ever seen was Lake Michigan, and that was from the shores of Chicago. I had crossed the Mississippi, because my grandmother lived in Moline, Illinois, and I went over to Davenport a few times, but I had never been anywhere. I had never been in the state of Indiana. I had been in Iowa, as I say, across the Mississippi River, and that was all. So it was a big thing for a farm boy, like it was for almost all people in those days--there weren't airplanes flying over the Atlantic, and to go to Europe was quite a project. And you felt kind of cosmopolitan or whatever when you came back after having been there and experiencing it.

Q: How did the seagoing life appeal to you at that point?

Captain Cutter: I didn't think much about it. I liked everything about it. My four years in the Naval Academy were the happiest years of my life; they really were. I can remember going to the head at night. (I don't know why I bring this up. I don't know why I remember it so vividly.) It was quiet, nobody was up, and I would get up and go to the head. And I can remember thinking how lucky I was to be at the Naval Academy. That just about says it all, you know. In those days, there weren't very many options. I could have gone to Cornell, Western Maryland; those were the two schools that were interested in giving me a scholarship for football after going to Severn. But I didn't know anything about it, what college life would be like. But I thought the Naval Academy was the greatest, and I still do. In spite of these things they say about the graduates, I am talking about a particular time under certain circumstances.

Cutter #1 - 89

Q: What is your recollection of the leaders at the Naval Academy in those years, the Commandants, the Superintendents, and so forth?

Captain Cutter: Oh, they were great, they were great. We had some screwballs, but you can't help that. But even they were great, and we had some good names for them. Gosh, I'll never forget--when I was second classman, we were playing Columbia that afternoon at the Naval Academy, this being the football season. And Saturday morning at the training table, a guy by the name of Holman Lee was sitting next to me.* He was a 140-pound quarterback, about a third stringer, and he was all guts and smart. But his nickname was "Holy," and he was the most unholy person in the whole class. So here we are, and in those days when we would get up to leave breakfast, they would say, "Rise, parade rest." And at parade rest, we would say the Lord's Prayer in unison. Well, at the training table Holman Lee was saying the Lord's Prayer. I had never heard him pray--ever--and I looked at him--what the hell's going on? I didn't say anything to him; that's all there was to it. So we were dismissed, and I went to the first class. I came back, and there was a note saying, "Report to the director of athletics."

So I went over there, and there was the head coach. It was Rip Miller in my third class year; also there were Lieutenant

―――――
*Midshipman Holman Lee, Jr., USN, class of 1935.

Cutter #1 - 90

Commander Hall, who was officer representative for football, and Captain Wilcox, the director of athletics.* They were all there, waiting for me, for this terrible midshipman, and I was on report with a class A offense put down by a guy by the name of "The Beagle." R.H. Smith was his name; he is dead now.** Actually, he was trying to do a good job, but it was a lot of misdirected effort on his part. He had gotten into a hassle with Lieutenant Commander Greenman, who was my battalion officer.*** Lieutenant Smith was a company officer in the first battalion. The two of them would inspect each other's battalions when they had the duty and put midshipmen on report for "room in gross disorder" or something. This was it, really—just childish as hell—the two of them.

Q: Of course, you were the people who suffered.

Captain Cutter: Sure, we suffered. So R.H. Smith, here he caught Cutter in this situation where he put me down for a class A: "This midshipman was grimacing and apparently directing the grimaces at another midshipman." Directing a grimace—now how the hell are you going to do that? How are you going to direct a

---

*Lieutenant Commander John L. Hall, Jr., USN. Captain John W. Wilcox, Jr., USN.
**Lieutenant Robert H. Smith, USN.
***Lieutenant Commander William G. Greenman, USN. In August 1942, as a captain, Greenman was commanding officer of the heavy cruiser Astoria (CA-34) when she was sunk in the Battle of Savo Island near Guadalcanal.

grimace? So I'm on report—-class A—-which means I go to the ship, can't play sports, and we are playing Columbia in the afternoon.

Q: The ship being the Reina Mercedes.*

Captain Cutter: That's right, and we had a football game so we've got about ten good football players on the team. I'm not one of them, but I am the first substitute for the center who is going to get knocked out early in the game; that's for sure, and they've got nobody to put in after me. Of course, I'm not much, but anyway better than nothing, I guess. So they were upset; they gave me this talk about what a terrible thing but they'd gotten me out of the class A, and it was a class B, which meant instead of getting ten demerits and going to the ship, I was going to get 15 demerits and walk extra duty after football season. So I walked extra duty from the end of football season until the beginning of the boxing season. Every Saturday and Wednesday afternoon, I am out there doing my extra duty and every day, but I mean two hours on Wednesday, two hours on Saturday, one hour the other days, except Sunday. Well, we went out and played the game and the next blow came on Monday. Commander

---

*The Reina Mercedes was a former Spanish ship captured as part of the Spanish-American War of 1898 and taken to Annapolis as a station ship. For many years, midshipmen were assigned to live on board the ship for specified periods of time as punishment for various offenses.

Tisdale was my battalion officer and a very dignified and wonderful gentleman.* He called me to his office and said, "Cutter, I am terribly disappointed in you." He gave me this thing and then he started talking about, "When you get out in the fleet and standing the deck watch under the stars in the Southern Hemisphere [and all this stuff about how close you are to God and all this], You'll feel regret that you did this sort of thing..." Oh God, he made me feel like I was completely without religion, which was really quite true at that stage of the game.

So I stood at attention and said, "So sorry, Sir," and all that sort of stuff and I ended up with my class B with 15 demerits, which hurt on my aptitude more than the 10 demerits would. I didn't ever get to the ship, but I was eligible for the football.

Q: Your grease mark?**

Captain Cutter: Yes, the grease mark. Gad, that was funny.

Q: Tisdale was a guy who went on to become a flag officer. What do you remember about him?

---

*Commander Mahlon S. Tisdale, USN.
**"Grease mark" was a slang term for a midshipman's grade in military aptitude and behavior. It was part of the overall numerical grade upon which an individual's final class standing was based.

Captain Cutter: I didn't know as much about him afterwards, but I knew him as a midshipman. He was a great influence; he was a wonderful man.

Q: That's what I am interested in is, what you remember of him personally.

Captain Cutter: Yes, Tisdale and a guy by the name of Paro, who was my company officer; they were men you never forget.* They were great people; impeccably dressed all the time and they did everything they asked you to do---they set an example. I suppose they still do; I don't know. They were great. Then we had Tommy C. Hart, who was one of the real all-time greats in the U.S. Navy.** Tommy Hart was not beloved of the midshipmen until after they graduated and they realized the kind of man he was. He was cold; he really wasn't but we didn't know it. He was absolutely fair, and his wife was a great lady. But it was an entirely different environment when Admiral Sellers came there.*** He was very warm, so was his wife, and he had a big name in the fleet. Hart didn't; Hart came in there as a junior rear admiral, and Sellers was sort of winding up his career. Then Oscar Badger was

---
*Lieutenant (junior grade) Eugene E. Paro, USN.
**Rear Admiral Thomas C. Hart, USN, Superintendent of the Naval Academy from 1931 to 1934; eventually a four-star admiral.
***Rear Admiral David F. Sellers, USN, Superintendent from 1934 to 1938; eventually a four-star admiral.

Cutter #1 - 94

the executive officer, just a marvelous man.* I guess they've still got them in the Academy today, but they picked them very, very well back 50 years ago, and these fellows were great examples.

Q: I think that was part of the job, being an example.

Captain Cutter: Yes, and they were. But, of course, our instructors were something else. Not very many of our instructors were competent professors. They were graduates of the Academy themselves and didn't have any real academic training. They had gone to PG school and, I guess, had gotten some special training, but not much. Most of them had master's degrees.

Q: This was part of the philosophy--that a line officer can do anything.

Captain Cutter: I guess that is true, but also the thought at that time was that your education was continuing, and you would have to get it yourself after you got out into the fleet. And that's what we had to do at the Academy. There was no lecturing; you'd get into class, and the instructor would say, "Any

---
*Commander Oscar C. Badger, USN, eventually a three-star admiral.

questions, gentlemen? Man the boards."

You didn't dare ask any questions, because they couldn't answer most of them. So you manned the boards and the slips were made out by some Ph.D. assistant head of the department. An officer was the head. And you would draw a slip, and if it covered material you knew, you would do all right that day. That's where this roommate of mine I was telling you about was helpful. He was so good he could always tell what the slips were going to be. He could pick out the key things in the lessons; "You'd better know this, Slade."

And I would say, "Okay, fine." He would give me that dope, so I did all right in my daily lesson. But when you got to an examination, that was something else. You had a little trouble.

Q: What made you like Hart in retrospect?

Captain Cutter: Again, I think the example he set. For instance, we all had one-eighth of an inch of our collar showing, and he insisted on that. It never happened before--on a full dress, one-eighth of an inch, exactly one-eighth of an inch. Exactly, I think it was a half or a quarter on your cuffs. So what we did, of course--we cut off our shirt sleeves and sewed the buttons inside the sleeves to hold the cuffs into the sleeves of our shirts and put a button inside the collar in back and the two buttons in the front of the collar, to hold our full-dress

Cutter #1 - 96

collar in place. But we sure looked good out on parade. He had these standards that were very, very high, and he didn't go along with relaxing the rules--for instance, letting the midshipmen ride in automobiles. Nowadays they seem to every year have to give them another privilege, so now you've got the Naval Academy absolutely inundated with automobiles. It's terrible, I think. He would never put up with that. He wouldn't let us go out in town. He stuck to the rules, exactly what they were, and I think they should always do that. We took pride in being deprived.

Q: I think this goes back to what you said before about Admiral Holloway's philosophy, "We are teaching you discipline and tradition here."

Captain Cutter: Customs and traditions of the naval service, and you do your job. Like MacArthur, you know--duty, honor, country--and stuff.* You can laugh at it in a way, but that's what your country expects you to do in time of war, and that's what they train you for. Anybody who has got any brains at all gets scared. I used to say to myself, and I used to tell my wife, "Well look, honey, I'm more scared of not doing my job than I am of what's going to happen to me, because I've got to live with this."

---
*General of the Army Douglas MacArthur, who was fond of quoting the West Point motto.

And I think this is what training does. These aviators who came in and did their dive-bombing and then went along the tops of these trees strafing and getting shot down—they weren't very happy doing that; they were just doing a job. That was their duty. The Air Force people at the time, untrained, they were brought in very green, weren't given the basic training our people were given, and sent out to do something. You can't blame them; they weren't indoctrinated to do that. They didn't have the traditions and customs. You can't blame them.

Q: In a hazardous situation, did you take sort of a fatalistic approach? When your time comes you are going to go anyway, so you are not going to be bothered by that?

Captain Cutter: I don't think that. Every time I went out on patrol, I would say, "Is this one in five?" I would say, "I've got four out of five chances of coming back." That's number one. The only thing I can remember—it didn't bother me any—was when we dove in the early morning, before sunup really, before morning twilight, I remember taking a look at the stars and wondering if I would see them again. I can remember that, as I slammed the hatch coming down, but not with any foreboding. You never know what's going to happen today or if you are going to be able to see the stars tonight or not. I remember thinking that.

Cutter #1 - 98

Q: Was that a frequent thing when you would think that?

Captain Cutter: Yes, frequently I did that, because I still remember it.

Q: What was the effect when you were a commanding officer and you would hear about men that you had been close to, from the Naval Academy onward, who had not made it back?

Captain Cutter: I don't know whether it's callousness, but it didn't bother me at all. This one time we were due in Midway after my first patrol, and the Pompano was due in three days later to Midway for a refit, and I was looking forward to seeing them. Tommy Thomas, who had been my exec and skipper for one patrol in Pompano, and Tom McGrath, who was regimental commander as a midshipman and also on the football team when I was assistant coach--a wonderful guy, heavyweight wrestler and a great fellow.* He had worked up to exec from being low man on the totem pole. I was really looking forward to seeing them, and they didn't come in. I was worried about it, and then about a week went by and ComSubPac in the meantime had been sending messages for the Pompano, "report your position," and she hadn't answered. So they sent out the word that she was probably lost,

---
*When the Pompano was lost in September 1943, the commanding officer was Commander Willis M. Thomas, USN, and the executive officer was Lieutenant Thomas P. McGrath, USN.

but they didn't tell the next of kin. They waited for about three or four weeks to be absolutely sure. So I wrote to my wife, who was in Vallejo.* She and the skipper's wife were very good friends, because he had been the exec on this ship when I was fourth officer. I wrote and told her that she had better prepare Alice for bad news. Our letters were censored, so nobody knew who Alice was, but Frannie would know. Of course, she didn't tell Alice anything, but she was ready for it when Alice did get the word; then Frannie was able to console her and be with her and so on. It didn't worry me, and I didn't vicariously put myself in that position at all. I don't know. We lost so many of them.

Q: But you would be saddened for the person, wouldn't you?

Captain Cutter: Yes, oh yes. I think the one that I really felt terrible about was right at the end of the war. Early in 1945, Dave Connole, who had tried like the devil to get a combat command, finally was detached from his command of a training submarine at the submarine school in New London. Dave and I had served in Pompano for three and a half years and were close friends. He was a very good officer, and he finally got command of the Trigger. On his first patrol he was lost, in March of

---

*Vallejo, California, was the site of the Mare Island Navy Yard, which had built the USS Seahorse, the boat in which Cutter was serving at the time the Pompano was lost.

1945, and left a pregnant wife and had a baby he never saw.*
Dave and I were very close friends. That really got to me, but it was because the war was over. We knew the war was over then; it was just a matter of a very short time, and I felt terrible about that. There were several people. Jim Clark was a classmate of mine—I saw him off on his last patrol.** Dave Zabriskie, this football player—I saw him off on his last patrol.*** Joe Bourland—I was down at the dock when he left on his last patrol.**** I don't know; it's kind of hard.

Q: What about Dealey? How did that one strike you?

Captain Cutter: I expected it. The same way with Morton. Not that they were foolhardy; they weren't, but you can only get away with the stuff they did for so long.

Q: Then you run out of the luck, as we were talking about.

Captain Cutter: That's right. That's exactly right. It is a

---

*Commander David R. Connole, USN, was commanding officer of the USS Trigger (SS-237) when she was sunk by the Japanese on 27 March 1945.
**Lieutenant Commander James S. Clark, USN, was commanding officer of the USS Golet (SS-361), presumed lost on 14 June 1944.
***Lieutenant Commander David Zabriskie, Jr., USN, was commanding officer of the USS Herring (SS-233) when she was lost on 1 June 1944.
****Lieutenant Commander Joseph H. Bourland, USN, was commanding officer of the USS Runner (SS-275) when she was lost around July 1943.

matter of luck, the odds. Every time you do something, there are odds, and eventually the odds are going to catch up with you. And they caught up with them.

Q: Did you run into the Kimmel brothers at all? They were contemporaries of yours approximately.

Captain Cutter: Yes, they were. Manning--I was in the Pearl area, and he was out in the Southwest Pacific. He was lost in the Lombok Straits; the ship was mined.* Tom was out there too, but then when Manning was lost, because of what the family had gone through at Pearl Harbor and stuff, he was ordered back to the States.** Admiral King did that, and Tom came to Portsmouth. He was administrative officer or something like that. When I came back to put the Requin in commission in January of 1945--on New Year's Day she was launched, and my wife was sponsor for it. Tom was back there, and, as I say, we were very good friends and I was godfather of their oldest son, Tom, Jr., and of course I have kept in touch with him ever since. He lives here, you know,

---

*Lieutenant Commander Manning M. Kimmel, USN, a Naval Academy classmate of Cutter, was commanding officer of the USS Robalo (SS-273) when she was lost 26 July 1944.
**Lieutenant Commander Thomas K. Kimmel, USN, served in the S-40 (SS-145) and the Balao (SS-285), then was ordered to shore duty at the direction of Admiral Ernest J. King, USN, Chief of Naval Operations. He was the only surviving son of Rear Admiral Husband E. Kimmel, USN(Ret.), who had been Commander in Chief Pacific Fleet when Pearl Harbor was attacked in December 1941 and wound up being relieved of command shortly afterward.

he and Nancy. We were neighbors over in Providence until my wife got asthma real bad and we had to leave Annapolis.* We were here for a year and three months. We bought a house over there and had to leave, sold the house for what we paid for it, and I wish we had it back. I think I paid $49,000, and I got $49,000, and I suppose they are $159,999 now.

Q: Or more.

Captain Cutter: Or more.

Q: Did he seem somewhat frustrated there being up in Portsmouth when he had really been trained to be a submariner?

Captain Cutter: No, I don't think so. The war was winding down there, but he hadn't had command, though. He was '36. You know, Tom felt what happened to his father very, very much, and he still does, and I agree with him.

Q: Not surprisingly.

Captain Cutter: He should, but that bothered him very much. The

---

*Providence is the name of a prosperous housing development near the Annapolis naval station; quite a number of retired senior naval officers live there.

loss of his brother bothered him a lot, you know. His father was in a kind of retirement that you don't want to be in, and his mother, so he just felt, I think, that it would be best for everything if he survived. It would be too much for them if he had been lost, too. I think that's what he felt, really. Tom was a fine submariner, and he would have been a good skipper, but he didn't have a chance.

Q: Is there anything else to recall from your time as a midshipman at the Naval Academy?

Captain Cutter: I think I've given you the idea that it was a happy time in my life. I didn't do what I should have done. I mean I could have gotten a lot more out of it. It had a lot to offer that I didn't take advantage of. I was a pretty good midshipman. I got a letter of commendation from the Superintendent when I graduated. They pick out about six out of the graduating class for contributing to the midshipmen and stuff, so I wasn't really a dope. But academically I could have gotten a lot more out of it. I was a three-striper, and I could have gotten a good bit more out of the education if I had worked a little bit at it. But I had a good time; I enjoyed it.

Q: Was the leadership training you got as a three-striper valuable later on?

Captain Cutter: No, I don't think that had anything to do with it. Some of the best officers we had in our class didn't have any stripes at all. I don't think that has any bearing at all. I think actually probably the reason I got three stripes was because I was playing football, you know. People get to know you. Some of the outstanding people in our class didn't have any stripes at all; that had nothing to do with it. Except the five-stripers, the top ones; they stand out.

Q: Ned Beach was a five-striper.*

Captain Cutter: Oh, yes. I could never understand, I just don't know why he didn't make flag rank; I can't understand that. Outstanding in every way and a great leader.

Q: One hypothesis is that he was too visible. He wrote for publication.

Captain Cutter: I think what hurt Ned was that he ruffled some feathers when he was President Eisenhower's aide. He was right. He did what was right, but he was a commander and the people he was ruffling were flag officers. Then they sit on the selection board, so what happens? They have a chance to get back, you

---

*Midshipman Edward L. Beach, USN, regimental commander for the class of 1939. He became a well-known submariner and eventually retired as a captain.

know. That's human nature. I can understand that.

Q: It's not fair, but you can understand it.

Captain Cutter: Well, that's the way the ball bounces.

Q: Had you given some thought while you were at the Naval Academy in what specialization you might go to once you got into the fleet?

Captain Cutter: The first choice was Marines, and second choice was aviation, and I hadn't thought of submarines. In those days you drew numbers, and your selection--I don't know what it is now--was not based on class standing. It was based on pulling a number out of a hat, and only 26 could go to the Marine Corps. My number was too low, so I couldn't get in the Marines. I tried to get into aviation, but I was too heavy. In those days, 193 pounds was your top level. Well, I could never get to 193 and hold it. I could starve down to there, but I couldn't stay there, healthily. So I was in the Idaho, and I tell you we had some officers that left a lot to be desired in the battleship Navy in those days. The skipper was a tremendous guy.

Q: Captain Stott?*

Captain Cutter: Yes, he was marvelous. Billy Whelchel, who later became vice admiral---he was only a lieutenant commander then.** He was one of those guys who was held back by the seniority system. He told me, "You know, Slade, it is unfortunate that you came to the Idaho because you'll never have a skipper to match Arthur Stott."

Well, I think I did in the Pompano in Parks, who was an entirely different person. Stott was a perfect gentleman, absolutely fair in every way, just a wonderful man, and his wife. They knew I was married, and I wasn't supposed to be. They never called on us. They never indicated that they knew anything about it, but the day after I was married on the 6th of June in 1937 (officially)---I got married in Tijuana on the 4th of April 1936, and on the 6th of June, a year later. Officially I couldn't get married until the 6th of June in 1937. My father-in-law, who was very uneasy---getting married in Mexico, he didn't think his daughter was married, and he couldn't wait until we could get married in the Episcopal Church. So we got married on the 6th of June 1937. We didn't send out any invitations to anybody out there. Her mother was dead, and her father wasn't well. It was

---
*Captain Arthur C. Stott, USN, commanding officer, USS Idaho (BB-42).
**Lieutenant Commander John E. Whelchel, USN, communication officer of the Idaho.

a church wedding; my mother was there and my aunt and so on and my sister and a couple of close friends aboard ship. But the next day, Captain Stott and his wife called, very pointed, the next day. We were living with my mother then.

Q: What about his professional qualities, seamanship and leadership?

Captain Cutter: All those people were. The selection process was brutal. In those days, there weren't many billets. You see, they had those jobs for two and three years. It wasn't like they do now where you have it for just a few months and they keep rotating it around. Very few people got command of a major combatant as a captain, and the ones who did were very outstanding people. There was another one, Captain Delano.[*] He wasn't the warm man that Stott was, but he was certainly very competent and very fair and very capable in every way. I have nothing but admiration for him. I didn't have the affection for him that I have for Stott. But the rest of the officers, down the line, we had some real dum-dums.

Q: How would you account for that?

Captain Cutter: I don't know. Some of them were Naval Academy

---
*Captain Harvey Delano, USN.

graduates, too. I think maybe they were discouraged over the promotion. Some of these people had been commanding officers of submarines and were sent to a battleship as a turret officer—I mean, what a comedown.

Q: Or as chief engineer?

Captain Cutter: Yes, or assistant engineer, or head of the F Division. But I mean actually, turret officer—two of them. One, a fellow named Little, and the other guy had the AA battery, both of them lieutenants and both had been submarine skippers, and these guys were good.* Then, my division officer in the B Division hadn't been selected for skipper, because there the competition in submarines was very tough. In those days, the S-boats had four officers, maybe five. But only one could be skipper at a time, three of these guys would never get to be skippers. There is only room for one at the top, and, again, they didn't turn over every year. It would take them two or three years, you see. So the skippers were topflight, and some of those who didn't make it were topflight, but they just weren't good enough politicians or were not quite good enough. I had one of those; he was my B Division officer when I was in the B Division, and we would get down there standing watch in the engine room together. And he would tell me about submarine duty.

---
*Lieutenant Marion N. Little, USN.

He loved it.

Q: Who was this?

Captain Cutter: He was my division officer for about ten months, Scotty McCall, dead a long time ago—an alcoholic, got a general court-martial for drinking while he was aboard the ship; that was his problem. But he was very bright. Scotty McCall came from Boise, Idaho.*

Q: Is he the one who really inspired you to go into submarines?

Captain Cutter: Well, he talked about it a lot, and, yes, I would say he had a lot to do with it. But then there was this fellow by the name of Little, who was my division officer. Ensigns moved around in those days. We were on probation for two years, and we would be in engineering, in navigation, in deck, and in communications—you know, a little bit of everything. When I was in the deck division, I was in the third division, which was a turret division, and this fellow named Little was the turret officer. A very dignified fellow, he was a submarine officer, topflight. And all of the officers who had been in submarines were topflight people on the ship, every one of them.

---

*Lieutenant Francis B. McCall, USN.

J.R. Topper was another one.* I can't think of the names of the others; there were about five of them. So that's why I went into submarines. I couldn't get into aviation, I failed the physical. I was too heavy. And I couldn't get into the Marine Corps, so I went into submarines. It was due to those people.

Q: Why did you want to go into the Marine Corps?

Captain Cutter: Probably, when I was a kid, down on the farm, I guess it must have been the summer of 1917 I remember sitting on the front porch and a guy by the name of Arthur Lake, who was about a second or third cousin of mine, was in the Marine Corps.** He came in his uniform and he came out and sat on the front porch and he was going overseas. He was killed in the Argonne, not too long before the war was over. He was an only child, and it was a very sad thing for the family. I don't know--kids--I just wanted to be a Marine from that experience of seeing him. I applied. I wanted to go into aviation, probably for the pay, I suppose. I can't think of any other reason, because I didn't know anything about flying, and the submarines, as I say, was because of the submarine officers.

When I was 14 years old, I got diphtheria. And in those days you were locked up; they put a red sign on your door. Where I

---
*Lieutenant James R. Topper, USN.
**Private Arthur Lake, USMC.

got diphtheria was at my grandmother's house. I had gone up there for the weekend. You remember, I told you about the eggs when she brought me home. I was up there another weekend, and this time I got diphtheria, I had this terrible sore throat so Grandma got the doctor. In those days they made house calls.

"Hell," he said, "this boy's got diphtheria."

I don't know how he knew so quick, but I had all the symptoms, I guess. So they put a red sign on the door, so they were locked up for two weeks—everybody in the house. This is in December, as I recall, in 1925, and the S-51 was sunk off Long Island Sound in about 150 feet of water.* And for ten days or two weeks, they'd hear tapping on the hull, and they finally died; the tapping stopped. Every day the radio would come in; this was a big deal. And here I am—no television in those days—locked up in my Grandma's house with diphtheria, and the radio the only thing I had for diversion. I listened to all this stuff. I can remember saying, "How can anybody be so stupid as to get into one of those damn things?" How could he, you know, because he didn't have to? Why did he get into submarine duty? I guess I sort of used that to soften the blow of those poor devils down there in that thing.

Well, that was when I was 14, and by the time I was 23, I was

---

*On the night of 25 September 1925, the USS S-51 (SS-162) was rammed and sunk off Block Island, New York, by the merchant steamer City of Rome. Of the 36 men on board the submarine, only three survived.

Cutter #1 - 112

in it. I was never bothered with claustrophobia, never worried about it, never thought anything about it after that. That's how I got into the submarine forces.

Q: You mentioned that you served as assistant coach right after you graduated from the Naval Academy. What did that entail?

Captain Cutter: No, that was when I was out in the fleet.

Q: I thought you had stayed at the Academy.

Captain Cutter: No, I went out to the fleet first. I was coach of the Idaho battleship team, and we met the Army all-star team in Tacoma on Armistice Day 1936. We beat them, 14-0. As a result of my coaching on the Idaho, they ordered me back with Hank Hardwick--he was head coach--to be assistant coach.* And the first year I was line coach for the freshmen--plebes--with Oscar Hagberg.** Well, I was ordered to submarine school, and they diverted me to the Naval Academy. And instead of going to submarine school in August or whenever it was, maybe July, I went to the Naval Academy and entered the submarine school class of January in 1938. I got out in May and was ordered back to be

---
*Henry Hardwick was head football coach at the Naval Academy the seasons of 1937 and 1938.
**Oscar Hagberg was later head football coach at the Naval Academy the seasons of 1944 and 1945.

coach again. So instead of going to the West Coast, to the Pompano where I was ordered, they sent me down to the Naval Academy with the S-30, which was indoctrinating midshipmen. We would go out in the channel out here where the ships go up and down off Kent Island, and dive with the midshipmen aboard. We would take them out one time each, and every midshipman was taken out. So we would go out there and dive. You remember I said the first skipper I had—-Bob Rice, who said he wouldn't attack these boats, a very gentlemanly type—-and I was with him for three months during the summer until the academic year started and I went out with the football team.*

Q: He turned out to be quite a skipper during the war, too.

Captain Cutter: He was good; you bet he was. Not flamboyant—-he was just a good, honest guy. He saw the enemy and attacked it and he didn't do anything. As I say, he wasn't flamboyant at all; he was very good, very good. And a real gentleman, Bob Rice. He wouldn't shoot anybody in the water or do anything like that. I admired him very much, and, boy, he worked me hard. He was a funny guy. You know, we were out there diving the midshipmen one day and had a diving officer who was—-he didn't stay on submarines, they got rid of him—-but he was pretty

---

*Lieutenant Robert H. Rice, USN, commanding officer, USS S-30 (SS-135).

senior. He had the dive, and we had a controller man, electric--in the S-boats the controls for the motors that drive the propellers were in the control room, and you had levers that would either put them ahead or astern and then the rheostats would govern your speed, how much power you gave the motors. Well, the controller man had been on leave in Baltimore. It was his first day after being two weeks on leave. He came out there, so we made this dive and all of a sudden we got a big down angle, a real big down angle by the stern, not the bow---by the stern and finally we got almost to the bottom and the diving officer says, "Blow everything." So we blew all main ballast, but that didn't stop us from hitting. In the meantime, the midshipmen were sliding all over the place, and the trash cans that hadn't been emptied were all over, and it was one horrible mess. Bob Rice was standing in the control room. I was in the control room, too. I didn't know what was going on. I had no idea what was going on; in fact, I was kind of scared. Bob Rice didn't say a word. When we got down, hit the bottom, and he said, "Jim, do you know what happened?"

"No, I don't know."

He said, "You were going astern." What had happened was that the kid, instead of pulling the controllers forward, had moved them back. The S-30 had been overhauled in Cavite, and it came back from Cavite and everything was bass-ackwards.* They

---

*Cavite was the site of a U.S. Navy Yard in the Philippines.

couldn't transfer anybody off the S-30, because nobody else knew how to operate it. It wasn't like any other boat. The Filipinos had put the controls together backwards, so instead of going ahead when you were going to go ahead, you came back with the levers. And when you wanted to go down, you went forward with them. Well, this guy wasn't thinking. He had been on another boat before that and he had been gone for two weeks, so when they said, "Dive," he went ahead.

Q: Did the normal thing.

Captain Cutter: Sure, and he was going backwards, and then when the angle came on the boat, first we were diving two-thirds and the diving officer said, "All ahead, standard," then, "All ahead, full."

That just made it worse, because we were going back faster. Oh, that was some harum-scarum outfit. It was really the worst.

We had another fellow on there by the name of Close, who had graduated the class ahead of me, and he was a topflight fellow.[*] The skipper was excellent; the exec was a bum. And so was this guy, really. Neither one of them ever saw the war. They were kicked out before then, but they were the ones who were put off of this. I don't know why they put Rice in there; he was too good to be in that boat. But we did need it for the midshipmen.

---
[*]Lieutenant (junior grade) Robert H. Close, USN.

He would give me a lot of--when I happened to have the deck coming in one day and the ferry was going out--does the ferry still go over there?

Q: I don't think so.

Captain Cutter: Well, it used to go out, and there was the channel, so I was giving the ferry plenty of room. I was over on the right-hand side of the channel, and I was looking over the side at the buoy astern and the buoy ahead. I was sure we were inside the line of buoys, you know, like all good seamen do. And the first thing I know, we had a hell of a starboard list, and the captain didn't say a word, except, "Left full rudder," just quietly. And after a minute, he said, "Take charge, Slade."

And I put the rudder amidship and got back on the course, and he said, "You know what happened?"

"No, Sir."

He said, "You were aground."

What had happened--this channel had been silted up over the years, and our bilge keel on the starboard side dug into the bank of the channel and caused this heel. He knew what it was, and he didn't get the least bit excited or upset. I know a lot of skippers who would have just had a fit over something like that. We went aground, you know.

Cutter #1 - 117

Q: These are two instances where he remained very cool when others wouldn't have.

Captain Cutter: Absolutely. He was imperturbable, a great guy. He married a gal, Eunice Willson, who was Captain Willson's daughter and he was head of the seamanship department when I was a midshipman.* They lived in the yard there. I knew Eunice quite well; we used to go over to her house. Bob married her. She was a real intellect and became one of the top people in the Black Chamber during the war in Washington, breaking Japanese codes. She was pregnant, and she told this story later. She would go in there in the morning, and everybody had to pass two Marines stationed in as you come in there. You had to show ID cards, and the Marines would say, "Good morning, Miss," "Good morning, Miss," and they kept saying it right up until the time she delivered.

Q: This was Russell Willson's daughter?

Captain Cutter: Yes. And they didn't want to let her go until she had the baby. They needed her there, so she kept going to work every day until she had the baby. That was funny. She was a great gal.

---
*Captain Russell Willson, USN. Later, as a rear admiral, Willson was Superintendent of the Naval Academy from February 1941 to January 1942.

Cutter #1 - 118

Q: How would you compare Hardwick as a coach to Hamilton and Rip Miller?

Captain Cutter: Oh, Hank is dead now, he was an alcoholic---just a great, loyal, fine friend. He was head coach only in name. We had Keith Molesworth, who had been quarterback for the Chicago Bears; he was in there as backfield coach and Rip, line coach---they carried the team. There were times when Hank wouldn't show up until Wednesday; after a game we lost, he would go off on a drunk and come back on a Wednesday.

Q: That was one of the disadvantages of the active duty coach thing.

Captain Cutter: That was ridiculous; coaching is a profession, and you can't mix them. Tom Hamilton did, but Tom did a lot of coaching. Every football season he coached and he was a student of the game and a very bright guy. He was a hell of a good football coach, coached at Pitt, you know, did a good job at the Naval Academy. But football was so much less complicated then than it is now. My goodness, all we had were two defense formations on the line, a seven-man line or a six-man line---no variations at all. With a seven-man line, you had a diamond backfield---one linebacker, two halfbacks, and a safety man. If you had a six-man line, you had a center and the fullback, backing up the line, always the center and the fullback—not a halfback, had to be a fullback—and then two halfbacks back there and the safety man. And nobody ever thought of doing anything different until, I guess it was Red Sanders at UCLA came up with a four-man line.* I don't know who got the five-man line; it was Sanders came up with the four-man line, the four-three defense. He was the guy at UCLA. First one who ever used it, and he could have done it all the time. If they had ever done that to us, we would just have had to walk off the field; we wouldn't have known what to do. I knew where my man was going to be opposite me in a six-man line. So I had to learn my plays for two situations, the seven-man line and the six-man line. If they had ever thrown a four-man line in there, forget it. Football went on for years and years like that, and the rules had always permitted variations, but nobody ever thought to implement them.

Q: How were you as coach of the Idaho team—pretty much going along with whatever you had done at the Academy?

Captain Cutter: Of course. I wasn't innovative. No, I did the same thing everybody else did.

---

*Henry R. Sanders was head football coach at Vanderbilt University for six years in the 1940s, then head coach at the University of California at Los Angeles from 1949 until his death in 1958.

Cutter #1 - 120

Q: What were some of the experiences that have stayed with you from your years in the Idaho, other than athletics?

Captain Cutter: Not much.

Q: That was pretty much a transition period?

Captain Cutter: Yes, and football took up an awful lot of the time. We would start our season in about May, working out physically; then football would go on through until around Thanksgiving. And then in the winter I had the boxing team. I was mixed up in athletics. As a matter of fact, they kept me assistant navigator for much longer than I should have been--more than half the time I was aboard. That was because when we were in port, I had nothing to do. This gave me time to discharge my sport duties. They were a duty; I was assigned by the skipper to these jobs.

Q: Fleet operations were far different, because you couldn't do that sort of thing today the way the ships are deployed.

Captain Cutter: No way. The battleships were together in San Pedro Harbor in the Long Beach area along with the aircraft carriers. They were all there and all in port during the weekends except during fleet exercises, which were conducted in the spring so it didn't interfere with the football season. Athletics was an important part. Then they had the baseball, which I didn't participate in, but it was also an important sport in the fleet. You see, some of those guys would stay their whole naval career in one ship, whole career, enlisted men. They were loyal, and they were good sailors.

Q: Do you remember anything from fleet exercises in those years?

Captain Cutter: I didn't know what was going on most of the time; we never knew. In maneuvers and stuff all we were worrying about was standing watches and keeping 500 yards from the ship ahead at night, and watching the fuel oil consumption. The emphasis was on--take Rickover, Admiral Rickover. He was on the New Mexico; he was a lieutenant.*

Q: And K.G. Schacht was there, too.**

Captain Cutter: Oh, he knew, I should say so. Well, Rickover was doing his job. I mean, it was dishonest. For the fuel situation he bribed the oiler who came alongside, give him a bottle of booze or something so he would give them 100 extra

---

*An account of Lieutenant Rickover's severe fuel consumption measures is provided in Norman Polmar and Thomas B. Allen, Rickover (New York: Simon and Schuster, 1982), pages 83-85.
**Ensign Kenneth G. Schacht, USN, a Naval Academy classmate and football teammate of Cutter.

gallons and take them away from the next ship or something. Turned off all the lights and turned down the ventilators so people would be miserable, but it would save oil—anything to win that efficiency pennant for engineering. I don't think Rickover did it for his career so much as the fact that he was a competitor, a great man. I have always admired that fellow. I don't think we would be where we are today if it weren't for him, in the nuclear power business. I think the civilian world could take a little lesson, too; there wouldn't be any Three Mile Islands if Rickover had been in charge.* The nuclear power plants in the ships are much more difficult to maintain in a safe manner than they are when they are sitting in a stable environment ashore. The ships are moving around and changing from full speed to stop, and these other people have constant power loads, no problem. But in civilian nuclear plants, people just aren't trained properly. We have never had a nuclear accident in the U.S. Navy. Amazing, it really is, and we wouldn't in the civilian thing if they had somebody like Rickover, who was very demanding, very unreasonable to a lot of views, and he is to mine in some ways. I'll never forget that guy.

---

*On 28 March 1979, a major nuclear accident occurred at the Three Mile Island reactor near Harrisburg, Pennsylvania. Radioactive gases escaped through the venting system, and a large hydrogen gas bubble formed in the top of the reactor containment vessel.

I was with Lew Parks for three and a half years.* When I graduated from submarine school, we were supposed to be qualified in submarines within one year, or else the skipper had to explain to the Bureau of Navigation why you weren't qualified. One year went by; two years went by; two and a half years went by, and I wasn't qualified. Neither was Schneider, who was ahead of me in sub school, nor was Connole, who was after me in sub school; the three of us were not qualified.** The reason was, Parks said, that as soon as an officer is qualified--and this was true at that time, and we're talking about 1940 and '41, and we were building a lot of submarines--and as soon as an officer got qualified, he was pulled off that submarine and sent to new construction. Or another officer was pulled off, so that you kept a lesser number of qualified officers in the operating boats and filled the empty billets with reserves. So Parks said, "If we don't qualify you guys, you won't get pulled off. We're going to war, and I want to be ready." So he just poured this stuff into us, worked our tails off, see, and, he wouldn't qualify us. And he said, "The bureau will never check up on us."

This was a Rickover trick, you know. Rickover would say, "You don't submit the report, and they will never check up on you." You know the bureaucracy. Well, this is true. Parks said

---

*Lieutenant Commander Lewis S. Parks, USN, was commanding officer of the USS Pompano (SS-181) from 1939 to 1942.
**Lieutenant (junior grade) Earle C. ("Penrod") Schneider, USN; Lieutenant (junior grade) David R. Connole, USN.

they wouldn't check up, and they didn't. But my colleagues, peers, were going around with submarine pins, and here I am with a clean chest. Kind of hurt my ego.

Q: Couldn't you initiate something on your own?

Captain Cutter: Whoa! With Parks? My friend, I should say not. No, we kept quiet. No, you didn't do that with Lew Parks. No, we didn't do anything. One day, for some reason, maybe the division commander or someone said, "You've got to qualify these people or else." So Parks made arrangements for a target, 12 to 25 knots, zigzagging. The target was the old destroyer Litchfield, and we were going out to fire exercise torpedoes. Now, he also taught us how to---and not too many people could do this---solve problems in our heads. We never used what is called an "is-was," which was an instrument to get distance to the track, the gyro angles, and things like that. It's like a slide rule.

Q: A circular slide rule.

Captain Cutter: Yes. And then you also had the torpedo data computer. Also, you had the banjo, which was the angle solver, which told you what angle to put on the torpedoes and so forth. We couldn't use that either; we could use nothing. We couldn't even use the stadimeter in the periscope. There were about eight horizontal lines etched in the lens of the periscope, about one-eighth inch apart. You know that when a target with a masthead height of 100 feet subtends one of those spaces between the notches, the range is 8,000 yards, and if it subtends four of those spaces the range is 2,000 yards. You would have to extrapolate if it was more than 125 feet or less. We could use a plot to determine target course and speed.

So we took our division commander, Commander Merrill Comstock, along to observe.* The division commanders in those days were unfamiliar with the then modern fire control equipment. So we went out for this day of firing. There is a lot more I could tell you about it. For instance, we would not say, "Come to a certain course." See, a torpedo problem is all relative. You don't need true bearings; all you want to know is your bearing in relation to the target; the range; and the angle between the target axis and line of bearing. The plot will give you target course and speed.

Parks said, "I don't want you to do anything except say, 'Make the tubes ready,' and then, 'fire.' You can say, 'Come right or left' so many degrees by compass, but don't give a course."

Schneider, out of the class of 1933, was first to fire. He

---
*Commander Merrill Comstock, USN, Commander Submarine Division 13.

fired, and he missed. The target zigged on him just as he fired—a tough break.

Q: Was this Penrod Schneider?

Captain Cutter: Yes, a great guy. I was with him all that time until he left the ship and got command of the one he was lost on. It was the Dorado.* His wife, you know, was on her way to the West Coast from New London. She heard it over the radio. She was driving across country with her son Butch; they had only the one child. That was a terrible thing.

Q: Especially being killed perhaps by a friendly aircraft.

Captain Cutter: It was, it really was, a PBY. But that guy, you can't blame him. There was a German submarine in the area. Penrod surfaced across the sea; he didn't want to get pooped, so he was heading in the wrong direction, the idea being (from the investigation) if he had been on the course he was supposed to be on—see, he had just surfaced. They had gone down apparently for a trim dive, which everybody did about once a day, and you don't surface with the sea astern. Because you are down

---

*The USS Dorado (SS-248) was commissioned 28 August 1943 with Lieutenant Commander Schneider in command. She sailed from New London, Connecticut, on 6 October 1943, and it is likely she was attacked and sunk by a U.S. patrol plane operating from Panama on 12 October.

in the water and if you open the hatch you get pooped, so you come broadside to the sea. You roll a lot, but the seas don't poop over you. So he was across seas, which unfortunately, was about 90 degrees to the course that all friendly forces had been told that this submarine was on. There had been a German submarine that had attacked a convoy in that area, and they were out looking for him, and they came across Penrod. You can't blame the fellow. Again, it was just luck, acts of God, you know.

Q: Very bad luck.

Captain Cutter: Yes. Penrod was really a splendid person, a fine officer and a wonderful sense of humor. I bet he had a good ship, too. They never had a chance.

Q: You were talking about Schneider firing and missing while in the Pompano.

Captain Cutter: Then Connole fired; he got a hit. I fired, and I got a hit. And Parks, showman that he was, said, "Make ready another tube for Mr. Schneider."

Schneider fired another one, and he got a hit. The division

Cutter #1 - 128

commander was sitting there, and he didn't know what the hell went on. He still doesn't know what happened. All he knew was that they signalled back a hit, but he didn't know how it happened. Normally, you'd get qualified in submarines, and then a year later or so, you'd get qualified for command. But Parks was a showman, you see. He turned to the division commander while we're all right there, and he said, "Commodore, I think these officers are ready to be qualified for command, too, don't you?"

And we were, so the division commander had to agree after our show. We were qualified for command the same day we qualified for submarines. Now that was Parks's moment of glory, too. And he deserved it, because he had worked our butts off and he taught us all these things. We had learned everything from him, not from submarine school. We got that from Parks. It helped out later on in the war. It helped me sink ships.

Q: He ran a PCO school up at Portsmouth later in the war, too.*

Captain Cutter: Oh, yes, he was outstanding. Well, after being with him three and a half years, we came back from our second war patrol, and we came through Midway right after the Battle of Midway. We had picked up a prisoner at Midway that somebody else had brought in, and we brought this prisoner back to Pearl

---

*PCO—prospective commanding officers.

Harbor. As we came in, we met the Litchfield, the flagship of SubRon Four, a little surface ship; it was a destroyer.* The skipper was a classmate of Lew's, and the exec was a classmate of mine. We had gone to a lot of social things before the war, with the staff of SubPac. Don Clay was my classmate's name; we were good friends, so when we came in they met us at the 100-mile circle early in the morning.** I was up on the bridge and the skipper was down below—I found out later—taking a shower. And the skipper on the destroyer got on the TBS (like the CB we have nowadays), called over and wanted to know how the patrol went.*** We were just batting the breeze back and forth, and I mentioned we had a prisoner aboard.

He said, "Mike Fenno came in here last week, and he had a prisoner aboard. It took an hour and a half before they could get the Marines over to take the prisoner off, and they wouldn't let anybody aboard until the prisoner was removed."**** And he said, "I will call How 2 [which was the water tower in Pearl Harbor with a big 36-inch searchlight on it, so we wouldn't have to break radio silence] with my 36-inch searchlight and tell them you have a prisoner aboard and they'll meet you down there."

---
*The Pompano's arrival at Pearl Harbor was on 18 June 1942.
**Lieutenant Donald N. Clay, USN.
***TBS—talk between ships, which was the name then used for the voice radio.
****Lieutenant Commander Frank W. Fenno, Jr., USN, commanding officer of the USS Trout (SS-202). On 9 June, in the aftermath of the Battle of Midway, the Trout rescued two Japanese from a hatch cover and delivered them to Pearl Harbor on her arrival there on 14 June.

And I said, "Fine, thank you very much, Sir."

So I called down and told the captain that I had exchanged messages with the Litchfield and they were going to inform How-2 that we had a prisoner aboard. Jesus, the next thing I know, up comes Parks, face covered with lather and a towel wrapped around his waist, no other clothes on than some sandals. And boy, was he fit to be tied. He really ripped me up one side and down the other and said, "What the hell do you mean by doing that?"

I said, "Captain, what would you have done?"

He said, "That has nothing to do with it. Do I interfere with your operating the internal mechanism of this ship?"

"No, Sir." He didn't either; he never bothered me a bit.

He said, "I don't expect you to interfere with the external affairs of the ship. That's my responsibility."

He was captain of the Pompano. He was the skipper of my ship, you see. We were coming in, and he had already gotten his orders to be detached. And we were on a first-name basis ashore, after all these years. Of course, aboard ship we were formal, but ashore he was Lew and I was Slade.

Q: You were exec?

Captain Cutter: I was exec, yes. So we got ashore that night, and as usual we got drunk as we always did just coming in from patrol. Most everybody else did. Anyway, I finally said, "Lew, what the hell would you have done?"

Then he gave me that same thing, "Goddamn it. That isn't the point."

Q: But he didn't really have an answer for your question, though.

Captain Cutter: No, he didn't. He would have done the same thing, of course, but that wasn't the point. The point was that I had overstepped my bounds. You know, you would almost think he would kind of overlook it since he was leaving the next day, but that's the way he was. That was good training.

Q: Clay Blair says you were a real terror on the beach.* What did he mean by that?

Captain Cutter: Oh, God. Well, one night, again after the same patrol--we got in that night and had a big night, of course. Then the next day, in the afternoon, we were in the officers' club. This is after the Battle of Midway. We had been in Midway just two or three days after the Battle of Midway. And we had come back into Pearl. We went in there and Parks bought a

---
*On page 677 of Silent Victory, Blair writes, "...Cutter was sometimes a terror while unwinding on the beach. But at sea he was awesomely cool and able, ... For years afterwards, whenever submariners gathered to recount the war and spin yarns, the name of Slade Deville Cutter ... would soon surface."

whole--they had these mess trays for the crews, you know, the mess table with the big aluminum trays--he got one of those with one or two cases of beer on it and passed it around--on him. He was in a very expansive mood. So everybody had some beer, but he was well on his way then. He had had plenty to drink, too, of course. There were two Army guys there--these were second lieutenants--and they had been enlisted men just before the war hit. They were enlisted, and now they were officers. One of them had been aboard our ship, because he was a friend of our cook. We were trying to get a ride out to the Royal Hawaiian, where we went for our rest and recreation.* Parks's wife was still there. He lived out in Diamond Head beyond the Royal Hawaiian and was trying to get out there. So we were trying to get a ride and we couldn't get a ride. They had a curfew in Pearl Harbor then at night. So one of these guys spoke up and said, "Well, that's the trouble with the Navy. You have no morale. Here we are, we are just second lieutenants, and we have a command car." And they did. But they made a mistake. They stayed in the bar. And the second mistake they made, they left the keys in it. So we came out and there was the command car with the keys in. So Parks got in. Of course, he was the skipper, so he got behind the wheel. And the exec was a guy whose name was Thomas and who later was lost as skipper of the

---

*The Royal Hawaiian was a plush hotel on the beach at Waikiki. During World War II, it was used as a rest and recreation haven for submariners between war patrols.

<u>Pompano</u>, Connole, and myself.* So Parks tried to get the thing in reverse. It had about five speeds ahead, and the reverse was somewhere in there. He didn't know where it was. We kept inching ahead as he tried to find the reverse gear, so we went through the hedge which was right in front of the officers' club on the circle there at Pearl Harbor. Finally, he got her into reverse, backed out into the street, and we went out on the highway into town, on Dillingham Boulevard. He did get the darn thing into high. Approaching town, there were sodium vapor lights up over the road. Tommy Thomas was in the back seat. The curtains were up in this command car, and a rifle was back there with a bandolier of ammunition. It had common, tracer, and armor-piercing bullets. Armor piercing had black, common had nothing on the nose of the bullets, and red was tracer.

So he said, "See if these are the same as the Navy's, Slade." I was sitting on the front seat, and he handed me the rifle and the shells. So I loaded them, and what the hell was I going to shoot at? Well, I tried to hit those sodium vapor lights, I remember, as we went through. None of us could have seen the tracer anyway, if they had any. Then we got into town and right as you make the turn onto Beretania Street, Dole Pineapple had a water tower made like a big pineapple. That was a good target, I thought, so whammo, whammo as we were going by. The next thing

---
*Commander Willis M. Thomas, USN. Lieutenant David R. Connole, USN.

Cutter #1 - 134

we knew, a Marine car, a green Marine car—I'll never forget it—with MPs in it had pulled up alongside and motioned us over. Well, the traffic was very, very thick. The navy yard was just changing shifts or something, I guess—anyway, lots of traffic. And you come to Beretania and King, well, one goes along the waterfront and the other one goes the other way; it's about a 45-degree angle. And we are in the lefthand lane, and the Marines are left of us, so we got to Beretania, and the only place they can go is up King Street and we went down Beretania. Gee, they couldn't get us. So we got down to the Aloha Tower place there, and they had the territorial guards stationed there, you know. So they stopped us and Parks took out his wallet. We didn't have ID cards in those days. I don't know what he showed them, member of the Elks or whatever. That was enough for these guys, and they waved us through. We thought if we went in there that we would be safe. About this time, I was worried with these damn Marines after us.

I said, "Captain, let's get out of here."

"No, we'll not get out of here." It was beneath his dignity to walk to the Royal Hawaiian from Aloha Tower. It was pretty far, about four or five miles, I guess, along the Ala Wai, the yacht basin. So we just drove down to the Aloha Tower and turned left and went on out the Ala Wai, out the gate along the waterfront. I hadn't been able to spot my shots yet, see, but now we've got a yacht basin with these white balls for anchors, and now I could spot them in the water. Boy, here I was; we were going along and whammo, whammo. Christ, the next thing I knew we were up over the curb and into a palm tree. We didn't hit it but stopped by the tree. There was this same Marine car, a Jeep, and another Marine vehicle. There were three of them, and they came out with guns drawn. Christ, we put our hands up. "Don't shoot," or "We're not mad," Parks says. And they loaded us in the paddy wagon, and down to the police station we went. We got into the station, and there was a cordon of cops there, and they just walked us right through there. You see, all this gunfire going on in town---these dangerous characters out there. So they took us up to the second floor, and there we were. I don't know, a lot of things happened. Dusty Dornin heard about it somehow, and he called and talked to the sergeant or whoever it was and offered to bring down bread and water to us.

He said to Dornin, "You come down here, and we'll lock you up, too."*

Anyway, finally Parks---and this is really quite a coincidence. The military governor was in charge of Honolulu and the military government. And he was a graduate of West Point, class of 1925, a colonel, and he was a neighbor of Parks, across the street out on Diamond Head. The federal prosecuting district attorney was Parks's brother, John Parks, who later became a

---
*Lieutenant Robert E. Dornin, USN, a Naval Academy classmate of Cutter. Dornin was then executive officer of the USS Gudgeon (SS-211).

federal judge in Honolulu. Of course, Parks got hold of his brother and he got hold of the other guy. So these birds were in a quandary; they wanted to let us go, but they didn't know how to do it. So finally they wanted to know where the evidence was; they needed some evidence. Where are these shells? Well, I had some in my pocket, empties—two, as I recall. Before anything had happened I had gone to the toilet and tried to flush them down the toilet. But .30-caliber cartridges won't flush down the toilet, so I fished them out and threw them out the window, which was over the parking lot. They wanted to know where the empties were, and I said, "I don't have any." Well, that was true.

"Where are they?"

"I don't know," and that was a lie.

So Dave said, "Christ, you had these things. Why don't you give them to them? What did you do with them?"

I said, "I threw them out the window."

I'll never forget this, a guy named Detective Paul was a lip reader. Hell, he sat 30 or 40 feet away, and he read my lips and he said, "You threw those away, whereabouts?"

Well, I figured the jig was up, so I said, "Out in the parking lot."

So they gave me an MP, and down I went, walking down there and got down on my belly, at this sergeant's direction, underneath a car and got only one. I could only find the one. It was underneath one of the vehicles, and I got it. Came back up and gave them the evidence, and they let us go, subject to being recalled the next day. In the meantime, Parks had left; he was going back to the States. The next day, Thomas, who succeeded him as skipper of the Pompano, had to go down there and they gave him a bad time, because we had gotten out of it without punishment. It made the shore patrol officer very mad. He was a Navy commander. He was skipper of the Lurline, and was angry as hell at being called to active duty and being senior Navy shore patrol; he just hated it.* So he wanted to make an example of us or something, and he said if he ever caught us again we would pay for it. He said, "Parks is no longer around, and you won't have the protection of his brother and the provost marshal." So we got out of that, and we were very careful from then on in Honolulu. Parks never wanted anybody to know it, and he was worried that people were going to find out about it. Hell, everybody knew about it. You can't keep something like that quiet.

Q: Dornin was probably spreading it far and wide.

Captain Cutter: Well, everybody did, I guess. Yes, Dusty was there; Dusty was a great guy. They told him, "Come down and

---

*The SS Lurline was a Matson Lines passenger ship which regularly operated on a run between Hawaii and the West Coast of the United States. Command of the liner was certainly a more prestigious job than running the shore patrol ashore in Hawaii.

we'll throw you in, too."

But, you know, we didn't give a damn. In those days, I didn't care at all what happened. But we weren't as bad as maybe Clay Blair said we were. We played golf, and normally these things would happen just when we came in from patrol. We would get unwound, and then we would settle down and be reasonable.

Q: Why do you think you were to that "don't give a damn" stage?

Captain Cutter: I didn't expect to survive the war. I don't think anybody did, really. That's why I never kept a diary, never took any pictures, never kept any pictures of anything. I wish to goodness I had now, but I didn't. A lot of people felt that way. Some didn't; some kept really detailed diaries and kept pictures and stuff.

Q: Were you thinking that after what you had been through, that this is nothing compared with that?

Captain Cutter: Well, they were not going to keep us in port. We were going to sea. I was just sure they were not going to lock us up. I didn't worry about it. I got a kick out of their discomfort; they didn't know what to do either.

So that was a story that was widespread out there—nothing to be proud of now, but fun to look back on.

Interview Number 2 with Captain Slade D. Cutter, U.S. Navy (Retired)

Place: Nimitz Library, U.S. Naval Academy, Annapolis, Maryland

Date: Wednesday, 1 December 1982

Subject: Biography

Interviewer: Paul Stillwell

Q: In covering your educational background last night, Captain, I believe we missed one school that you attended. Would you discuss that now please?

Captain Cutter: After I graduated from high school, I stayed out one year and then got a music scholarship to Elmhurst College.* And I spent one year there playing in the orchestra, and I took German and religion. It was a religious, pre-theological school, and now it's quite well known and a good liberal arts college, I think. Then there were were all boys there and about 300. Somehow or other, they were trying to build up a football team, and they did a lot of recruiting. And some of the people they got in there were not students at all. They got me interested in football. I went out for the team, but I didn't get a chance to play. It was a nice year. It was the following year that I went to Severn. I remember Professor Stanger, who taught German. It

---
*The college, then affiliated with the Evangelical denomination, is located in Elmhurst, Illinois, one of the western suburbs of Chicago.

was a very nice experience, but that was the end of my music. When I got out of Elmhurst, I just dropped the flute and never played anymore.

Q: Had you intended to go all four years there until Mrs. Loomis intervened?

Captain Cutter: I didn't have any plans. It was during the Depression; we didn't have any money to go to college. I had this scholarship at this little school, and I was just there; I didn't learn anything to help me at all in the courses I took: algebra, religion, and German. The English was good, but I was always good in English; I really didn't need that. That was about all I took. I just killed the year is what it amounted to. Then Mrs. Loomis intervened, fortunately, and I went to Severn and on to the Naval Academy.

It is strange how little things will change your life, a complete change in direction in every way. I have noticed all through life that you make a minor decision, and the first thing you know, it has a major impact on which way you are going, what your life remains.

Q: Well, certainly submarine school did that for you, picking up now where we left off. What was your wife's reaction when you decided to go into submarines? You had just officially gotten married at that point.

Captain Cutter: Yes, well, Frannie was for anything that I was for. She was a tremendous support always. Anything I wanted to do, she wanted to do. Even in the war, she was a tremendous support. I told you about the time I took Pleatman out in the Seahorse for one run, and he had been married for three months, and he was very anxious to get back to his bride.* Incidentally, that fellow Pleatman stood number one in the submarine school. Of course, he was not a Naval Academy graduate and had had only three years of college at Colorado School of Mines. I don't know how he got into the reserve officer program, but they made a good decision in taking him. Anyway, I wrote and told my wife about it and how sorry I was that Ralph had been denied this chance to go back. She wrote back and told me, "For goodness sake, be careful. Don't let anything happen to Ralph."

Q: She wasn't worried about you?

Captain Cutter: Well, she never did worry much about it. So many of the wives would write to their husbands to be careful, don't take any chances, and all that. They had that feeling, you know. Only once on one patrol I felt that way. I had a boy whose name was West, and he was about 18 years old. He came

---
*Lieutenant Ralph F. Pleatman, USNR, who is discussed in some detail in the first interview.

aboard from the relief crew and was all steamed up about going on his first war patrol to get his combat pin. I got a tragic letter from his mother. He was an only child, she was a widow, and he was her whole life. She didn't want him to go out in the submarine and she wanted me to take him off. I got the boy in my cabin and we talked very confidentially, and I showed him the letter. I let him read it, and I said, "Now you can get off. I'll transfer you back to the relief crew." Well, he broke down and cried. He wanted to go that bad, so we took him out. I was worried about him, you know, and that was the patrol that sent us to Saipan. That was my third war patrol as skipper.* Admiral Lockwood called me in before we went and told me what we were supposed to do.** We were going to Saipan to draw off the antisubmarine units in Saipan, keep them occupied so that the Greenling could go in with the UDT people to survey the beaches on the southern coast of Saipan.*** Of course, I knew nothing about us invading Saipan.

I'll never forget, the admiral said, "Slade, you will not be taken prisoner," for the information I had about this. At that time, they were going to go in in May. Actually, they went in on

---

*This patrol began from Pearl Harbor in March 1944 and lasted 56 days before winding up in Brisbane, Australia. The Seahorse was credited with sinking five Japanese vessels with a total tonnage of 19,374.
**Vice Admiral Charles A. Lockwood, Jr., USN, Commander Submarines Pacific Fleet.
***UDT--underwater demolition teams, which were swimmers who exploded underwater obstacles in advance of the arrival of a U.S. amphibious assault force.

the 15th of June. But we caught hell out there. We drew the ASW forces off all right and we sank a submarine.* And when we hit that submarine, this kid absolutely went to pieces, screamed and fell to the deck and was out of it. From that time on, the pharmacist's mate, every time we went into an attack situation, would give him a sedative of some kind. He would knock him out so he would be quiet. But he was worrying about his mother.

Q: And she was worrying about him.

Captain Cutter: Yes, it was tragic.

But getting back to Frannie, she was a tremendous support in that she never caused me any anxiety. I was free to do my job.

Q: Were there other submarine skippers that you think had a diminished effectiveness because of that sort of input from home?

Captain Cutter: I don't know, but some of them had something working on them. They weren't very aggressive.

Q: It was a pretty select thing to be chosen for submarine school at the time you were, wasn't it?

---

*On 20 April 1944, the Seahorse sank the Japanese submarine RO-45 off Saipan.

Captain Cutter: Yes, it was. You see, there were only 30 men in each class, and there were two classes a year, which meant 60 total, and they were a very select group. There were a lot of very good students in there, and I don't know how I happened to be selected really. Dick O'Kane was another one.* Dick O'Kane was not very smart. As a matter of fact, the best submarine skippers weren't too smart. Fluckey was good, but Fluckey came in late.** He had read a lot of patrol reports; he had learned a lot. He studied many war patrol reports, and he came out and profited from his observation and studying what others had done. So Gene did a good job. He was a very flamboyant person, and I used to like to read his patrol reports, because they were written like a thriller novel instead of just a narrative of chronological events of what happened.

Q: What about Pete Galantin? He was a very smart one, wasn't he?

Captain Cutter: Yes, Pete was very smart, and I don't know just what he did, really.*** I never followed his record; he was out

---
*Lieutenant (junior grade) Richard H. O'Kane, USN, who won the Medal of Honor as a submarine commanding officer in World War II.
**Lieutenant (junior grade) Eugene B. Fluckey, USN, who won the Medal of Honor as a submarine commanding officer in World War II.
***Commander Ignatius J. Galantin, USN, was commanding officer of the USS Halibut (SS-232). He was one of only three World War II submarine skippers who eventually rose to four-star rank, the other two being Bernard A. Clarey and John S. McCain, Jr.

there the same time that we were. As a matter of fact, Dusty Dornin and I hit a convoy the same night, unbeknownst to the other, and Pete Galantin was there, too, but he didn't make his presence known.* The reason I knew there was a U.S. submarine there—I didn't know which one it was—was because I was ahead of this convoy, getting ready to go in and attack. This was a couple of hours after dark, and I was on the surface; a dark night is a beautiful opportunity. And all of a sudden, all hell broke loose in the stern of the convoy—gunfire and depth charging and all that. So I knew that a U.S. submarine was in there, but I didn't know who it was. It was Dusty Dornin. I was in a waiting area; we were going into the East China Sea, and at that time that was a very productive area, and they wanted it occupied. So they would send a submarine going in there to the waiting area, which was off Kobe, southeast of Kyushu about 160 miles, as I recall, off the coast. And then, when the submarine came out in the East China Sea, you in the waiting area would move right in; that was the idea. Most submarines didn't stay there for the 30 days that you were normally allotted for patrol. We didn't either. I don't know what Dusty was doing there; I never did find out. I guess he was on his way to the Japanese

---

*Commander Robert E. Dornin, USN, commanding officer of the USS Trigger, (SS-237). For a description of his supposed rivalry with Cutter, see Clay Blair, Jr., Silent Victory: The U.S. Submarine War Against Japan (Philadelphia: Lippincott, 1975), pages 519, 569. The incident referred to here took place the night of 1-2 November 1943.

coast or coming back; he had command of the Trigger.

Q: Clay Blair said this is what started the legend or the rumor that you and Dornin were poaching on each other's territory.

Captain Cutter: Some idiot on the staff of SubPac thought he was going to be cute. We sent in our report on the sinking and the time we sank it and so forth, and Dornin sent one in. I got two ships out of that convoy; we should have gotten more. And Dusty, I think, got two that night. And that was my first attack as a skipper. Somehow, our attacks were very close together, and there was some confusion in SubPac as to who got what—whether we were claiming the same ship. That is what they were worrying about. When they sent a dispatch out to a submarine, they didn't send it to a specific submarine. It would be in the heading. It went to all ships in the sub force on the same frequency. But in the title it would be "For Seahorse," or "For Trigger," or for whomever they wanted to receive it. Then the ships that received it weren't supposed to break down the rest of the message. Of course, we all did, you know, just to find out what was going on. So they had this thing--"The first liar doesn't have a chance," was in that dispatch, and goddamn, that made me mad. So I sent a dispatch back that we had seen the torpedoes leave our tubes, we had followed the tracks, we were on the surface, and they hit the ship, and we saw the ship sink and so on. I don't know what

Dusty sent back, but there is where they got the idea that we were mad at each other. Not at all. I was provoked at SubPac, the people who released that silly message that went to all the doggone submarines in the Pacific area, making us look like liars. You were a little neurotic under those circumstances, you know.

Q: That's understandable.

Captain Cutter: Yes, we really are.

Captain Cutter: We were talking about submarine school being a selective thing. Do you think this football business we talked about last night played a factor in you getting in---that you were known?

Captain Cutter: Well, it was based on your fitness reports, and I guess I got real good fitness reports, which I didn't really deserve for what I did in the <u>Idaho</u>, except my job as football coach. I did a good job with that, and I guess there were certain qualities of leadership that came out in the fitness reports. So I was selected. The same thing for Dick O'Kane. Dick O'Kane stood in the bottom half of his class at Annapolis, but he worked real hard at sub school, and then he went with Mush Morton. Mush Morton was his first skipper, and Mush Morton was one of the best.* He was lost in the La Perouse Strait—mined, they think. Dick had a good mentor like I did in Parks, and Dick went on and did a tremendous job. There again, I think that sometimes the very bright people—I don't like to say bright or dumb, or anything like that—but some people are more creative than others. And the creative type has imagination, and you can't have too much imagination in that business. Imagination on how to carry out an attack and that sort of stuff, but then you start worrying about the fringe areas and what they are going to do to you and all that, and you can get all tied up in it. I used imagination on getting contacts. I always found ships. I would put myself in the place of the Japanese skipper. Where would he go, knowing there was a submarine in the area, and what he would probably do to avoid us. We were in the East China Sea, and we didn't get any contacts for several days. I thought that I knew where the ships were; they were going into the Strait of Tsushima south of Korea—between Korea and Japan. But they were going in very shallow water, and we couldn't go in there. Then they would have to make the run across the East China Sea from Korea into the Strait of Tsushima. And that was deep enough water for us to dive in if necessary. I knew there were going to be ships there, but it was also mined. I mean, we were told it

---

*Commander Dudley W. Morton, USN, commanding officer of the USS Wahoo (SS-238), was lost with his submarine on 11 October 1943. He was credited with sinking 19 Japanese vessels for a total of 55,000 tons.

was mineable waters. So we got desperate—we had to sink some ships, so we went in there. I figured if we picked up a convoy and followed it in, it wouldn't go through mineable waters. We decided to go in at night on the surface so we would not have to dive where the mines might be at about 150 feet or something. We would follow them in, and then after we made the attack, come right out the way we went in, and we would avoid any mines. That's what we did and we sank two tankers that night, doing that.* But I was chicken about going in there until I just had to. Time was running out, and we wanted to do our job and get out of there.

Q: It sounds like you felt a compulsion to produce that your predecessor McGregor didn't have at all.**

Captain Cutter: Well, I don't know what his compulsion was. No, he didn't really. One night off Toagel Mlungui Pass in Palau, we picked up a convoy coming out, and I'll never forget—they had a big, three-stack transport in it. And that ship we could positively identify; it was about a 15,000-ton transport. And it

---

*On 26 November 1943, the Seahorse sank a 4,000-ton cargo ship at 33-36N, 128-57E and early on 27 November sank the 7,309-ton tanker San Ramon Maru at 33-38N, 129-05E. On 22 November, the Seahorse had sunk another ship in the vicinity, the 3,322-ton cargo ship Daishu Maru at 33-36N, 128-35E.
**Lieutenant Commander Donald McGregor, USN, was commanding officer on the first patrol of the USS Seahorse. That patrol left Pearl Harbor in August 1943, lasted 55 days, and was credited with no sinkings.

was heavily escorted, and they were heading out towards the Philippines. They went past us. We could have attacked, but we didn't. That was all right with me. The captain said, "We'll get more of them on the surface at night. If we attack now, they will hold us down, and we'll lose them." So we surfaced and went up ahead; we had gotten way ahead of them. The captain went down into the wardroom, and there he stayed, and he let me maneuver and keep ahead of them.

So I would keep going down there, "Captain, we are in position to dive." And he kept delaying it. There was a moon, partial, a quarter moon or something; finally I said, "Captain, it's getting toward daylight, and we'd better dive now. The moon is going down." He wasn't even dark adapted, didn't have on red goggles, which you are supposed to do at night. He was sitting down there just like you and I are here in this lighted room. So finally I said, "The moon is set, Captain. It's two hours before sunrise, [or whatever it was] we've got to go now."

So he said, "All right, dive." So we dove. Then he came to the conning tower, not dark adapted, put up the periscope and said, "I can't see anything. Take her down."

So we went down to 300 feet, and the convoy went right over us, and we didn't do a thing about it. I mean, it was terrible. We let them get away; I was sick. We surfaced, and again he went below. And all that day they were on a sine curve, that type of a zigzag. And when they would come on our side, there they would be, and we would ease over a little bit. We were keeping contact through our high periscope. They couldn't see us. We could just see the tops of them. We followed them and finally, around 11:00 o'clock in the morning I had been up all that previous day, all night until 11:00 A.M., and I was exhausted. So I went down and Spud Lindon, a man out of '39 and a very fine officer, had the deck so I felt confident that I could go to sleep.* So I went down there to sleep. After I had gone down there, the skipper came up and gave a different course and didn't continue to maintain contact. So Lindon sent for me and said, "We have lost contact." I couldn't believe it; the captain deliberately lost contact. So we returned to Toagel Mlungui Pass, and then he sent a message to SubPac that we had lost the convoy we were pursuing.** We had 33 convoy contacts on that patrol. He had said that on several occasions.

He got a dispatch from SubPac: "Proceed to Toagel Mlungui Pass at best speed. Remain there for the remainder of the patrol." In other words, knock off this stuff. And this shook him up. He called me in while he was writing up the patrol report; he wrote up the patrol report. I, like most people, let the execs write it up. It was just a narrative type; we didn't put ourselves into it. So he was writing the darn thing. He called me in, and I don't know why he did, but he said, "You

---
*Lieutenant Elbert C. Lindon, USN, a 1939 graduate of the Naval Academy.
**SubPac—Commander Submarine Force Pacific Fleet.

know, you'd have to be a Philadelphia lawyer to write this patrol report." Because he had an awful lot of explaining to do, and it just couldn't be done. On the basis of those reports that were going back, Captain Babe Brown, whom I had known when he was graduate manager of football, was then training officer for ComSubPac and was in charge of assigning skippers and relieving them.* So he knew me well. He knew I had been with Parks, and he knew there must have been a lot of fireworks, which there were.**

Q: You said that he was a perceptive individual.

Captain Cutter: Oh, yes, and that was why the first piece of paper that came aboard the Seahorse when we tied up in Midway was a radio dispatch, me relieving McGregor. So I tore up a letter that I had typed, putting McGregor on report. You see, he put me under hack, relieved me of all duties coming back on that patrol and made Lindon acting exec. He did it in a nice way, really. He said, "You just stay in your room, Slade. Let Spud get some training; he will do the navigating." But, in effect, he relieved me of all duty. The crew knew it. It was a very difficult situation, and I felt very depressed.

---

*Captain John H. Brown, USN.
**Lieutenant Commander Lewis S. Parks, USN, who was commanding officer of the USS Pompano (SS-181), in which Cutter made his first war patrols.

At the same time, he gave me an unsatisfactory fitness report, but he didn't make it below 2.5. I never saw it until years later, and I never paid any attention to it. In 1951, I got back to BuPers on duty, and my good friend John Sidney McCain was the director of the officer records.* And one day, after I had been there for several months, Jack and I were batting the breeze having a cup of coffee, and he said, "Slade, have you ever seen your fitness reports?"

I said, "No, I haven't bothered to go down and get them out and study them."

He said, "I think you'd better."

When I saw that, I was really upset, because McGregor recommended that I be relieved of submarine duty and be assigned to duty in connection with athletics at the Naval Academy. That was the only comment made on that, which is the kiss of death. McCain said I should consider this unsat and send it through regular channels. I don't know the exact procedure. I think I sent my comments first to McGregor, who was still on active duty. He was professor of naval science at the University of California. It went to him, and then it went to Admiral Lockwood for comment. Admiral Lockwood's comment was, "Commander Cutter, while skipper of the Seahorse [and he listed what was done in the Seahorse] and while McGregor was in command of the Gar for four

---

*BuPers—Bureau of Naval Personnel. Captain John S. McCain, Jr., was a fellow submariner.

war patrols and the <u>Seahorse</u> for one war patrol, sank one ship for 1,500 tons. I think the record speaks for itself." That's all he said, but, you see, those fitness reports stay in your record. You never look good when you take any action against what a senior has done.

Q: Well, I think you would have a real problem in terms of loyalty, too, in the expectation to support a skipper.

Captain Cutter: Yes, oh, my goodness. I really had no use for McGregor then, but later on, as I look back, and knowing his background and his age---he was approaching 40; he was too old, and it wasn't too long after that that anybody reaching his 35th birthday was no longer a skipper.* They got younger and younger and younger, as they gained experience. And also he had been in charge of the communications department at submarine school; in fact, he had been one of my teachers there. During the middle of our submarine school, McGregor relieved a fellow named Kirk Patrick.** Anyway, he believed all this stuff about the underwater sonar. He was a proponent of it in the school, and I think he really believed that it was impossible for anybody to successfully attack a convoy protected with a supersonic

---

*Donald McGregor was born 26 October 1903.
**Lieutenant Merrall K. Kirk Patrick, USN.

screen.* This is what I told him. I said, "Well, Captain, in the Pompano we went right smack underneath, and they didn't pick us up." And we did. A ship had passed right overhead off Okinawa. The sonar operators picked up so many schools of fish and whales and all sorts of things that they became slap-happy, ping-happy listening to that ping going out. They didn't pick us up.

Q: Who were some of your fellow students when you were at submarine school?

Captain Cutter: Well, there was Johnny Eichmann and Dusty Dornin, Dick O'Kane, a guy named Lautrup, Tucker, and the number one man in the class was named Warren Walker.** And Bub Ward and Johnny Hack, Keats Montross.*** Eichmann and Montross were lost during the war.**** Hank Monroe, Elliot Loughlin.***** It was a good class.

---
*Supersonic here refers to a frequency above the sonic range.
**Ensign John H. Eichmann, USN; Ensign Robert E. Dornin, USN; Lieutenant (junior grade) Richard H. O'Kane, USN; Lieutenant (junior grade) George W. Lautrup, Jr., USN; Lieutenant (junior grade) James F. Tucker, USN; Lieutenant (junior grade) William W. Walker, USN.
***Ensign Norvell G. Ward, USN; Ensign John A. Hack, USN; Ensign Keats A. Montross, USN.
****Lieutenant John H. Eichmann, USN, was lost with the USS Triton (SS-201) on 15 March 1943. Commander Keats A. Montross, USN, was commanding officer of the USS Swordfish (SS-193) when she was lost on 10 January 1945.
*****Lieutenant (junior grade) Henry S. Monroe, USN; Lieutenant (junior grade) Charles E. Loughlin, USN. Loughlin's oral history is in the Naval Institute collection.

Cutter #2 - 156

Q: Was it a really competitive class?

Captain Cutter: Very competitive—Sam Loomis was in it, and so was Myers Keithly; the two of them stood at the bottom of the class.* What happened was your assignment was based upon class standing and nobody wanted to go to China, because you couldn't take your family with you. Loomis and Keithly had been ordered out there. Everybody fought like the devil to stay out of the bottom of the class, because two people had to go to China, and then some had to go down to Panama, where they didn't particularly care to go. So there was keen competition, but it was all aboveboard. Everybody liked everybody else, and we were just in there cutting wood, you know, to do the best we could and learn as much as we could. We knew war was coming, and that's what we were training for. It was serious, very serious business.

Q: You were probably a good deal more pushed to succeed than you had been at the Naval Academy?

Captain Cutter: Yes, and I was in very fast company. Fellows like Ed Fahy, who became a naval constructor, Johnny Eichmann,

---

*Ensign Sam C. Loomis, Jr., USN; Ensign Roger Myers Keithly, USN.

Johnny Hack; they were star men at the Naval Academy.* Dusty Dornin was practically a star man. Bub Ward stood very high in the class. Most of them did. I was down in the bottom half of the class at the Naval Academy, in the third quarter of the class. Sam Loomis and Keithly were down at the bottom of the class. Dick O'Kane didn't stand very high; I don't know exactly where Dick stood. He worked his butt off at submarine school, and he ended up standing ten, as I recall; I stood 15 out of 30. I felt very proud of myself in that company. We worked and we took things that were worthwhile: diesel engineering and we learned all about batteries, and all about torpedoes and torpedo fire control; it was a fine course.

Q: Was there any training in leadership, per se, how to run a crew?

Captain Cutter: No. Most of them were just good leaders, topflight people. Fahy was the brigade commander out of the class of '34. Johnny Eichmann had four stripes; he was a battalion commander. And Dusty Dornin had a company; I had a company at the Academy. Practically all of them were stripers, showing leadership as midshipmen. They were good men.

---
*Lieutenant (junior grade) Edward J. Fahy, USN.

Q: Was there much training in tactics in submarine school?

Captain Cutter: Oh, yes, we went to the attack teacher, and we got the basics of torpedo approaches, but then a lot depended upon what boat you went to, who your skipper was. There is where it made a great difference, more than the submarine school.

Q: What was the balance of time between classroom study and in actual boats?

Captain Cutter: Mostly classroom study. We would go out once or twice a week for a morning or an afternoon. It was mostly classroom stuff. I remember those people, Webb, a fellow who taught the diesel course.* Peterson taught electricity; Brady taught tactics.** Kirk Patrick was the communicator, and he taught communications.*** We all had to learn Morse code--you had to learn it, too; you had to be able to send and receive messages. I had taken it in the Naval Academy but hadn't learned it well. I got it at submarine school, and by golly, I could take pride that later on I was better than any signalman that we had aboard taking Morse code by blinker or searchlight. In submarines, the same man had to be quartermaster and a

---
*Lieutenant Richard C. Webb, Jr., USN.
**Lieutenant George E. Peterson, USN; Lieutenant John H. Brady, USN.
***Lieutenant Merrall K. Kirk Patrick, USN.

signalman. Mostly they were rated quartermasters; signalling was just a sideline with them. In fact, I was a better typist than any of my yeomen. We were more worried about a yeoman being a bow planesman or sonarman than whether he was an expert typist.

Q: Was there any screening done for psychological factors, to see if people would have problems or claustrophobia or that sort of thing?

Captain Cutter: You know, that's a strange thing. That's a good question. Never were the officers. All the enlisted men were, and the enlisted men would get screened psychologically after every patrol. When I got down to Brisbane, we lost nine men that were taken off the boat. And I had one officer who was very shaky. In fact, I had to relieve him of all duty on the way down there to get him to rest, because he was so shaky. He was the navigator, exec---and he couldn't plot his position, his hands were shaking so bad. He was a fine officer, but it had just been too much, what we had undergone off Saipan---the constant contact with the enemy ASW forces and the large number of depth charges we got.* This is the same patrol when the man fell apart, the fellow named West; and the crew was shaky when we got down there, but they recovered. Nine had to be transferred off. We had to transfer one-fourth of the crew, anyway, so these were just part

---

*ASW---antisubmarine warfare.

of the 25%. But I had only that one fellow, West. In the
Pompano we had one fellow go berserk. As I understand, in the
German submarine force, it was common. Of course, they went
through a lot more than we did.

Q: The Germans sort of put their submariners out there until
they got killed.

Captain Cutter: Right, and they weren't trained. They took them
from the air force, the Luftwaffe, and put them in. They lost
900 and some submarines, and they just didn't have enough
people--not enough volunteers, and they were up against a lot
more proficient ASW than we were. Let's face it. The Japanese
were not very good in antisubmarine warfare, not nearly as good
as we gave them credit for, I don't think. Parks had utter
contempt for them; he didn't pay any attention to them.* That
was one extreme.

When the war started, from the very first day of the war--we
went on patrol the 17th of December, we left Pearl Harbor on
patrol, and we didn't dive until we got almost to Wake Island.
The other submarines, practically all of them, would stay
submerged all day long and run on the surface only at night. Of
course, that was stopped very soon, because it took too long to

---

*Lieutenant Commander Lewis S. Parks, USN, commanding officer
of the USS Pompano, in which Cutter was serving at the beginning
of World War II.

get to the patrol area, staying submerged all day making two knots and then getting up at night. Parks didn't pay any attention to it; off he went.

Q: What about escape training? Was that part of the submarine school course?

Captain Cutter: Yes, there was a water tank 100 feet high at the submarine school. All students, officer and enlisted, had to go from bottom to top using the Momsen lung. I think there were nine men below in the Tang who escaped from 180 feet of water with Momsen lungs.* But those were the only ones I know that ever used it. We all had the training. I guess it gave you a little sense of security. When you are out there in the Pacific with the bottom at 2,000 fathoms, you don't worry much about Momsen lungs.

Q: You mentioned that when you had diphtheria you had heard about these fellows in the S-51. Was this in your mind when you were going through submarine school?

Captain Cutter: No. That's the beauty of being young; you don't worry about things like that. It isn't going to happen to you

---
*Nine survivors, including commanding officer Richard H. O'Kane, escaped when the USS Tang (SS-306) was sunk by a malfunctioning torpedo she had fired on 24 October 1944.

what happened to the other guy.

Q: Any other recollections about submarine school?

Captain Cutter: No.

Q: Then perhaps one of the luckiest breaks you got was going to the Pompano under Parks.

Captain Cutter: Yes, it was. He was a taskmaster. He was a hard man to please, very tough, and not very popular, because he was extremely competitive. And all these little tricks that he had, they were all his. And he didn't want us to divulge them to anybody else, and he didn't tell us--I am talking about his officers--until we had been aboard for, golly, we had been out in Pearl Harbor for a year, I guess, before he said, "War is coming, and I am going to divulge these secrets, but don't you tell anybody else."

Such as how to conduct an approach from beginning to end without using any of the instruments. That helped one night, I was on a convoy. The tankers were in the center, so I was going in to get the tankers and I had passed the outer screen and the outer column of them. We had about a 60-track. I had to come toward, because the range was so short, and I had to shoot; if I had waited until the 90-track, it would have been too close for the torpedoes to arm. So while I was waiting for him to come to the firing bearing, I looked up ahead and I saw a blurb on the horizon. I didn't know how far away it was. I knew it was the same course as the convoy that we were tracking and at the same speed, but I didn't know what the range was. But I saw that it was just on the starboard bow, which meant that we would have about a zero gyro angle. And if you have a zero gyro angle, solving the triangle, you use the same angle to get a ship at 500 yards or 5,000 yards; it is just a similar triangle. So just instinctively I said, "Shift the setup. Do not change range. Bearing, mark, stand by, fire"--like that. I didn't care what the range was; all I had to do was get the bearing in there because we had the zero gyro angle--the same solution as we would have for the ship that was coming up. We got both of them. The tanker blew up and burned furiously, and Tony Gallaher--we were in a wolf pack with Tony, who was a very fine submarine skipper.[*]

Q: Was this your last patrol?

Captain Cutter: It was my last; it was my fourth patrol; you are right. Tony was way off; I knew where he was when we picked up this convoy, and I knew where they were going, what course they

---

[*]Commander Antone R. Gallaher, USN, commanding officer of the USS Bang (SS-385) and commander of the wolf pack which was made up of the Bang, Seahorse, and Growler. The incident described here took place on 27 June 1944; the Seahorse was credited with sinking the 5,000-ton tanker Medan Maru.

were on. There was no way he could make contact with that convoy, so I didn't tell him. Well, when this ship blew up, it looked to Tony like he was just next door. Of course, he was over the horizon, but it looked close, because he burned for hours. Hell, he was still burning in the morning. This was 3:00 o'clock when I sank him, and he was still burning at daylight. Anyway, I rendezvoused with Tony that night, and he was really angry with me. He thought that I had deliberately said nothing to him. That was not the case. He made a contact three or four days later, and I always thought he just deliberately did not let us know about this contact. I don't know whether we could have gotten in or not. I don't know; Tony and I were very good friends, but I think he was whizzed off at us that one time.

Q: Why didn't you notify him about this ship?

Captain Cutter: He couldn't have gotten in. He was too far away. I knew where he was, and it was going away from him. He would have to overtake, and there was no way he could get up there. Later on, we were at the Academy together. He mentioned it a couple of times, and he realized that then but, you know, the pressure of the time and so forth. He was having a hard time making contacts. I was in the area about a week, and all my torpedoes were gone, and I was heading for home. Poor Tony hadn't gotten a ship, and he spent 30 days and asked for a

Cutter #2 - 165

seven-day extension, so he spent 37 days in the area. I don't know that he got anything. Just that there were no contacts. But we were just lucky in the Seahorse. We ran into them, got rid of our fish, and headed for home.

Q: Was Parks the skipper of the Pompano when you reported?

Captain Cutter: No.

Q: Who was your first skipper?

Captain Cutter: Hanson, a very fine man.* He was in the class of 1921; Parks was 1925. Pop was too old. I was only aboard about three months with him, and I liked him very much. We were in the navy yard when the ship was being built. We were with Parks for about a year before the ship went to sea.

Q: Why was this first skipper not allowed to see it through?

Captain Cutter: Because they had to take the engines out and send them back to the factory--it was just too long. Parks was the resident inspector at the factory where these engines were being built, Hooven-Owens-Rentschler Company in Hamilton, Ohio.

---
*Lieutenant Commander Ralph E. Hanson, USN. Hanson had been a lieutenant when he put the Pompano (SS-181) into commission as her first commanding officer on 12 June 1937.

So they sent Parks out with the engines; when they sent the engines back to install in the ship, they sent him with them. In other words, you live with your problem. Parks was a very competent engineer. Those engines were absolutely no good; eventually, they were taken out of all our submarines. They were in about seven of them: Salmon, Seal, Skipjack, and three others had them, plus the Pompano. They were terrible.

Q: What was the problem with the engines?

Captain Cutter: They were double-acting, which means it was like an old steam engine. They had an upper cylinder head and a lower cylinder head with one piston. The piston rod went through a stuffing gland into the lower cylinder head. Diesel engines generate a lot of heat, and the stuffing glands in the bottom cylinder head would get full of carbon and would freeze. This would eventually cause an engine breakdown. There were just all kinds of problems with those engines.

Q: What were your duties in connection with the outfitting of the Pompano?

Captain Cutter: I was the "George," being the junior one, you know. They had only four officers on the ship—the skipper, the exec, Penrod Schneider, and myself, when I first went there.* So I was the commissary officer, the communicator, the assistant engineer, and all the odds and ends that "George" gets in a submarine. Then Connole reported aboard; he was out of the class of '36.** And, later, Thomas, who was the skipper when she went down.*** Warner Edsall, who later was skipper of the Missouri—as a matter of fact, he dropped dead out at Sasebo, coming into port, on the bridge.**** His widow is still alive at Vinson Hall.

Q: Did you have any duties in connection with actually outfitting the ship or getting her ready to go?

Captain Cutter: Oh, just routine things, getting provisions aboard and stuff like that. I had no great responsibility.

Q: The fact that Parks of the class of '25 would relieve a guy four years senior would suggest that already at that point they were trying to get more youth into the submarine force.

Captain Cutter: I don't think so. We had people like Admiral

---

*Lieutenant (junior grade) Earle C. Schneider, USN.
**Lieutenant (junior grade) David R. Connole, USN.
***Lieutenant Willis M. Thomas, USN.
****Lieutenant Warner R. Edsall, USN. He died 26 March 1953 of a heart attack while conning the USS Missouri (BB-63).

Crawford (we used to call him "Turkey Neck"). He was a nice guy; he was skipper of the Perch, and he was of the class of '21.* And Weary Wilkins, who was from the class of '24.** As a matter of fact, he relieved me as skipper of the Seahorse, took it out on one run as commander of a wolf pack. I don't think they were going for the youth at that time. Actually, most of the skippers were PG engineers, and the reason for it---we were having a lot of trouble with diesel engines, and they wanted skippers who knew about the diesel engines. Parks knew more about those engines than anybody aboard. Most all of them were engineers. They didn't turn out to be particularly proficient when the war hit. But, of course, they were handicapped by the terrible torpedoes; we can't condemn any of those men. You go out there and fire something that you just know isn't going to go off. It was a great comfort to me--I took out one of the first two loads of the good torpedoes from Midway. I think Dusty Dornin got the other load.*** We both left at about the same time on my first run. Admiral Lockwood came to Midway Island and brought an exploder with him.**** He had the skippers, the torpedomen and the torpedo officers of the boats meet with him and personally demonstrated what was wrong with the torpedoes and

---

*Lieutenant Commander George C. Crawford, USN.
**Lieutenant Commander Charles W. Wilkins, USN.
***Lieutenant Commander Robert E. Dornin, USN, commanding officer of the USS Trigger (SS-237) in October 1943 when she and Cutter's Seahorse went on patrol from Midway.
****Vice Admiral Charles A. Lockwood, Jr., USN, Commander Submarines Pacific Fleet.

how they had been corrected. I guess you have heard all that story. It gave us tremendous confidence, because we believed in Admiral Lockwood, and it made a lot of sense what the problem was. On my first patrol, the first ship we sank was at night and we were on the surface. It was a great satisfaction to see the first torpedo we fired hit, explode on a 90 track, and see that ship break up in two and go down.* If we made a successful attack submerged, I didn't worry much about depth charges, because I would always go right in where the ship was, very close to it, figuring that with the survivors in the water, they were not going to drop a lot of depth charges, and they didn't. Then, when things cooled off, we would ease on out. But if you missed, you caught hell. They didn't have to worry. They had you there, and they would get you. There was a destroyer we fired at off Hong Kong on my last patrol--just as an afterthought--and I missed; we fired at a couple of other ships from the stern tubes and had the bow tubes left, so we let go a couple of fish at this guy, even though we didn't have a proper setup on him. But, anyway, I had what they called pillen werfers aboard. Now pillen werfers were what the Germans used. We released them through the signal tube in the after torpedo room. They would effervesce and create a stream of bubbles in water that would be a stationary target for active sonar. Well, some of the Japs were pretty

---

*A 90 track meant that the torpedoes were fired to hit the target ship at an angle perpendicular to her course.

good. I have said they weren't very good as a whole, but there are always some exceptions to any general rule. With a moving target you get what is called doppler effect. If the ship is moving toward you, when that sound wave hits, the returning sound wave will come back at a higher frequency than it went out, even though the target is making only a knot and a half. And if it's going away, you get a lower pitch coming back. If it's a 90-degree track, the returning sound wave is without any doppler effect from the target, and you had better be suspicious that the target is stationary and not a ship. Anyway, I had been carrying these things for two war patrols. Now this is what I was talking about previously. If you make too many patrols, you get careless. You become contemptuous of the enemy. So, the hell with it. Let's fire one and see what happens. We didn't have to, but we fired one. Well, that destroyer skipper zeroed in on that stream of bubbles. He came right through it and started searching, and he picked us up. And we had one of the best depth charge attacks we had during the war from that guy.

Q: And probably unnecessary in retrospect.

Captain Cutter: Unnecessary! It was stupid. I had been carrying them for two war patrols and never used one, and I don't

Cutter #2 - 171

know of anybody else who used them, but I just did it for the hell of it. He didn't have contact with us. Of course, he could turn and come down the torpedo tracks, but by that time we could have moved on out. But we showed him exactly where we were when we let go that pillen werfer from our submerged signal gun.

Q: You said Parks very jealously guarded those secrets of attack. That strikes me as a very selfish thing to do when you could benefit the whole submarine force.

Captain Cutter: He was very competitive. Parks was going to make admiral come hell or high water, and he did. Everything he did was geared to making flag rank. He was a paradox. One of my very best friends, and I admire him, as you can see, but like all human beings he had frailties. And one of them was a terrific ego and tremendous ambition. He wouldn't walk up over anybody else; he did it on his own. He didn't make anybody else look bad to gain his, but he wasn't going to share things that he felt were unique, that he had discovered and were giving him an advantage over his peers. He just wouldn't divulge those secrets. I guess I told you about the time that we were attacking the battleships?

Q: You told me about it in a letter, but I would like to get it on the tape.

Captain Cutter: This is evidence of the stodginess of the high command we had in submarines before the war. They were well intentioned. They had good intentions, but they really didn't know much about modern submarine warfare. At the beginning, I am talking about---the ones we had. One was Tommy Withers, a very fine, old gentleman; we all loved him and so on.*

We were sent out on a fleet exercise in which the battleships were protected by a destroyer screen. We were ordered to attack using only sonar to obtain data to fire exercise torpedoes. Our sonar throughout the war was never really good, but in those days it was really bad. Here was all this noise around us, all these ships around there and we are supposed to go in and get sonar bearings and ranges and fire torpedoes. We were using exercise torpedoes to fire at the battle line. We couldn't get a thing; it was just a madhouse of noise from all those ships milling around above us, so Parks came up to take a look. He fired, and we got a hit, and nobody else got any hits. In the endorsement, Parks was accused, in a nice way, of cowardice---losing his nerve was the way they put it---by coming up and taking a look. Actually, and they should have known it, he was damn brave to come up and take a look from the information we had, which was very little.

---
*Rear Admiral Thomas Withers, USN, Commander Submarines, Scouting Force, U.S. Fleet.

Q: Did he hazard the boat in coming up for a look?

Captain Cutter: No, but he took a calculated risk. We weren't exactly sure where the rest of the ships were. There was too much noise on the screen. So he caught the devil for that. During this same period, he believed that the magnetic exploder was too theoretical; he wanted a practical demonstration. He had never heard of one. The way they demonstrated its effectiveness was to set one up in the torpedo shop—I was torpedo officer at the time, so I was privy to this—and pass a charged wand over it. It would go "click," and they would say, "See, it works." That was supposed to simulate a torpedo going through a magnetic field. Well, it didn't work during the war, and finally they inactivated it, you have probably heard that story. Admiral Christie insisted they were good, but finally they were just made inactive.*

Q: But Parks was skeptical already?

Captain Cutter: Sure. So he wrote an official letter and wanted

---
*Lieutenant Ralph W. Christie, USN, conducted torpedo experiments in the 1920s, as recounted by Clay Blair, Jr., in Silent Victory: The U.S. Submarine War Against Japan (Philadelphia: J.B. Lippincott Company, 1975), pages 54-56. By World War II, Christie was a captain—and later rear admiral—in command of U.S. submarines based in Australia. He was defensive about the performance of the torpedoes he had helped develop and thus reluctant to concede shortcomings. See Blair for further details on the controversy.

a demonstration—fire one with a warhead through a magnetic field and see if it works. And he told them where they could do it—off of East Loch inside Pearl Harbor. They wouldn't do it, because they said there weren't enough torpedoes in our arsenal. He asked for two torpedoes, and I think they said at the time that two and a half torpedoes per week were coming out of Newport, and that was the only place they were being built. And we couldn't afford the luxury of firing, so we didn't.

Q: How many dozens and dozens were wasted after that?

Captain Cutter: And lives were lost. I believe it was Chuck Triebel who sent a letter to the Secretary of the Navy demanding that Admiral Blandy, Chief of Naval Ordnance, be court-martialed for culpable negligence, or whatever he called it.* And then he listed two or three submarines that he felt sure were lost because of the faulty torpedoes. One of the submarines fired a torpedo that failed to start when fired and just went out and went straight down. It was armed and went off when it hit the bottom. It really shook up the submarine. It went off way down deep. But they were horrible at the beginning of the war. That was an electric torpedo that did that, but I had very good luck

---

*Commander Charles O. Triebel, USN, commanding officer of the USS Snook (SS-279); Rear Admiral William H.P. Blandy, USN, chief of the Bureau of Ordnance. According to Blair in Silent Victory, page 588, Triebel's letter was intercepted by Admiral Lockwood but had its effect. Triebel was assigned to the Bureau of Ordnance to help deal with the problem.

with electric torpedoes.

Q: Did you have the option of inactivating that magnetic warhead and using a contact warhead?

Captain Cutter: By the time I got to be skipper, it already had been done.

Q: I mean when you were in the *Pompano*.

Captain Cutter: As a matter of fact, we didn't have them in the *Pompano*, because they gave us old Mark 10 torpedoes. They didn't have enough Mark 14's, which were the new ones, and we made our patrols with Mark 10's, which were 36-knot torpedoes. But they didn't have a magnetic exploder mechanism, and their exploders worked. We were the only navy in the world that had the firing pin vertical. There was a ring sitting on these four supports for it, and if it got bumped in any direction, the ring would be released. It would fall off, and a spring would take the firing pin up. And there were two fulminate of mercury caps in the booster. There were two tits on the firing pin that would hit these caps and explode. And they would set off the booster, which would set off the main charge. In theory this was fine. But, because the firing pin moved vertically, driven by a spring, it would not strike the caps with sufficient force to explode them under certain conditions. When the torpedo hit the target at a 90-degree angle, the negative G force would cause the firing pin to get bound in its guide and not strike the caps with sufficient force to detonate them. When the impact angle was small, all was well.

Then, later on, after we got that solved, we weren't getting real, high-order explosions, because as the warhead crushed, part of the TNT or torpex or whatever we were using would fall out, and all of it would not be exploded by the booster. The Germans, the Italians, the French, the British--all of them had their firing mechanism in the nose in a horizontal position, so it went straight back and the impact helped the spring set off the caps. There was no question about it going off. We had copper warheads, because they didn't deteriorate. They would last forever, made out of copper. Then during the war they became steel because you didn't have copper; copper was going into electric wiring and stuff. The warheads weren't going to have to last that long anyway, to rust through. The steel warhead didn't crush like that. When we started to use them, I was startled the first time I fired a steel-jacketed warhead and heard the explosion. It was much louder than the ones with copper warheads. They found that out at Kahoolawe Island, Hawaii, where they fired live torpedoes into the vertical cliffs and then sent divers down where they found these pieces of unexploded torpex on the floor of the ocean underneath these cliffs.

Q: Didn't it become at one point that skippers were trying for a shot less than 90 degrees?

Captain Cutter: We were told to do that by SubPac, a glancing blow. But many times we didn't have the luxury of choosing what angle we were going to use to fire at a target.

Q: Do you have any more observations on Parks as a teacher?

Captain Cutter: No, no more. He was an outstanding teacher, because he was very demanding, and he was in an environment where we were all highly motivated. He was a great leader, and the war was coming on. He used to send me, as torpedo officer and fire control officer—when the Tatsuta Maru or one of the big ships came in from Japan to go down to the docks at Aloha Tower in Honolulu and look them over. He wanted me to see if there were any features or anything on those ships that was unique that would help estimate the angle on the bow. The angle on the bow is the angle between the fore-and-aft axis of the ship and the line that runs from the submarine to the ship.

Q: The target angle?

Captain Cutter: Not target angle—the angle on the bow. The target angle is the angle between your torpedo track and the

Cutter #2 - 178

course of the ship. The angle of the bow is how we determine the course of the ship; this is all relative to you.

Q: Where were you operating out of then, Pearl Harbor?

Captain Cutter: Yes, in those days we were operating ten days at sea, and then we would come in for three days, and ten days out. Sometimes we would be in during the week, sometimes on the weekend, just however the days hit.

Q: So Japanese merchant ships were coming through Hawaii then?

Captain Cutter: Oh, yes, they would come through and stop on the way to San Francisco. They were beautiful ships.

Q: Could you place the event chronologically, the war game in which you got the hit on the battleship?

Captain Cutter: I would say early in 1941. We got out there in May of 1940, and I think this was early in '41.

Q: By that time, the battle fleet was stationed there also.

Captain Cutter: Oh, yes, they had come out from the East Coast in the spring of 1940. But they had been there for quite a while before we had this exercise. I remember the first time we ever heard about radar. That was a well-kept secret. We went in on the California at night. We were on the surface, and what a shock it was when all of a sudden they opened up with 36-inch searchlights on us. This was before the war.

Q: I think she was the first ship to have a CIC.*

Captain Cutter: Yes, California was the first one. It was a great big bedspring sort of thing, quite crude, I guess, but they were able to pick us up. They didn't get us until we got in to about less than 2,000 yards, but when they did they were right on. So that was very unnerving.

Q: They had a radio officer named Henry Bernstein, who was one of the very early radar experts, so they were quite capable.**

Captain Cutter: Yes, they were, with rather primitive equipment.

Q: I take it you were surprised when the light picked you up.

Captain Cutter: We sure were. God, what happened? Normally we could go in at night and would never get picked up. Those Japs

---

*CIC—combat intelligence center.
**Lieutenant Henry E. Bernstein, USN.

could pick us up, though. They didn't have radar, but they had much better night glasses than we did. I got picked up several times at night where I just couldn't believe that they could see a submarine.

Q: How would you know that you had been seen?

Captain Cutter: The angle on the bow of the nearest destroyer would be zero. That was all the evidence we needed.

Q: How did the crew regard Captain Parks?

Captain Cutter: They liked him. Parks was tough. We were down in Tahiti--the kind of leader the guy was, he wanted everybody back aboard before midnight and no fooling. He was very public relations-conscious, and this was a French possession at the time. They were at war, and they wanted all U.S. sailors off the street by midnight. They had a curfew there in Papeete, Tahiti, so we had liberty expire at midnight. Well, we had a second class electrician's mate, a little Portuguese fellow, a real good man, and he was on report. He had gotten in late, about 12:30. It was at mast, and I was his division officer. (That was before I became exec). He came up to mast and the captain said, "What's the story, Ortez?"

"Well, Captain, it's this way. I had gone up to town and had a few beers and I was coming back, and you know where that coal pile is in the lumber yard and the path coming through there on the way down here to the dock?"

And the captain said, "Yes, I know."

"Well," he said, "as I was walking down this dark pathway, this hand reached up on the lumber yard side and pulled me down. So, Captain, you know how it is, Sir, but the trouble was I had had too much to drink, and it just took me longer than it should have."

So the captain said to him, "Case dismissed."

That was one of the few times he excused a man at mast; he could understand that. He excused the fellow. Parks was a great guy.

Q: Sometimes, an ambitious skipper will burn out his crew to further his own career.

Captain Cutter: He never did that, never. He protected his crew; he protected his officers and men. He was like a mother hen. Nobody ever better criticize anybody in the *Pompano*; that was a criticism of him. He wouldn't tolerate that.

Q: In what sense did he provide protection?

Captain Cutter: Well, if anybody got into trouble with the shore

Cutter #2 - 182

patrol or anything, he would go to bat for them; he'd say, "I'll take care of that; that's my problem, not yours."

We all knew he was behind us, and we had a very high _esprit de corps_, in spite of the fact that he was tough. A lot of tough skippers didn't have any _esprit de corps_. They didn't have the qualities of leadership that Parks had.

Q: You have referred to him as a sundowner. That's not the usual sort that inspires loyalty and high morale.

Captain Cutter: Maybe I chose the wrong word. He had the same qualities a lot of sundowners have, but he was more than that. He was a stickler for the regulations and detail. Like I told you about, when I was exec and he gave me hell for answering a legitimate request from another skipper.

Q: Would it be fair, then, to call him strict but not mean?

Captain Cutter: Yes. He wasn't mean at all. No, he didn't have a mean bone in his body. And he was always very loyal, and he expected loyalty, too. It was up and down, both ways with him. Then, that's how I got into public information business, which was the biggest mistake of my life, because I was completely unsuited for public information. You have been in PR. You know what you need. You have to keep your mouth shut lots of times and don't say all you know and don't be frank and aboveboard. You've got to hedge and all that. Well, I wasn't any good at that. For instance, when I was director of athletics, I didn't care for basketball, I never liked basketball and Ben Carnevale was the head basketball coach and a great guy.* Every Wednesday, he would have a luncheon for the sportswriters, the *Baltimore Sun*, *The Washington Post*, and the *Evening Star*. This particular time, he asked me if I would come up. I never went to them, but he said, "Would you come up and have lunch with us?"

And I said, "Sure." We were sitting at card tables in the fieldhouse, right on the basketball floor, and he was giving this spiel about the basketball team. As I was talking during lunch, I said, "You know, [this is exactly what I said] these whistle blowers are making a sissy sport out of basketball. They blow the whistle all the time. The kids just can't do anything out there—this personal foul business."

The next day, in the papers, it came out, "Cutter says basketball is a sissy sport." The Superintendent wanted to know about that and so did a lot of other people. Oh, boy! And that was after I had been on public information duty for two years, and I hadn't learned.

K.G. Schacht said, "If somebody could put a clothespin on

---

*This refers to Cutter's tour of duty at the Naval Academy in the late 1950s. Carnevale served as the Academy's basketball coach from the 1946-1947 season to 1965-1966, compiling a record of 308-169.

your mouth, you'd be a hell of a lot better off."*

Q: What difference did it make for you when you made the transition from division officer to exec?

Captain Cutter: None. I had more responsibility. I was ready for it. I had been on there for so long. I had been on there two and a half years with Parks by then. We had gone through Edsall, Thomas, Schneider—three execs—and I just moved up until I got to exec. Then Connole, who was beneath me, relieved me.

Q: Was that pretty much the standard practice in submarines at the time?

Captain Cutter: Yes. It was very seldom that they pulled an exec off another ship. It was very seldom that someone would be ordered to a submarine as exec, except, of course, in new construction. Instead, we would fleet up.

Q: Well, you took over as navigator at that point, didn't you?

Captain Cutter: Oh, yes.

---

*Captain Kenneth G. Schacht, USN. He and Cutter were Naval Academy classmates and also went through submarine school together. At the time of this incident, Schacht was chairman of the Naval Academy's department of seamanship and navigation.

Q: Were there two or three officers under you then?

Captain Cutter: Well, everybody, internally in the ship, is under the executive officer; he runs the whole show. The executive officer has to be pretty hard-nosed about everybody doing their duty and all that. The skipper, Parks, would have none of that. The crew really worshipped the guy; they didn't know how tough he was. They didn't know what he was giving me. You used to say that the exec has always got to be a son of a bitch; you have heard that. He doesn't have to be that, but he's got to lay down the rules and see that they are observed, and arrange for the training schedule and all that sort of stuff.

Q: I am just wondering if it made a difference from going to being one of the guys as a division officer to then having to be an intermediary between them and the captain?

Captain Cutter: No, I don't think so. I didn't feel any difference. I was very comfortable with Parks by then, and I had tremendous respect and admiration for him. There was no problem.

Q: I think it would help also, in a wardroom that small, that people are very close to each other.

Captain Cutter: Oh, yes. We got in to Pearl Harbor on Tuesday morning after the attack. And on the dock was a fellow named Thomas Patrick McGrath who had been brigade commander at the Naval Academy and a football player.* He was on the football team when I was assistant line coach my second year, when I was with the varsity. The first year I was with the plebes, and second year I was with varsity. So I knew Tom real well. He was a guard and a real good one, and he was also a heavyweight wrestler, a very handsome fellow from Tucson, Arizona, and a good student—just an all-around, all-American boy. Well, he was on the dock when we pulled in to Pearl Harbor on Tuesday morning. All he had on was a .45 strapped on him, a pair of khaki shorts and sandals, open sandals. That was all he had. He was signal officer on the *California*, and he was up on the signal bridge firing his pistol at the Jap planes. The ship sank; all of his clothes were there, and he had been sleeping up in the submarine base grounds with a lot of other survivors. So the *Pompano* was coming in, and he came down and met us as we came in. He knew I was aboard the *Pompano* somehow or other—I don't know how—and he came aboard. I invited him down in the wardroom to have lunch with us, so he came down. He was a scrappy Irishman, and he said, "I want to go out on the first ship that's going out after those bastards." That's the way he talked.

The skipper was in his cabin, which was just aft of the

---

*McGrath, who had been graduated from the Naval Academy in the class of 1940, was an ensign at the time of the attack on Pearl Harbor in December 1941.

wardroom, and he said, "Young man, do you mean that?"

"Yes, Sir," said McGrath.

With that, Parks got up and went to headquarters. He wasn't gone 15 minutes, and back he came, "Son, you are a member of the Pompano crew."

He had gone up there to Admiral Kimmel's headquarters; he had seen the personnel officer and had Tom assigned to the Pompano.* So he started out at the bottom.

Q: He had had no submarine training previously?

Captain Cutter: No, he never did go to submarine school, and he went down as exec.** And he was really a great guy. I'll never forget--he was in the control room, and I don't remember what his job was. He wasn't diving officer, but we were under depth charge attack and the man on the trim manifold, which is the one that pumps the water around the ship to even it off and to pump water out if you get heavy or flood water in if you are light. It's called the trim manifold and had about ten valves there. And the guy tending it just crapped out; I mean, he just couldn't do it, just froze. I'll never forget McGrath manning that trim manifold--I mean very efficiently and very quickly he opened and

---
*Admiral Husband E. Kimmel, USN, Commander in Chief Pacific Fleet until he was relieved in mid-December.
**McGrath was a lieutenant when the Pompano was lost in September 1943.

closed the valves and his knees knocking together. But he was functioning 100%, scared as hell; we all were. But he functioned and did the right thing. I'll never forget that.

Q: Admiral Withers, I think, was Commander of the Submarines Scouting Force at that point.

Captain Cutter: Yes, in the early part of the war.

Q: Did you have much contact with that staff?

Captain Cutter: None. They were kind of cold, nothing like we had during the war with Admiral Lockwood. And Admiral English was a good man, too.* He was younger. They brought him in, and he brought a good staff, but they were all killed--a plane crash. That's when Lockwood came out. Then Lockwood and Voge and Grenfell; they were really fine people.** Voge and Grenfell had been skippers right at the start of the war and they were too old; they were from the class of '25 and '26. They both had some war patrol experience, and we needed that kind of person in operations and in personnel.

---
*Rear Admiral Robert H. English, USN, was Commander Submarines Pacific Fleet from 14 May 1942 until his death in an airplane crash in late January 1943.
**Rear Admiral Charles A. Lockwood, USN, later promoted to vice admiral, succeeded English. Lieutenant Commander Richard G. Voge, USN, was SubPac operations officer; Lieutenant Commander Elton W. Grenfell, USN, was the SubPac strategic plans officer.

Q: You mentioned Voge. He is almost a legend as far as the submarine force is concerned. What are your recollections of him?

Captain Cutter: Well, my recollections of him are all very pleasant, because when I went out on my first war patrol I went out from Midway, so I didn't see him. I got my operation order, and off we went. But we came back to Pearl Harbor, after completing the best patrol of the war up to that time. I came into port, and when I went up to see the admiral for the debriefing or whatever—every time you came in from patrol, you would go up and see Admiral Lockwood. And somehow I got to see Dick Voge. And he said, "What were you doing on the 27th of November?" And I told him, because he hadn't seen our patrol report; we had just gotten in there. We had sunk a tanker that absolutely disintegrated. It was a tremendous explosion; they were carrying gasoline.*

"Well," he said, "what happened to that destroyer that was nearby?"

I said, "He started signaling at us, sending a recognition signal, [this was going into Tsushima Straits that night] and that's why I had to fire at such a long range. I fired a torpedo run of 4,200 yards, [which is really a long way off] and the

---

*This was the San Ramon Maru. Cutter discussed this incident earlier in the oral history. See page 149.

reason I did was because he was signaling at us. And all we had left were torpedoes aft. All we had were in the aft torpedo tubes, so I made a 180-degree turn and fired as soon as we steadied up, because I figured this destroyer was coming after us." We bailed out of there at full speed, and I called for the cameraman to come up and take a picture. If this thing went, I wanted to see it. It did. I was starting to swear, because so much time had gone by. It seemed forever. At 47 knots, for 4,000 yards it took about two or three minutes. I don't know the math of it, but it just seemed like forever. Finally, the kids below heard it, which you always did through the water--an explosion hit--and I heard the cheering from below, so I knew we hit him and then fingers of flame the whole length of that ship. Red flames came out, and all of a sudden it went up in a mushroom. Just like a huge mushroom, and it was sort of a dark beige, lighted from beneath, I guess. And that thing hung there in the air, and in the end turned into a brilliant blue white. You could read a newspaper. We saw pieces of this ship falling into the ocean. We were then two miles away, more than that. So I said, "Radar, get on that destroyer. Watch him, because we want to get out the same way we came in." We didn't want to get in any minefield. Radar and plot reported, "Speed zero," and he never bothered us. Well, I sort of forgot about him. We had other things to do.

Voge told us that 26 people had been killed and the ship was immobilized; it had wiped off the topside apparently. If 26 were killed, that meant just the guys topside, I guess.

Q: In the destroyer?

Captain Cutter: Yes, in the destroyer. He had gotten this from Japanese intelligence, and he knew about it.* He knew we had sunk two ships out of that convoy. He wanted to know the details of what had happened, so I told him the story. Then, when we got ready to go out that time, he called me up and wanted to know where I wanted to go.

Q: This was after your first patrol?

Captain Cutter: Yes.

He said, "Where do you want to go on patrol?"

And I said, "The Seahorse has unfinished business down in Palau." Where we had these 33 convoy contacts our first patrol. I said, "I want to go back there."

"Okay, you can go."

In fact, he held the area open for six days to let us get in. That was another hot area that wanted a submarine there all the time. We never got there. We picked up a convoy before we got

---

*Voge was being supplied with Ultra—decrypted versions of intercepted Japanese radio messages.

there, and we messed around with that, got a couple of ships out of it. And then, just before we got to the patrol area in Palau, we picked up another convoy, and we were in contact with that for 82 hours. We sank only three ships—should have done better than that, but it was pretty heavily escorted.* After I wrote to you, I read that patrol report, and it was kind of hairy.** They had air cover during the daytime, and it was awfully hard to get up ahead of them. Then they had good escorts; they didn't pick us up, but they were always maneuvering back and forth across in front of the convoy. We couldn't get in a good position until the last day, and we sank two of them that last attack. Then our torpedoes were gone and we headed for home. That was the night the pharmacist's mate gave me the Old Crow whiskey.

Q: Where was the Pompano at the time Pearl Harbor was attacked?

Captain Cutter: We were coming back to Pearl Harbor from Mare Island, and that's an interesting story. We were with the Pollack, Plunger, and Pompano—a division of submarines that had been sent back to get degaussing gear installed and to get the

---

*This incident took place from 28 January 1944 to 1 February. Cutter discussed it previously on pages 53-54.
**Copies of Cutter's patrol reports are on file in the Operational Archives Branch of the Naval Historical Center, Washington, D.C.

conning tower doors removed.* We had, believe it or not, glass windows in our conning towers, and they were taken out and welded shut with steel. The degaussing equipment was put on, and we were there for two months.

Q: Where, Mare Island?

Captain Cutter: Mare Island. So we left, I think it was the 1st of December, for Pearl. In the meantime, just before the end of November, I got a letter from my wife, and she said, "Admiral Kidd stopped by with a driver on a Sunday and said, 'If you ever want anything, get in touch with me.' I wonder what he means."**

People talk about flag officers not knowing war was imminent--they did, and they were ready for it as much as they could be. Admiral Kidd was commander of Battleship Division One, and Arizona was the flagship. He was aboard the Arizona; he went down with her and was lost. The way Frannie and I got to know him---when I was a midshipman I was heavyweight boxer there, and he had been heavyweight boxer at the Naval Academy when he was a midshipman. And he had a boy, Isaac C. Kidd, who later became a four-star admiral and was then just a little fellow. He brought him down to meet me and stuff, and I got to know the family. I

---
*Degaussing gear is designed to reduce a ship's magnetic signature in order to lessen the likelihood of setting off magnetic influence mines or torpedoes.
**Rear Admiral Isaac C. Kidd, USN.

got to know Mrs. Kidd, and she was a delightful person, and the admiral. Although he was on duty in Washington, they lived in Annapolis. They had a house on King George Street, the one that goes right past Alumni House. So she wanted to know what it was. Anyway, we left, and on the morning of the 7th, at about five minutes of 8:00 or five after 8:00 the radioman---I'll never forget---the guy came up through the conning tower and reached up and handed to the officer of the deck a dispatch which read, "Air raid on Pearl Harbor. This is no drill."

We had aboard two officers we were bringing out for transportation. They were coming out to take command of submarines; they were lieutenant commanders. One was named De Tar; I forget who the other one was.* And they had all served in China, including Parks, and they got talking about the Japs: "That's just like those yellow bastards. They'd do something like that." And they believed it right away. So we rigged ship for dive to get down. The Pompano had had engine trouble. We were supposed to be in that morning at 6:00 o'clock at the entrance buoys in Pearl Harbor, which would have put us right there at the time of the attack. But we had engine trouble; those damned engines that we had gone back there and worked on had held down our speed. We had the division commander aboard, so it held the other submarines back, too. So we weren't due in

---

*Lieutenant Commander John L. De Tar, USN, who took command of the USS Tuna (SS-203).

until that afternoon. We were 135 miles from Pearl Harbor, northeast of it on the great circle route from San Francisco to Pearl, when we were attacked by the Japanese aircraft. We couldn't get under, because as soon as this word came in, to make as much speed as we could, we had pumped out all of our variable water, to lighten us to make more speed through the water.

As a result, as soon as this message came in, Parks said, "Rig ship for dive and compensate. Get the water back in so we can dive."

Well, we weren't done when we got attacked by the first wave coming back. And we were strafed; the other submarines went under. We weren't damaged. We came up. Norman Ives was the division commander, and Parks sent a message to him over voice radio saying, "You should tell Pearl Harbor we were attacked by enemy aircraft."[*]

And Ives said, "They've got too much on their mind." You know, the air was just filled with fifth column stuff--enemy ships off Barbers Point and all this crap that went on the airwaves. And it was very confusing, and everything was in plain language; all the communications broke down. So we never told them. And a good thing, I guess, because if anything had been sent after the enemy, it would have been sunk. We didn't have anything left really, so it was just as well. Admiral Kimmel's

---

[*]Commander Norman S. Ives, USN, Commander Submarine Division 43. See Clay Blair, Jr., Silent Victory, pages 100-101.

Cutter #2 - 196

staff thought the Japanese came from the Marshalls; they were looking for them in that southwest area. But, of course, they weren't there; they were up in the northwest. So then we got a message to proceed to Lahaina Roads, submerge, and stay submerged until the following night when we could surface and would receive a message telling us what to do. And they told us to meet the McFarland, which was the destroyer that escorted us in.

We met the McFarland, and the three of us were escorted into Pearl Harbor. All forces were very trigger happy, and they were told not to bother us, and we weren't bothered at all. We didn't know anything that had gone on; we had no idea of the damage. The first thing we saw, going into the entrance to Pearl Harbor, on the reef was a Navy fighter. It had been crash landed, but didn't look like it had been damaged very much. I'm sure the guy walked away from it. That was the first thing. Then as we got a little farther in, Hickam Field, as I recall, was to the right, and it was just burning. Then we got to Ford Island; that was burning. And right ahead of us was the Nevada, which was beached—she couldn't make the turn at Hospital Point. She went straight ahead and grounded; and, of course, the damage on Ford Island was still smoking. Then we turned the corner and saw the battleships, this way and that way—the masts—all of them didn't sink on an even keel and we passed the floating dry dock, where the Shaw had been blown up, so we saw the Shaw there. Then, when we came closer, there was the Oklahoma upside down; the Utah was upside down, and, of course, the Arizona was still burning, and it looked like there were six inches of oil on the water. I guess it wasn't that much, but it was a very depressing sight. Then we got into port and tied up. There was a bunch of people on dock, but we couldn't get people to handle our lines. It was like they were all in a daze. We had had one of our boys by the name of Reed, whom the captain had put in the brig when we left Pearl. I don't know what he had done; he was always doing something bad ashore. Parks had disqualified him for submarine duty, and he was through. When we got back, two months later, Reed was on the dock and he was the one guy who handled the lines. They had let him out of the brig and he was functioning. So he was back aboard.

Q: Requalified for submarine duty.

Captain Cutter: Quick. But poor Reed, he was the kind of guy-- he would go ashore, and he just followed his natural impulses. Aboard he was a perfect sailor, and he got to be torpedoman's mate first class eventually, during the war. He was always impeccably dressed when we had inspections. He was just a good sailor, but he would get out on the beach and, boy, I'll tell you, he was something. After Parks left, we went back to Mare Island for overhaul, and I left and went to the Seahorse. When the Pompano was in overhaul, and I was still aboard as exec and we sent Reed and three or four other fellows down to Montara, south of San Francisco, for gunnery school. The school had .50-caliber machine guns, and men would go down there for a week's course. Send them down on a Sunday, and then they would come back the following Friday; we sent them down in a bus. Well, we got a call from down there that the other fellows arrived but not Reed, and he was in charge of them because he was a torpedoman's mate first class. So that was typical Reed. Anyway, he finally came back, and we took him to mast, and, "What happened?"

"Well, Captain, it was like this. [That's the way they always start.] I got down there in the bus and was waiting for the bus at the foot of Market and Third [or wherever it was] to go to Montara, and there was a couple of schoolteachers there from San Jose. And, well, you know how it is, Captain, they were going to San Jose, and so I went to San Jose instead of Montara."

So then, the captain--this was Thomas, who had relieved Parks after the Pompano's second war patrol. Thomas didn't know what to do. "Well," he said, "Reed, I hate to do this, but you were in charge, and you don't demonstrate ..." I don't know what his speech was, but the net effect was that he busted him.* You know what Reed said?

---

*Captain's mast is the term used for commanding officer's nonjudicial punishment, which is less serious than a court-martial. To "bust" a person is to reduce him to a lower pay grade.

"Thank you, Captain," and he meant it. He didn't like the responsibility of being in charge. He didn't like responsibility. He was a follower, and he would work his head off and do anything anybody told him to do, but he didn't want to be in charge. That was Reed.*

My family was in Pearl, and we were allowed to go home that night. Things were pretty chaotic. A good thing the ships couldn't get to sea. Then we went out on the 17th of December, and, as I told you before, Parks always started right from the beginning of the war to run on the surface. So we were heading west toward--we were supposed to be going to Ponape and Truk, which was headquarters of the Japanese fleet, they thought at the time. And while we were heading for Truk, we were diverted to go to Wake Island, because they hadn't gotten any word from Wake, and they wanted to see if the Japs were there. So we changed course and headed for Wake. We were steaming along about 2:00 o'clock in the afternoon, and in the morning we were sighted by a patrol plane, PBY, obviously from Pearl Harbor. We were then about 600 miles out, I guess.

Q: Did you use recognition signals with the plane?

Captain Cutter: No, we dove. You see, a submarine is fair game.

---

*G. Russell Reed was in the crew of the *Pompano* when she was lost in the autumn of 1943. He was then a torpedoman's mate second class.

You are on your own, and you expect to be attacked by any aircraft. You can't attack a submarine after making recognition signals. You've just got to get them by surprise. Well, about 2:00 o'clock in the afternoon, I was below and the diving alarm went and shortly after—WHAM! WHAM! WHAM!—three bombs. What had happened, the Enterprise was coming back from Wake.* A classmate of mine was the leader of this section of aircraft. They picked us up. They came out of a cloud. We hadn't seen them, and didn't have any radar then—no aircraft radar—or any radar, as a matter of fact. They picked us up, and they had come out of a cloud. They figured where we were, and they overshot us. And the bombs dropped on the far side, but they were close enough to open seams in our main ballast tanks, which were carrying fuel oil. Two of our main ballast tanks were converted to carry fuel. It split a seam there, so we left a trail of oil wherever we went for the rest of the patrol.** We went off Wake, and the Japs were there. Parks, of course, got in real close to look it over and he saw the Japanese and the flag flying over the Pan Am building and all that sort of stuff. He was going at dead slow speed; it was a flat calm sea and with just a little bit of periscope up, and we started to go down below periscope depth and Parks said, "Bring her up, bring her up, goddamnit, bring her

---

*The Enterprise was then west of the Hawaiian islands to serve as protection during the ill-fated U.S. attempt to relieve Japanese pressure on Wake Island.

**For more on this incident, see Clay Blair, Jr., Silent Victory (Philadelphia: J.B. Lippincott Company, 1975), pages 114-115.

up." He didn't want to speed up, so he said, "Put a bubble in negative tank." This was the tank amidships, not the auxiliary but the emergency tank; anyway, it had high-pressure air connected to it. Two tanks had high-pressure air, negative tank and bow buoyancy, which is up in the bow. Both were connected to high-pressure air, 3,000 pounds. The valves to open the tanks were one above the other with identical cranks. In blowing negative tank, the auxiliary man would grasp a handle, turn it, and then look at the gauge recording the number of pounds of water going out of the tank. Instead of blowing water out of the negative tank, he had his hand on the crank for the bow buoyancy tank. The diving officer ordered him to blow out 500 pounds to lighten the submarine and bring us up. He was cranking the high-pressure air and looking at the negative tank gauge, and nothing was happening. So he gave it more and gave it more. He was blowing bow buoyancy by mistake. The next thing we knew, we were on the surface, right off the damn island; we weren't 400 yards off the beach. So we vented bow buoyancy in a hurry and went all ahead full. We got under, and nothing happened to us, of course; they weren't looking for it. That brought about a change; they changed the handles. They were both the same, so later on we were ordered to get a ball on one so they had different shapes so we wouldn't make that mistake again.

Q: That's the way a lot of changes came about, from mistakes happening.

Captain Cutter: Oh, I should say so, you betcha.

Q: This was about mid-December, and that's when the relief expedition was sent out to Wake and then came back.

Captain Cutter: They never got there. The Japs were there in force.

Q: Was that part of your job---to give a report on how much strength they did have on the island and in the area?

Captain Cutter: Oh, yes, and how active they were, any aircraft there, any ships we could see. They wanted to know what was there, as best we could see. That's why we got in so close. We had a good look.

Q: I guess you did.

Captain Cutter: We went from there down to Wotje, which is in the Marshall Islands. We didn't have enough fuel.

You see, everything was theoretical. Before the war, they never tested these things. They never sent ships out to really see---can you do it? So as soon as we started on patrol, Parks kept a graph on our fuel consumption and how much we had left, and also on our food—how long we can endure out there. Well, we couldn't possibly get to Ponape and Truk and get back to Pearl Harbor, no way.

Q: Especially not with that leaking tank.

Captain Cutter: Yes, but even without that. We didn't leak an awful lot; you don't have to leak much fuel oil to leave a slick. Parks just told them you can't do it; it was unrealistic. These theoretical things didn't work out. Instead of that, they sent us down to Wotje in the Marshalls to reconnoiter for Admiral Halsey's raid, which took place on the 1st of February 1942. That was the first offensive act against the enemy.* They came down there, and we reconnoitered Wotje, and Parks did a good job. Then we cleared out of there. They came in the next day after we had sent our report in. I don't know how much damage they did, but it gave a boost to the morale of our forces and the people back home.

Q: Did the submarines have any offensive mission at that point? It sounds like you were mostly on scouting missions.

---

*Vice Admiral William F. Halsey, Jr., USN, Commander Task Force Eight; Halsey was embarked in the USS Enterprise (CV-6).

Captain Cutter: Well, we were supposed to get any ships we could and we fired at the Kamakura Maru, which was a big transport. It was a big luxury liner before the war. It came out of there, and we reported sinking it, because we heard—we didn't know what a torpedo hit sounded like—again, not knowing any better. We heard the hits and saw the splash of water, so Parks assumed that it was going to be sunk. Because when we came up after the depth charge attack, there was no Kamakura Maru around. She just bailed out, that's all; she hadn't been hurt at all. Two duds bounded against her and caused the splashes along the side that Parks took to be hits.

Then we would come in every day and patrol right off the entrance. I was navigator, and the charts we had were 1895 or something. They were plus or minus five miles, I think the hydrographic office said. Parks said, "I want to be two miles off the breakwater in the morning."

Well, he almost made a nervous wreck out of me, taking sights at night, you know. So I would have the sonar, the listening gear, lowered and would stop every little ways and listen. We could hear the reef, and when we got close I wouldn't go any more. We would always be pretty close to where he wanted to be in the morning, because he didn't want to have to run in submerged; he wanted to be there. They had two destroyers out one day that we thought were looking for us. I don't know whether they were looking for us, but they were patrolling the entrance. So Parks maneuvered all day long, trying to get in position to hit them, but they never settled down to get a good firing position. I was operating the TDC, and he was up in the conning tower.* So finally, in desperation, he decided to shoot. He took a 60-degree gyro angle, which was much too much for those torpedoes at that time. And we fired two torpedoes, and both of them prematured. Jeez, I'm on TDC and I got from Parks, "Range 1,200 yards, speed 25, angle on the bow two degrees port, stand by." And I put on the solution light, "Fire!" About this time, Parks came down, "Slade, did you ever have so much fun before with your clothes on?" And over the loudspeaker system. I'll never forget it.

Well, I wasn't worrying about having fun with clothes on or off about that stage of the game. Looking at this thing on the torpedo data computer, here was this target at 1,200 yards, and he'd be over here in a minute or so. He came, and that's the first depth charge we ever heard. We had never had one fired in practice; I didn't know what they sounded like. Well, a barrage came over, and I know what is was like to face death, right then, because we heard the water rushing through the superstructure. As we learned later, that is normal, but we thought we had been holed. So I thought, that's the end and you don't feel anything. I guess you're not thinking. I don't know what it was—we didn't

---
*TDC—torpedo data computer.

think. It was so fortunate, and we realized very shortly that we hadn't been holed. And then it was a matter of maneuvering to get away from this guy. We abandoned the conning tower, and to this day I can see Lew Parks—he got on the annunciator controls in the control room and the wheel. He did it. The skipper maneuvered the submarine around, all ahead full, starboard back full and port ahead full, to cut down the turning circle to evade these guys up above dropping their depth charges. God, it was funny.

Q: This is what he had been waiting for and preparing for.

Captain Cutter: Oh, he was ready, he was ready! Then he shifted to hand steering to reduce our ship's noise and had two men turning the steering wheel by hand. Well, that was our baptism of depth charges. And Parks thoroughly enjoyed it apparently. He was having a hell of a time.

After that, every time we went out on patrol, one of the pre-patrol training exercises was to have a destroyer drop one or two depth charges 100 yards away so everybody could hear what they sounded like.

Q: Was there generally a sense of fear in the crew at facing this unknown thing at that point?

Captain Cutter: I don't know. They were conditioned for it; they were good men, and they expected it, I guess. I don't remember any talk about fear. I said previously that West and another man went to pot, or broke up. It was that patrol; the other man was a chief petty officer. The fellow was sitting there, and he had a very responsible position. He was the hydraulic manifold operator—that was his battle station—which is the guy who opens and closes the valves. Parks was gentle with him, just took him off. He would sit there and stare. He didn't scream or anything like that; he was just immobile. That's the way it affected him.

Q: It sounds as if Parks was really exceptional among his contemporaries for this sense of bravery and aggressiveness.

Captain Cutter: He could have been a top skipper at age 50, and it's just a crime that he didn't have a good submarine with good torpedoes, because he would have made a killing out there. But he had this old submarine with these torpedoes that weren't worth much. He was aggressive.

Q: But most of the COs of his vintage didn't have his outlook, did they?

Captain Cutter: I don't know. I can't say that for sure. I

don't know. But from the results and reading the patrol reports and reading what happened to some of them, I think they did not.

Q: It sounds as if it was more of the caution that you talked about---if you don't risk anything, you don't have a chance of making a mistake.

Captain Cutter: Well, you know there were several of those skippers there---the Articles for the Government of the Navy that we were governed by said that, "You shall attack any ships at any opportunity."

There was no question about it. You were offered no discretion. If you saw a ship, you attacked. A lot of these peacetime skippers who had been brought up under the Articles for the Government of the Navy, which you had to read part of at every inspection, and that was the bible and what you would do. Several of these people---I don't know how many of them---turned over command to their execs, because they weren't able to do that. A hopeless situation---they felt they didn't measure up. Well, discretion became the better part of valor to us who followed. I mean, if it looked impossible, we would say, "Well, we will live to fight another day and avoid this particular situation."

Now the judgment came on which situation you decided to avoid. We all avoided some, and some avoided a lot more than others. It was just that sort of thing. But it wasn't so much a matter of bravery as a matter of judgment. I don't think any man is really brave facing fire. You do things that afterward you wonder how did you do them. I remember the mouth is dry, so dry that you are conscious of it. That's being scared, but you don't let anybody else know it, because it is contagious. You've got to put on a front. It is very important for the skipper.

Q: You were the beneficiary really of timing in a couple of senses in that you got a modern submarine, you got good torpedoes, and by then there was the experience to know how you do face these situations.

Captain Cutter: That is right. And another thing, that we had tremendous confidence in that submarine.

We got a young fellow named Bill Budding, out of the Naval Academy class of '43, fresh out of sub school, to the new construction, the Seahorse, and his father was the shipbuilding superintendent of the Seahorse.* So he was in charge of the construction of the ship, and I'll tell you nothing was too good for the Seahorse.** I mean, we had all the radiographs we were supposed to have, checking all the welds for flaws. I mean, we got everything. I'll never forget, one thing--I forget the

---
*Ensign William A. Budding, Jr., USN.
**The USS Seahorse (SS-304) was built by the Mare Island Navy Yard, Vallejo, California, commissioned 31 March 1943.

details, but it had to do with squeaking propeller shafts. As the submarine went deeper, you could hear the propeller squeak. It would squeak and make noise that sonar could pick up. I think it was the lignum vitae that they used at that time, and then they came out with rubber. I'm not saying this is exactly accurate, because I don't recall, but this much is accurate—that what he installed was not authorized by the Bureau of Ships. They knew at Mare Island that this was the answer to our problem. So they asked the skipper—this fellow McGregor—and they sold him on the idea that this was good, and they put them in.[*] We never had a squealing propeller in the Seahorse. The father was looking after his only son, Bill Budding, and Bill later became one of the youngest execs in the submarine force. When I left the ship, he was exec. He was 23 years old. I told Weary Wilkins that I apologized that he was getting such a young exec.[**] But I said, "He is awfully good, and he is a hell of a TDC operator. I used him on that, and he has the respect of the crew, and he can do a job for you. He is an excellent navigator—very bright." So he took him and afterwards, years later, Weary told me that he was the best exec he ever had in submarines. Now I think he was kind of maybe pouring it on a little bit. But the exec he had prior to Budding was in the

---

[*]Commander Donald McGregor, USN, first commanding officer of the Seahorse.
[**]Commander Charles W. Wilkins, USN, relieved Cutter as commanding officer of the Seahorse in August 1944.

submarine he commanded at the beginning of the war, and that guy was in the class of 1932, 11 years earlier, and later became a good skipper.*

Q: What a difference.

Captain Cutter: Budding was really good. He later became a naval constructor. He is now an officer at Electric Boat Company.

The Seahorse was really tight. I took her down to over 600 feet. Her test depth was 412 feet. We were depth-charged at a depth of over 500 feet. One time all of our lights on our depth charge indicator lighted up. You have heard about the depth charge indicator. That was a box about 10 inches long, 3 or 4 inches wide, and about 6 inches deep, and it was connected to microphones, one in the bow, one in the stern, starboard, port, above and below. And they were hooked up so that if a depth charge went off to starboard, it would hit the starboard microphone first and that would cut out the port microphone, and it would light up starboard. If it went off ahead, it would get the one forward, and if it was above you it would hit that first and would block out the one below. That's the way it worked. Anyway, in one depth charge attack off Saipan, all six lights

---

*Lieutenant Frank D. Latta, USN, was executive officer when Wilkins was commanding officer of the USS Narwhal (SS-167).

Cutter #2 - 212

went on. We had been bracketed by a barrage of depth charges. We would use that as a criterion of how good the guy up there was, but that was a very tough submarine that could take that punishment. And it was also a tough submarine that would be below those depths. It was very foolish; we would never have done that later when I realized what pressure does to a submarine. I don't know why, but I didn't realize that the pressure at 500 feet is tremendous. Of course, your depth charges generally went off above you, and they vented up so you didn't get too much of a shock from depth charges above you. And that's why we went down there, because we didn't get the knocking around that we got when we were at shallower depths.

Q: I guess it was a point of judgment with each CO how far he would go, and some went too far.

Captain Cutter: Well, I don't know; nobody told you. I'll never forget--you would go out on training exercises, and I would be trained by division commanders that didn't know anywhere near what I did. They weren't competent to be my training officer, because I had been under a real expert. We would go out during these exercises, and it annoyed me to have these people tell us just what to do. I knew what I wanted to do; I knew what I had to do to get ready. We would leave for patrol and would be escorted out, I think it was 100 miles, by a destroyer. And then at sundown they would signal to us that we were leaving and, "Good luck and good hunting," and all that sort of stuff. And off we'd go, and I always felt relieved, because now nobody can tell me what to do. Now I'm on my own. That's a great feeling, but to some people it is a very lonely feeling. It depends upon your attitude and your outlook.

Q: Some people want rudder orders and some don't.

Captain Cutter: Yes, and I guess it's better for the long haul and your profession and so forth if you are better at taking orders than being kind of a renegade, I guess they think. I don't know.

Q: But for the time and the situation, you were in exactly the right place.

Captain Cutter: Yes, I was trained for that. I was seldom happy in the Navy after the war. I had some pretty good jobs—skipper of a cruiser and squadron commander, a submarine division commander, on staff and stuff, but I don't know. It seemed kind of empty.

After the war was over, we went down to Key West, Florida. And before the war, inspections were kind of farces. In an administrative inspection the name of the game was to bury all your problems under the rug and hope to God the inspectors don't find out about them. Well, I thought the war had changed everything, because in the war it was all aboveboard in everything. If we had any problems, we told them, because we wanted them cured; we wanted them corrected. Even though it might be our mistake and we had done something wrong, we wanted it fixed. So, the first administrative inspection I had was just before going to the shipyard for the first overhaul for the Requin. This was in 1946, and a good friend of mine, Bub Ward's crew---he was the senior member, but his crew were the inspectors---came aboard the Requin to inspect us.* And I told my crew, "This is a new ballgame. Now the Navy has learned a lesson, so tell everything that's wrong. Open up the engines. Show them everything, so they can help us getting our work requests through the shipyard. We've got the backing of the force through the administrative inspection."

Well, when that thing came out, it sounded like we were the most derelict bunch of people in the world. All these things that we had told them about, they wrote up as deficiencies. I was absolutely furious. Well, Bub Ward was a skipper and a very good friend, a very fine man, who made admiral and he very well should have made admiral. A fine submarine skipper, too, and he was skipper of the boat. He and his wife are very dear friends

---

*Commander Norvell G. Ward, USN, commanding officer of the USS Irex (SS-482).

of ours to this day and came out that afternoon to call on us at our house. We just didn't do things like that. We would get together at the club or something, but they really made a formal call, came in the late afternoon, 5:00 to 6:00 something. We didn't say anything about the inspection at all, but that's why he was there, and I knew that's why he was there. I guess he wanted to see how much I was whizzed off, which was plenty, but I wasn't mad at him. I was mad at the system. We were reverting back to what we did before, and they are still doing it, still doing it, I'm sure, because they were doing it when I left the Navy in 1965.

Q: You talked about getting attacked by one of your classmates in the <u>Enterprise</u> squadron. Did you ever get together with him later and compare notes?

Captain Cutter: Just vaguely; he didn't remember it. He didn't remember the incident. Eddie Outlaw was his name.* He made admiral, too. Eddie was a good man. He stood down at the bottom of the class, very few were from the bottom. He wasn't much of a student but a good leader and smart; he just probably didn't apply himself, interested in other things.

We got attacked several times by our own forces, by air, and never by the Japanese, never close. We'd always be well under by

---

*Lieutenant (junior grade) Edward C. Outlaw, USN.

the time they got over there. Their tactics weren't as good; they flew too low, and they didn't have radar. Our people had radar and would come out of the clouds, or they would come in out of the sun when you didn't have your radar in operation, which we wouldn't do if we were close to enemy areas. One Sunday morning in May 1944, just before Mitscher's second raid on Truk, we were off Hall Island, which is near Truk.* It is a satellite island, and we had evidence of radar on the island. We figured they had radar detectors. I was not using our aircraft warning radar, so they wouldn't be able to DF us.** I was in a safety zone proceeding to Satawan Island, and all forces had been warned that we were there and we were right on our PIM---your moving point, you know. We were right on the center of this safety line. Sunday morning, had a big flag flying, and we had carrier planes in the area and all of a sudden---I happened to be in the control room, and WHAMMO. A bomb went off before the diving alarm. God, I was really upset about that, because my exec had eight lookouts up there because of the situation and two officers of the deck. One of them was this Frank Fisher, who, as I told you, was president of Arco later, an excellent officer. And he came down, and, boy, I gave him the business, "What in the hell are you doing up there with that watch asleep? What was it?"

"It was a B-24." (And that was a big airplane.)

---
*Vice Admiral Marc A. Mitscher, USN, Commander Task Force 58.
**DF---to locate a ship's position by means of radio direction-finding.

"How in the world did he get in on you?"

Later on, after we got on the surface and were steaming along, then everybody was a lot more alert. I was up there, and they picked this guy up way the hell and gone over---I guess about 20,000 feet, working around to the sun. And he got into the area where the sun would be when he got near us. He was below it, of course, at that great range, coming right towards us. So he got to about ten miles, and we pulled the plug and went down, but that's how he got in. In the meantime, I drafted a dispatch and sent it to Pearl Harbor, in which I said, "<u>Seahorse</u> to blame. The watch was asleep," and I reported the incident.

A stupid thing to do, and I caught hell from Admiral Lockwood, in his nice way. He said, "That was a gratuitous comment. For once we had those bastards dead to rights. They don't brief their people. They don't have navigators that know where they are. This is what we are trying to catch them and stop them from doing. And you blew it."

Well, that wasn't all I did on that run. Then we got down to Satawan island (I think I told you about that; we were going through a safety lane). We were tasting that beer down there in Brisbane. We were very anxious to get to Brisbane, Australia. We were supposed to go to Majuro Island and after what we had endured in Saipan---Dick Voge told me later when we got back---that they felt we would need recreation, and they sent us to Brisbane, Australia, for refitting, which is a long way away, instead of

Majuro.* There was a blind bombing zone south of Satawan Island; as I recall it was 4 degrees north of the equator and about 200 miles to the west. It was north of New Guinea, and anything in there was fair game, surface or submarine, no recognition signals or anything. We never paid any attention to recognition signals anyway; you'd always dive before exchanging. So we were directed to proceed due west to the safety lane and then proceed to Manus for refueling and on down to Brisbane.

After this episode, we started west, and as the day wore on I started to cut into the blind bombing zone, cut the corner, and by 3:00 or 4:00 o'clock in the afternoon I was heading almost due south. I was going to get into the safety lane sometime that night. We got picked up by a B-24, with radar. We picked him up, too; we had our radar on, so we dove. I stuck the periscope up after about 10 or 15 minutes, and as soon as that periscope broke the surface, this guy turned toward us. He had radar and good radar to pick up the periscope, and he was five miles away. I went down again and stayed down for half an hour or so, and when I came up, he picked us up a second time. Then I stayed down for about an hour, figuring he would run out of gas eventually and he'd head back toward New Guinea. And he did, so we got on the surface and were proceeding merrily on our way and we got this message from General MacArthur's headquarters ordering us to proceed directly to the safety lane and stay there

---

*Commander Richard G. Voge, USN, operations officer on the staff of Commander Submarines Pacific Fleet.

and speed of advance was to be 12 knots, all the way to Brisbane, and we were not to get more than 15 miles ahead of our PIM or more than 30 miles astern.* If we did, we had to report to them, so we stayed on it. Since we were going to Manus for fuel, we had plenty of fuel to make 18 knots, and here we were held to 12 knots. And that held all the way to Brisbane; that was really quite a bit of punishment. We got down to Brisbane and started a very good recreation period.

Q: Who was MacArthur's submarine operations officer then?

Captain Cutter: He didn't have any, but Admiral Carpender was down there, and if you have read Clay Blair's book there was a continuous battle going on between Carpender and MacArthur at the expense of the operating forces.** A very childish situation existed between these two senior officers. Both of them, I guess, had pretty good egos, and they didn't want to cooperate with each other. It was a kind of messy affair. I don't know who, on MacArthur's staff, sent that, but we got that from the Army.

When we got down there, the Lennon Hotel is where MacArthur's

---

*General Douglas MacArthur, U.S. Army, Supreme Commander, Southwest Pacific Area.
**Vice Admiral Arthur S. Carpender, USN, Commander Naval Forces Southwest Pacific. See Clay Blair, Jr., Silent Victory (Philadelphia: J.B. Lippincott Company, 1975).

headquarters was located. This was the biggest hotel in Brisbane and a very nice one. They took it over, and they had a nightclub down below and stuff. And naval officers were barred, couldn't get in. A guy named Claggett, a classmate of mine, was skipper of the Dace.* Anyway, he was in port at the same time we were. Claggett was a great guy; we were having a lot of fun together. We decided to go to the Lennon Hotel; we didn't know about this barring of naval officers. So we got down there and there were two MPs. One of them said, "You can't go in, only Army personnel, unless you are the guest of an Army officer."

This captain, or first lieutenant, came up and heard it, and he said, "These gentlemen are my guests," and with that he took us in---we had two girls---and left us. But we were in, and we had a great time and felt real good about beating the system.

Well, in 1978, I'm in San Antonio, Texas--moved down there from Tucson, Arizona--and I joined St. Francis Episcopal Church. One of the guys on the chapel committee was this same fellow.

Q: The lieutenant?

Captain Cutter: Yes. And there is one house between his house and my daughter's home in San Antonio. Isn't that a coincidence? He was a retired general. I forget his name but a very great guy. My wife and I called on him, and we talked about the

---
*Lieutenant Commander Bladen D. Claggett, USN.

Cutter #2 - 221

incident, and he remembered. Then he remembered something that I had forgotten. When we went out on our training--all our training consisted of down there was going out and diving the boat to see if it was tight; there was no area to fire torpedoes or anything at Brisbane. There is a quite long channel you have to come up, so we did our training up off Manus. I invited him to go out with us, and he did. He remembered that; it was the only time he had ever been in a submarine. Some of the boys had met some Army nurses and we took them out, too. We had a good time, a lot of fun.

Q: What were some of the escapades in that liberty?

Captain Cutter: Oh, well, they are better left unsaid, I think. I'll tell you one of them. We had--Bill Holman, God rest his soul, he was a great guy--and Bill had a little problem with drinking.* We were at a place called Harwood House, which was where the skippers spent their time. And we had an engineer officer who was in charge of the refit. Shorty was his name, and he also had a drinking problem.** Claggett and I took on a load of beer. We were pretty bombed, I guess, and Shorty was sound asleep. He had passed out. We had a cigarette lighter, and we lit the hair on his chest, and it started burning. The

---
*Lieutenant Commander William G. Holman, USN, executive officer of the USS Dace.
**Commander Stanley G. Nichols, USN.

way it works—it goes out like a saucer, until the center gets in there. He'd wake up and scratch it. Then we'd light it in another place, and he'd scratch again. Finally he woke up—Shorty Nichols was a great guy and had a wonderful sense of humor. He said, "Ah, you want to play, huh?" With that, he was wide awake, and we didn't go to bed the rest of the night; he wouldn't let us. He kept us up all night long until we were absolutely exhausted. Well, that was a lot of fun.

So, the next night Bill Holman passed out, and he is very hairy on his chest, so we lighted him off. Well, he was scratching and scratching, but he never woke up and we burned almost all of the hair off his chest, and it left blisters. God, these are terrible things to relate. Looking back on it, how can reasonably mature people in their early 30s do such a thing? Holman got sent back to New London as a submarine school teacher or something like that; anyway, his wife was a very proper lady and a very lovely person and a good friend of my wife's. When she was with him, he behaved himself. He didn't drink around her, because she wouldn't put up with it. He got back there, and here he is with all these scars. And he's got to account for them, which is pretty hard to do. He told her what had happened, and she was absolutely furious at me and Claggett and kind of took it out, of course, on Frannie. She gave Frannie hell for what her husband had done to her husband down in Brisbane, Australia, after I got back to new construction training school in New London.

Claggett said, "Let's go down to Sydney."

And I said, "The hell with that. I'm not going down to Sydney with you," because I had heard a lot of things about Sydney, so I stayed there. He went down, and two days later he was back. He ran into some of his crew down there, and they almost killed him with kindness, and he couldn't take the activity. So he came back to Brisbane to do his drinking there for the rest of the refit period.

I mention these things that happened early in the refit; that would last about two weeks. We got completely unwound, and then you got ready for sea, and it was all business then. You were checking all your equipment, and everybody was very serious; all the foolishness stopped. It was really very interesting.

Q: Was there a tendency on the part of some of the married men in these crews to be geographical bachelors--to sort of have amnesia about their wives?

Captain Cutter: Oh, yes. Oh, yes. I think the wives knew about it, and I think most of the wives understood the thing. There were no love affairs or anything like that--just one-night stands.

For instance, I had a driver. Being a skipper, I got a driver down there and a car and the officers were at a place called Surfers' Paradise. They had cottages out there reserved for crews of submarines—I mean the officers only. The crews were sent to rest camps. There was on Paradise Beach, beautiful white, sandy beach for miles there; it's a famous beach and these houses were there. On a Sunday, I went out to see how my officers were being taken care of and how they were. I got there, and most of them were still in bed. One of them was in bed with a gal, but the gals were there and these girls stayed there. When one submarine's gang moved out and another moved in, there they were. They kept the house clean, they were lovers, they cooked for them—it was beautiful, a real good setup. This one officer on the ship who was a very, very proper man, married to a very proper girl. He was the one in bed with this girl, and I couldn't believe my eyes. He said, "Hey, Captain, come on in."

I went in, and there he was in bed with this gal, and on the dresser was a picture of an Australian soldier. And do you know who that was? Her husband, and he was a rat of Tobruk. Did you ever hear of the rats of Tobruk?*

Q: I've heard of Tobruk.

Captain Cutter: The rats of Tobruk were the Australian division or whatever it was that was in Tobruk and the Germans couldn't

---

*Tobruk, a port in Libya, North Africa, was useful to the British as a means of getting supplies to their desert armies.

drive them out and they were there for something like nine months living in underground shelters, and they called them the rats of Tobruk, and he was one of them. She was a good woman.

Q: So it was a case of two sets of loneliness encountering each other.

Captain Cutter: Yes, and that's the end of the relationship. When you went back to the ship, that was it.

Q: Was this officially sanctioned, that there would be these women available for the crews?

Captain Cutter: I don't know about the rest of the boats, but I do know they were there for the submarine ahead of us, and these girls had been there for several submarines coming in.

Q: Were they mostly married women?

Captain Cutter: I don't know about the others; the only one I knew about was this one.

Q: Going back to the time when you were in the _Pompano_ and reconnoitering in the Marshalls prior to Halsey's raid, how did you communicate the results of the intelligence you picked up?

Cutter #2 - 226

Captain Cutter: It was by radio.

Q: Did it go directly to Pearl Harbor, to the <u>Enterprise</u>, or what?

Captain Cutter: To Pearl, and then it was relayed. Those things went to CinCPacFlt.* The amazing thing--sometimes, when you would send a message to Pearl Harbor and they would pick it up in Annapolis--here in Annapolis at the radio towers, and they would send it out to Pearl Harbor. It is interesting what happens, and also sometimes some of our very important messages would be picked up in Australia, and they would send them back. Many times we couldn't reach Pearl directly. Probably one of the most important things the <u>Seahorse</u> did during the war was at the time of the "Marianas Turkey Shoot."** There were two Japanese forces; one was at Halmahera. CinCPacFlt knew where that was. The Japanese fleet was in two parts; one was at Halmahera, and the other was somewhere in the South China Sea. Our people did not know exactly where it was, and they were looking for it, because they knew, through intelligence, that action was coming up. The Japanese were coming out after our fleet, and CinCPacFlt wanted to know where the other half of it was.

---
*CinCPacFlt---Commander in Chief Pacific Fleet.
**The "Marianas Turkey Shoot" was an air battle on 19 June 1944 in which U.S. carrier planes shot down more than 300 Japanese aircraft while supporting the invasion force on Saipan.

I was on the way from Australia. I was going into the South China Sea between Luzon and Formosa, through that pass there. We were about 150 miles off Mindanao, going north in the afternoon of an overcast day, and we sighted a carrier-based aircraft on our port beam. We dove. He didn't see us, so we came back up shortly and resumed our surface running with our high periscope manned in order to cover more ocean area. Well, the periscope watch, a fellow by the name of Lessard, who was the engineer officer, picked up what he thought was a small boat on the horizon, like a patrol boat.* I was up there and reversed course, and immediately it disappeared, which meant that it was way over the horizon, so I knew then that it was the tops of a big ship. Then we poured on the coal to get as close as we could. It was getting late in the afternoon, and it became dark. They were making 17 knots, and there was no way that we could get in on them or to go ahead, but we could maintain contact. We made a contact report, and it was picked up by CinCPacFlt. Boy, then the air was full; they wanted all sorts of information. They wanted to know types of the ships, the number of ships, the course, the speed, whether they were zigzagging and all this information they wanted. And for us to maintain contact at all costs. Which we did. We had Fairbanks-Morse engines on there, which produced more power than the generators and motors were designed to handle. The generators were made by a company in

---

*Lieutenant Lester J. Lessard, USNR.

Beloit, Wisconsin. Anyway, they were good generators, but they were not rated for that amount of power. So I told them to make 150% of the main motor capability, because full power on the engines was about 150% of the rated load of the motors and they started to spark. We were making 18 knots; otherwise we would make only about 16-1/2. We were keeping up pretty well, but we were off on the flank. Finally the brushes on the main motors burned up, and we had to stop and spend the next two days replacing the burned brushes. In the meantime, we were able to give the course and speed of this force, and they projected it forward, and they knew where they were going to meet. And that was where the Cavalla with Herman Kossler sank the carrier.* They positioned Herman Kossler up ahead, and he was another good skipper, and Herman sank the carrier. That's probably really the best contribution we made to the war because it helped them tactically to get arranged for that Marianas Turkey Shoot. That is written up in Blair's book and in Roscoe's book.**

Q: You came back from the Marshalls. Where did you head then in

---

*Lieutenant Commander Herman J. Kossler, USN, commanding officer of the USS Cavalla (SS-244), which sank the Japanese carrier Shokaku on 19 June 1944 at 11-50N, 137-57E. See Samuel Eliot Morison, New Guinea and the Marianas, Volume VIII of History of United States Naval Operations in World War II (Boston: Little, Brown and Company, 1953), pages 280-281.
**Clay Blair, Jr., Silent Victory (Philadelphia: J.B. Lippincott Company, 1975), pages 657-658. Theodore Roscoe, United States Submarine Operations in World War II (Annapolis: U.S. Naval Institute, 1949), pages 381-382.

the _Pompano_?

Captain Cutter: The next patrol we made was to the South China Sea, between Hong Kong and the Philippines. I'll tell you the kind of guy Parks was--we got done with the navy yard overhaul. We went in for work in the Pearl Harbor Navy Yard; they had to do some work on us. We went out and made a trim dive, just below periscope depth, and everything was tight. We surfaced and went back in, loaded, and out we went on patrol. Parks would never take a trim dive once we got under way. He said, "I want to keep the diving officer on his toes." Well, when you are going all the way from Pearl Harbor to east of the Philippines, almost ten days to two weeks is involved. And without a trim dive, it makes the diving officer nervous, because if you are not reasonably in good trim, you might not be able to go under, or you might get under too well, go too deep or something. Anyway, Parks wouldn't let us make a trim dive. He was the only skipper I knew who did that. I never did that; I made them take a trim dive every day. It only takes five minutes. Well, we got off Wake, and an enemy plane sighted us. He came in and dropped one bomb, and we went down to 250 feet or whatever it was. In the after battery compartment we had two toilets, and the discharge for them went through the ballast tank outboard, and air pressure would blow the waste out. Well, where this went through the hull was a flange with a gasket, and these rascals in the shipyard had put in a split gasket. They had done that, because it is easier to put on; they didn't have to take the toilet out, so they just cut it and slipped it around there. A split gasket won't hold under pressure; it opens. So we were down there at 250 or 300 feet, whatever it was, and water was coming in the after battery compartment where the batteries are, below that. It was serious, and we had to do something about it. We were not far off Wake, at night, on the surface, unable to dive, because we had to remove the pipe going through the hull and put a blank flange over the hole with a proper gasket. So we had only one toilet for all the crew after that, which was a problem, too.

While we were on the surface, there was a guy by the name of Calcaterra, and they called him "Chainfall" because you didn't need a chainfall with him aboard.* He was strong as an ox, and I was pretty husky in those days, too. So he and I were the ones who sawed through that monel discharge line, which is tough metal, with a hacksaw blade held in our hands with a rag, because we couldn't get a hacksaw in there. So here we were leaning way around there in back, putting all we can into it, and boy, we were motivated because we couldn't dive, and were in enemy-controlled waters. We finally cut through it, and they put the correct flange on, and we went on our way. So we got out there in the South China Sea, and we were on the surface one

---

*Motor Machinist's Mate First Class Herbert A. Calcaterra, USN.

night and we picked up a contact. So we shut off our engines and put our stern toward it. We didn't want to be picked up, but the contact saw us and turned toward us. So we turned away again, and he turned toward us. Parks sent for me to man the .50-caliber machine gun which we had aft, so I got the thing ready.

And he said, "Put it on them." So we made another course change, and the guy turned toward us again, and Parks said, "Let him have it." That was his—instead of "commence fire," he would say, "Let him have it," so I pulled the trigger. Well, something I think about lots of times—after the first burst, they had tracers on, you know, and they were going right into it, and I guess he was about 300 yards.

Q: How big a vessel was it?

Captain Cutter: It was a fishing boat, stack aft, and the bridge was aft—good size, probably 20 men aboard. And after that first burst of probably 50 rounds put into it, a guy held a lantern up to show the rising sun on their flag. He thought we were the Japs. The captain said, "Let them have it," so I opened up again, and that time we just kept firing. And finally the thing caught fire, I guess the tracers set off the fuel or something, and it burned and we got out of there. It was a fisherman. That's one of the terrible things of war. He was harmless, and he thought we were friends. He was coming over to exchange information or whatever.

Q: That probably planted the seeds for your later distaste for the gun actions.

Captain Cutter: Probably. I was quite upset about that afterwards, after I found out what it was. But that didn't bother Parks. They were enemy, anybody. He said, "Don't worry about that, they're feeding them, and they are fair game."

Q: Your sighting at that point was still entirely visual, wasn't it? You had no radar.

Captain Cutter: We had no radar. We didn't have the radar on that patrol. The interesting thing about it--the Bendix Corporation was on strike, and they made a particular tube that we had to have and we didn't have it. The radar was installed, but we didn't have this tube, and none of the other submarines had it either. This is what we had gotten back in the Mare Island shipyard, another of the things we had installed just before the war to help us, but we didn't have this tube, a magnetron tube or whatever it was, and it was a key part of the radar. After we had gotten an airplane coming in and bombing us and this happened several times, the crew was angry. And I'll never forget getting down there in the control room and talking to them and saying, "Look, we are out here to protect our country." I was trying to get them over this anger at Bendix Corporation and at the United States that it would tolerate such a situation when we were out there risking our lives for people who didn't care. My point was, "Well, your family cares. Your mothers and brothers and sisters and grandparents all care, so you are fighting for them. To hell with the rest of them." Making it like a family affair. They bought that. Eventually, the strike at Bendix was over, and we got our tube. We got the piece we needed, and we had radar.

Q: How big a difference did that make in your operations?

Captain Cutter: Really not much, except peace of mind. I would never use it around enemy bases for fear of getting DFed. It was of relatively low frequency, and it was easy to DF. I don't know the wavelength of it. The 10-centimeter radar was our precision radar we used for fire control, and apparently they couldn't DF that as far away as they could the other, which was a lower frequency.

Q: What about radio communication? What precautions did you take to minimize DF-ing of that?

Cutter #2 - 234

Captain Cutter: Well, the shortest transmission that you could, but we couldn't do anything about it. A very interesting thing happened during that night of the Marianas Turkey Shoot, that night we were sending in our contact report. We had a tremendous amount of jamming. This is very interesting, I think. We had a chief radioman on there by the name of Hoffman, who was absolutely outstanding, and he still is.* He became a commander; he was commissioned and retired a commander. He was manager of a bank in Vallejo, California, before he recently retired, a topflight person, also a sonarman. He was the chief radioman. He had been on Radio Washington stationed there several years before, as a chief petty officer. He was communicating with Radio Washington--this was Annapolis--and he recognized the man at the other end; he recognized his fist.** I never got proficient enough to recognize a fist; they say it is just as recognizable as handwriting.

Q: I've heard that.

Captain Cutter: Well, I saw it happen. What they did--we had frequency changes. You had procedures to go through in changing frequencies, so when we got jammed on a certain frequency, they would shift to another one, but the one during wartime was so

---
*Chief Radioman Roy L. Hoffman, USN.
**"Fist" was a term used to describe the particular way in which an individual used a Morse Code key.

damn ponderous, it was in a code. It took time, so he reverted back to old peacetime procedure signals, which were very quick. And nobody else knew them except him and this other guy. I am sure some other old-time, experienced radiomen knew it, but the Japs didn't know it. As soon as the Japs would catch up with his frequency, they would shift to another frequency, and they kept the word going in. Isn't that interesting? That was Roy Hoffman.

Q: Petty officers before the war apparently were extremely skilled professional people.

Captain Cutter: They were. They were. Some of them weren't too well educated, but the ones who were very bright and had at least a high school education, they became officers, and they were tremendous. Hoffman, as I say, was one of them. I commissioned two of them, a fellow named Anderson and a fellow named McGrievy. McGrievy, who later retired as a commander—he settled down later but he sure wasn't settled in those days.* His commission came in when we arrived in Brisbane. I had already commissioned him, and it came through, so he was an ensign. Anderson was his sidekick; he was chief fire controlman and he got a commission as an ensign. Anderson was responsible for the TDC, which was the guts of the fire control system and it was down. We had to get

---
*Chief Quartermaster Joseph L. McGrievy, USN.

it fixed and back in 100% commission. McGrievy was a signalman and quartermaster, and his responsibility was to keep the charts up to date and all that sort of business. So they both got my permission to go over to Perth, where they had been stationed early in the war, to visit some of their old friends over there, civilian friends—female mostly. They bummed a ride on a plane over there. When we got ready to go to sea for training and they were not there, two officers were AOL.* The torpedo data computer wasn't back in commission. They didn't have the talent in Brisbane to fix it, and Anderson was that talent. He wasn't there. I'll tell you, I was pretty mad at these two characters. They both came in, you know, full of apologies and full of excuses. What little training we had there—as I told you, we didn't fire any torpedoes—just went out and saw that it was tight. But to button up the ship and test all the equipment to be sure everything was in working order—it wasn't done, so I wasn't very happy.

Q: So much for making them responsible commissioned officers.

Captain Cutter: Oh, boy, they got off to a bad start. But they were so great—McGrievy had marvelous eyes at night; he was like a cat, and I made several attacks during the war at night at periscope depth so I could get in closer and didn't have to worry

---

*AOL—absent over liberty.

about escorts. So I would do it at night, and I would put him on the periscope. I couldn't see anything, but he could see those black hulks through the periscope. The way he did it, he told me—he moved the periscope from this blurb until he could see a star which meant he was ahead of it. Then he would move it back and say, "Fire." Then he would move it astern till he could see stars and move it back and say, "Fire." He was inside the stern and inside the bow, and then he would fire one right where he judged was the middle of the blurb. Boy, he had eyes like a cat. That was when he was still an enlisted man, and that's why I made him an officer. And he was also officer of the deck, my officer of the deck, mind you, as a chief petty officer, at night during our battle stations. When we made night surface attacks, I was in the conning tower where I had the TDC.* He was feeding the data such as bearing and disposition of ships down from the bridge. He was invaluable and absolutely fearless; nothing bothered McGrievy. He was great. When you are just looking at the TDC, it becomes a problem rather than a threat. You are not looking at the escorts, only the target, and that only as a symbol on the TDC. I would go up there and check every once in a while, and I didn't like what I saw. It looked awful close to me. Then I would go down and check my TDC, and they were 2,000 yards or 1,500 yards or something.

---

*TDC—torpedo data computer.

Q: This bears out what you said before—that it is a tremendous team effort.

Captain Cutter: Oh, yes. On my last war patrol, in the South China Sea, we were trying to get on this damn convoy, and they were maneuvering just so much so that I couldn't reach a firing position. We would get ahead of them, and just about the time they would close up enough that we would want to shoot, they would change course. I said, "What I am going to do this time, I'm going to get ahead of them, and I don't care how much they change course. We are going to shoot."

So we were steaming along there, making about eight knots, they were making eight knots and all of a sudden WHAMMO, a forward gun opened up on this ship astern of us. And, hell, we were only 1,000 yards away. He was pretty close, but the shell fell on the port beam. The port lookout was a guy named Max Martell, who was my chief gunner's mate, and Martell was cold as a cucumber. He was a great guy.

He said, "Captain, they got point-detonating fuzes, too." In other words, they went off when they hit the water. We had point-detonating fuzes and anything they hit, even a sail, would cause them to go off.

Q: He must have been calm to make that kind of observation under fire.

Captain Cutter: Yes, and I was getting the hell out of there, boy. We didn't get a ship out of that convoy. We had only two torpedoes, and they were aft. We reported our status, and Admiral Lockwood told us to return.

Q: How much longer did Parks remain as skipper after you had made that patrol to the South China Sea?

Captain Cutter: That was his last patrol. We came back via Midway, as I told you before, and came to Pearl Harbor and he was detached, and he went back to the staff of SubLant in New London.*

Q: Then your new skipper was Commander Thomas?**

Captain Cutter: Yes. He had been with us before, and the poor guy was one of those who were taken away from the sub force and sent back when we gave the 50 destroyers to Great Britain, the Lend-Lease thing. Put them in commission out of mothballs, and Tommy was one of those people sent back to command one of those destroyers. After they were delivered to the British, he was free, and they ordered him back to submarines. But he hadn't made a war patrol. That was in 1940 when they gave those

---
*The staff of Commander Submarines Atlantic.
**Commander Willis M. Thomas, USN.

destroyers to the British, so he came back and a funny thing happened. Mush Morton reported aboard the Pompano as relief for Lew Parks, and he was aboard two days.* He was going to be our skipper, and we weren't very happy, because Mush did not have a good reputation. He had been passed over for executive officer in a submarine; he hadn't even gotten to be an exec in peacetime. That isn't a derogatory criticism of Mush; it is a criticism of the system.

Q: That's exactly right.

Captain Cutter: That's a criticism of the system, but we were going by reputation. And he hadn't made it, so we didn't want him. Somehow, somebody got sense enough to recognize his potential, and they ordered him to the Pompano. They ordered him to the Pompano, I think, because we were pretty experienced--for those days. I was getting ready to command, and Connole was one year behind me.** And the other officers aboard were McGrath, and Pleatman was aboard--we had some talent on there.*** And I think they figured that if they put Mush there with that talent, that he would have a better chance. Then Thomas showed up on the scene. We were all good friends. Thomas knew us, we knew

---

*Lieutenant Commander Dudley W. Morton, USN.
**Lieutenant David R. Connole, USN.
***Lieutenant (junior grade) Thomas P. McGrath, USN. Lieutenant (junior grade) Ralph Pleatman, USNR.

Thomas, we all respected each other, and it was perfect for him to be assigned as skipper. He went out and relied heavily on Dave Connole and me, because he hadn't been out there. I deeply regret that we didn't have good torpedoes and a better area. We didn't have a good area, and we didn't get anything. But he was aggressive, and he tried, but he just didn't have the opportunity. We picked up a contact with a patrol boat—this was an enemy, manned. He had guns; he killed one of our men, as a matter of fact. We dove and went in and battle surfaced on the guy about 100 yards off. He opened up with that gun, and Tommy was up there on the bridge with everybody else. One of our men got creased, and another got killed by their return fire. We had received a message from ComSubPac to look for enemy patrol boats on the 600-mile circle from Japan. Intelligence had learned that the Japs had placed a number of boats 600 miles from Japan after the Doolittle raid.* We were ordered to sink them. It was a Sunday morning that we reached the 600-mile circle and proceeded up along the circle, because we hadn't gotten anything out in the patrol area. We wanted to come back with something, so we went looking for them and we found one. After sinking it with a 3-inch gun, we put a rubber boat in the water to bring somebody back aboard. Our men in the boat would approach them, and the

---

*The raid by a force of B-25 bombers led by Lieutenant Colonel James Doolittle, U.S. Army, against Tokyo on 18 April 1942. Doolittle launched from the USS Hornet (CV-8) earlier than planned because of detection by a Japanese patrol boat.

Japanese would just open their mouths, and down they would go. These were all naval ratings; they were not civilians. Finally one of them—this fellow Pleatman that I visited in Cincinnati on the way east here—he hit this guy over the head with a .45. I don't think the guy was knocked out, but he acted like he was. We hauled him aboard. He was stretched out over the gunwale of the rubber boat, and they brought him alongside. We took him down below, and the crew started knocking him around. They didn't actually hit him, but they were shoving him around, up against the gyro table and against the hydraulic manifold until one of the officers got down there and stopped it. It was because of this kid that had been hit. We had to bury the boy at sea the next morning. As a matter of fact, he lived until about 11:00 o'clock at night. He got hit right in the shoulder and it didn't look like much of a thing at all, but apparently it went in and hit his lung; he was coughing up blood, and finally he died. One of the last things he said was—he cried, and he told Mr. Connole—Dave Connole was the gunnery officer, and he was up there with him. And he said, "Mr. Connole, kill that son of a bitch." This fellow was really a fighter.

This was "Chainfall" that I told you about, Calcaterra.* A destroyer escort was named for him later on.** His mother was a lovely person and she visited—when we got back to the shipyard

---

*Motor Machinist's Mate First Class Herbert A. Calcaterra, USN, was fatally wounded on 4 September 1942.
**USS Calcaterra (DE-390), commissioned 17 November 1943.

in the *Pompano* after that run, she came to visit us to hear about what happened to her son and about the burial and all that sort of stuff. He was an only child; his father was a doctor who died during World War I in the flu epidemic; he got the flu and died. She was a lovely lady, and I could understand why he was such a fine young man. Calcaterra was quite a boy. One time he got drunk out in the Royal Hawaiian, and the manager of the Hawaiian, a guy by the name of Herb Dollahite, came to me and said, "You've got to go up there and get this guy [up on the sixth floor, or wherever it was]. He's throwing all the furniture out." And he had taken all the damn furniture right through the window and everything. Boom---out it had gone.

Q: He was strong enough to lift it.

Captain Cutter: Oh, yes, and they were afraid to go in there. He saw me and he started to cry, "Oh, Mr. Cutter." And he was just as docile as a lamb. He didn't have any clothes to put on; everything was out of the room.

Q: What had set him off?

Captain Cutter: He had gotten drunk; I don't know what it was. We took him out to base and put him in the relief crew for the rest of the refit period, and then we went out, and that's the

Cutter #2 - 244

patrol when he was lost. But he was a gentleman, I mean the finer instincts. He was working off this, whatever it was, and he hadn't hurt anybody, throwing all the furniture out of the room. Then I went up there, and he just sort of gave in, just fell apart. That was the job of an exec; that's who they would turn to on those things.

Q: You have mentioned the relief crew. How did that arrangement work?

Captain Cutter: When we came in port, we would transfer 25% of our crew to the relief crew. And anybody who wanted to volunteer for the relief crew—I mean if they wanted to get off, we'd let them off. It was kind of a challenge to them and very, very few ever volunteered, although I am sure a lot of them wanted to. But they just didn't.

Q: It was a test of manhood.

Captain Cutter: That's right, that macho stuff in them. Anyway, we had to transfer 25% every time, and then we would take 25% new men. But the old men, the 25%—a cross section of your ratings—would go to the relief crew. And they would be there while your boat was being overhauled, for the two weeks. Then 25% would be made up from the members of the relief crew who worked on the boat, so the men working on the boat were motivated, because they were going out in it. The ones going off were interested, because a lot of their pals were going back out. We got marvelous work, really.

Q: Was this kind of a rotating pool then---the relief crew?

Captain Cutter: Yes, they would would be in there maybe two or three runs and then would go out again, or they would go back to new construction. It was just marvelous; it gave them a relief from this tension. We had some people whom we didn't transfer ever; Hoffman was one of them. I wouldn't go to sea without him; he was my eyes and ears through the sonar. He was absolutely terrific, and he would always say when we were clear to surface. We couldn't see anything, and we wanted to get the hell out of there. He would say, "The escorts are going away." The tendency was to be on the conservative side, but not Hoffman. When he thought it was safe, he would say so, and we would go on his word. He was really tremendous.

Q: I think you were probably pretty forgiving then, even though he did come back late, because you needed him so much.

Captain Cutter: Hoffman didn't do it. It was McGrievy and Anderson. Oh, nothing happened to them. I vented my spleen on them verbally, and that was it. They went right to work, and they were very chagrined. They were fine men. I don't know what had happened. They had trouble getting back or were bumming a ride. I never should have let them go to Perth; it was 3,000 miles; I shouldn't have let them go.

Q: In retrospect, I am wondering, how was the substitution made that brought Thomas in after Morton had already showed up? Who made that decision?

Captain Cutter: SubPac, somebody up there---I don't know who it was then. That was real early in the war, you know. Things were chaotic. I don't know who made the decision.

Q: It almost sounded as if the crew held a vote and decided they would rather have Thomas.

Captain Cutter: No, I didn't even know he was around until he reported aboard. He came in and was sent directly to the Pompano. And Morton---that was the last we saw of him. I guess he went back---he made a PCO run with somebody.* He made a practice run, and then they sent him back, and he got command of the Wahoo, and O'Kane was his exec.** And O'Kane later got the

---
*PCO---prospective commanding officer.
**Lieutenant Commander Richard H. O'Kane, USN. The Wahoo had a superlative record under Morton's command, sinking 19 Japanese vessels before she herself was lost in October 1943.

Tang.

Q: That would have been quite a combination of Morton and all the talent that you have mentioned in the Pompano, had he gone out with you.

Captain Cutter: Yes, but it was better off the way it ended, because he got a good boat. You see, the Wahoo was a good submarine. The Pompano---hell, we had a lot of problems with her engines, terrible problems with the engines all the time. The boat was old. It was the first of its class, the first of the fleet boats. It was smaller than the later fleet boats, and we had only a 252-foot test depth, and the propeller shafts squealed every time we went below depth. And the air-conditioning was an afterthought; it wasn't built into the ship. Office types were put in; we had one in back of the maneuvering room and one down in the pump room, and it was quite inadequate. Later on, they were built into the submarines, and they were good.

Q: This is one problem that the Germans had, I think---foul air. Was this a problem for you?

Captain Cutter: No. We didn't know any better. I guess we did have foul air, but we didn't stay down. I stayed down 16 hours once because of a very persistent depth charge attack, and the air that time was very bad. But that was the only time. We never had any problem with air. You didn't worry about smoking. You let them smoke because after a while, when they couldn't keep a cigarette lighted, you couldn't light a match.

Q: That problem took care of itself.

Captain Cutter: That took care of itself automatically, yes.

Q: You mentioned that you came back through the area where the Battle of Midway had taken place. What did you see at that point? Were there ships in the area still?

Captain Cutter: Oh, no, they had all gone. We got in, I believe, two days after the Battle of Midway, and there was a Captain Simard who was the commanding officer at Midway.* The skipper and I, Lew Parks and I, went to call. It was protocol to call on the commanding officer of the base, and Simard was taking a shower. He said, "Come on in." And he came out there bare-ass naked after his shower and we sat there while he got dressed. And he was very upset about the Army Air Forces because of the claims they had made about the Battle of Midway, which were false, and the fact that they were getting lost. And he had to put good Navy navigators in the Air Forces planes that were going

---

*Captain Cyril T. Simard, USN, commander of Midway Atoll.

out on search missions, because they couldn't get back to Midway without them. He told us all of these things, and it sounded terrible. His morale was really shot. The island was just leveled, you know. They even hit the hospital. That's where we picked up the prisoner that had been brought in by another submarine, and I guess that submarine was going to be refitted or something. I don't know why else they gave him to us, but we brought him back. Simard was really a fine guy.

I'll tell you a little story about Dick O'Kane. I'm a great admirer of his, as you know from what I have said before, but he was a hell of a bore when you got in port. We were in Midway. We came in together. I came in from the East China Sea, and he came in from the South China Sea. We both had good runs, and we rendezvoused together with a destroyer, and he brought us back. And we entered Midway together.

Q: This was some later period then?

Captain Cutter: Oh, no, after my first run.

Q: But I mean you were in the Seahorse then, as opposed to the Pompano.

Captain Cutter: Oh, yes, I meant back in Seahorse. So we came into port in column, into Midway. As we came in, there was a submarine on the reef; they had tried to get in a couple of days before, and they hadn't made it. Anyway, we got in port and as always the squadron commander, who lived on Midway—there were quarters there that had been taken over from the Pan Am people.* He had his quarters there with stewards and stuff and would have you up for drinks—that was the most important ingredient—and dinner. And you would sit around and tell sea stories, just like we are talking now. You would talk about your patrol. I didn't want to talk about the patrol after they had gotten everything out of me that I thought was of any use to them, but Dick couldn't stop talking about it. Finally, they wanted to get him the hell out of there. So somehow or other they convinced Dick he should go to bed, because he didn't drink. He didn't drink; he was all business. I couldn't believe it the next day when my officers came up and said, "Captain, you won't believe what we have just seen."

"What's that?"

"Captain O'Kane is down at the dock holding dry dives at 8:00 o'clock in the morning."

Here is the crew just in from the war patrol. He is going to lose 25% of them to the relief crew, and they are holding dry dives at the dock, which is something that you did only when the ship was first built, to test to see that all the valves worked

---

*Pan American Airways had established a series of bases on Pacific islands before the war to provide rest stops and refueling bases for Clipper planes going to and from the Far East.

and everything. That's how hyped Dick was.

Q: A little too serious?

Captain Cutter: Sure, that's what made him great, too. He didn't leave any detail unturned; everything was taken care of. But I thought that was carrying it a little far.

Q: I'm surprised that you said Captain Simard was so frustrated. You'd think he would be elated that he hadn't been invaded and so forth.

Captain Cutter: No, they were still having patrols out there. Oh, yes, he didn't have enough space on the landing strip there in Midway for all the planes that were sent out, and he had to keep them in the air in order to make room for the ones that were on the ground. And he wanted to get them the hell out of there. He said, "They are no good. They're not doing me any good, and they are using up my naval aviators as navigators." He was an aviator himself. And I remember he was highly indignant. That's a long time ago, 40 years ago.

Q: You gave a very good picture of coming into Pearl Harbor two days after the battle of Pearl. What do you remember seeing at Midway two days after the battle?

Captain Cutter: It was just levelled. It was not comparable to the devastation at Pearl. There wasn't that much there to start with, and there weren't very many buildings. Not all of them were knocked down. The residential quarters weren't bothered. There was more on the industrial part of the island where the tenders were tied up, but they weren't hit. Come to think of it, the tenders probably weren't there. I think they got them out before the battle. I don't know. But there were no ships sunk, and the damage was not that extensive. Captain Simard's quarters were still there, and he was taking a shower. But they hit the barracks, and they hit the hospital. I remember that.

Q: How much was there in the way of submarine servicing facilities at a place like Midway?

Captain Cutter: Nothing practically. Later on, they had a couple of tenders in there, and we got excellent service. They had fuel there and everything we needed. It was a heck of a place for recreation; there was nothing you could do except watch the gooney birds.

Q: What role during the war did submarine division and squadron commanders have?

Captain Cutter: None, I guess--administrative duty or something.

I really don't know what they did. They were training officers. They would go out. Just before you went on patrol, they would go out and ride with you to see how you were coming along. I guess they provided a service. There were some skippers that were relieved at that time. They would say, "He isn't ready," or "He's got an officer on there that should be replaced," or something like that. I guess it depended upon the individual. Parks would be wonderful. He could shape them up, but he might cause a few unhappy people doing it.

Q: But they had very little operational role, then?

Captain Cutter: None. All of our operations were controlled by Dick Voge.* They had nothing to do with it. I don't think they had anything to do with personnel. They were in charge of the relief crews, and they helped us get supplies and things like that. They were as helpful as they could be, and they wrote endorsements on our patrols, their comments. It didn't amount to anything.

Q: They made some patrols themselves, didn't they?

Captain Cutter: Later on, they did. They would go out as wolf

---
*Commander Richard G. Voge, USN, operations officer on the staff of Commander Submarines Pacific.

pack commanders, but generally that was later in the war when the division commanders had war experience. You see, our first division commanders had none, so they weren't very helpful.

Q: I remember Admiral Loughlin's oral history talks about Jimmy Fife going out on a war patrol.* Lockwood was denied that opportunity, and the irony of it was that Fife got a tombstone promotion to four stars, which Lockwood didn't.**

Captain Cutter: Because he got a combat award. You know, Fife also got his first baptism when he rode British submarines. Did you know that?

Q: No.

Captain Cutter: He rode British submarines in the Mediterranean before the war, and that was hairy duty. He submitted a report which was circulated through the force, which I read. Very interesting. Fife was a good one. I don't know why--well, he had the Southwest Pacific, didn't he?

---

*Rear Admiral C.E. Loughlin, USN(Ret.).
**Charles A. Lockwood, Jr., retired as a vice admiral, his highest active duty rank. Rear Admiral James Fife, Jr., USN, held a number of submarine billets during World War II, including Commander Submarine Squadron Two, Commander Task Force 72, Commander Submarine Southwest Pacific, and Commander Task Force 71.

Q: For a while, I believe, after Admiral Christie was there.

Captain Cutter: Yes, he was a good man, very good.

Q: How much sharing of experience was there, in an official sense and in an unofficial sense, about lessons learned from patrols?

Captain Cutter: Very wide to the skippers; we learned from each other and also from patrol reports. We read all patrol reports. A lot of them were better than others, some of them were very flamboyant--like we held our breath, and this or that--stuff like that. You remember that with Gene Fluckey, who was very, very good.* But Gene was very flamboyant and a good writer, and he wrote all his patrol reports because nobody else could do it that well.

Q: I think just the conversations in the officers' club, like you mentioned with Captain O'Kane, would tell what had worked and what hadn't.

Captain Cutter: Oh, yes, very much so. And what the enemy's capability was and what evasion tactics you use and how effective

---

*Commander Eugene B. Fluckey, USN, who won the Medal of Honor for his service while in command of the USS Barb (SS-220).

their antisubmarine screens or any evidence of radar on them. When you went out and there wasn't any evidence of any radar, that was reassuring. You would go out and plan your patrol thinking, "Well, I don't have to worry about radar at night. I can get on the surface and charge my batteries without having to worry about such things." This is the thing, you see. Everybody was so honest, and everybody wanted to help everybody else. It was a joint effort throughout the submarine force--very high morale and esprit de corps. Everybody loved everybody else, and really it was a very wholesome environment. We were very proud. We were like the Marine Corps and I think for good reason.

Q: This is sort of a contrast to the way you talked about Parks who wouldn't share, but that was the prewar period.

Captain Cutter: Oh, that was prewar. When the war was on, Parks shared everything; it all came in his patrol reports. Oh, no, that was altogether different. It was a new ball game at the start of the war. In fact, Parks was very happy--he did a lot of things you probably didn't consider too prudent at the time so he could impress people. Like this business of not making a trim dive all the way to Midway--getting caught at Midway without having made a trim dive.

Q: That was kind of foolhardy, as it turned out.

Captain Cutter: Well, sure it was. But I'll say this—when we dove, we had no trouble getting under, and we had no trouble maintaining depth. Connole, the diving officer, had meticulously kept the boat compensated in weight. For example, every time you used a gallon of fuel oil, you were one pound heavier, because fuel is seven pounds per gallon and salt water is eight. So for every gallon of fuel used, one pound of water had to be pumped to sea from a variable tank. Fuel was carried in main ballast tanks, open at the bottom. Fuel, being lighter than water, was in the top of the tank. As it was used, sea water came in from the bottom. So the main ballast tanks were always full but changed in weight as fuel was used. Food used had to be compensated for. The changes from one day to the next were not critical, but when a boat went several days without a trim dive it was difficult to stay in diving trim. It took some really careful computation and record keeping.

Q: I didn't realize that it had to be so precise, but I can see where it would be necessary.

Captain Cutter: Sure, when you are only going a knot and a half, you have very little force on those planes, and that is all that's holding you up, if you are heavy. We would get to a neutral buoyancy position where we could go dead stop, and just raising and lowering the periscope would make the difference

Cutter #2 - 258

whether we would go up or down. If we started going down, we would raise the periscope, displace more water, make us a few pounds lighter and we would come up, very slowly. But many times we did that—controlling our depth through the periscope; it was very precise.

Q: How long did Thomas remain? I guess you left before he did.

Captain Cutter: A good thing. Thomas never came back.*

Q: When were you detached?

Captain Cutter: I was detached in the navy yard in the spring of '43 and went to Seahorse.

Q: Was she at Mare Island?

Captain Cutter: Mare Island. The Seahorse was commissioned in March. We left in June; we were commissioned earlier than that, because it was a government-built submarine. And then we went directly to Pearl Harbor for our training period. McGregor did an outstanding job as training officer.** He was very careful

---

*Commander Willis M. Thomas, USN, was the commanding officer when the Pompano was lost with all hands in September 1943.
**Commander Donald McGregor, USN, the first commanding officer.

and took care of detail; he was good. I was absolutely appalled when we got on patrol, to see the difference. He recognized that I was good, from Parks. I wouldn't have been if it hadn't been for Parks. But I was better on approaches than he was, so he put me on the periscope. Incidentally, Mush Morton put Dick O'Kane on the periscope, for attacks.* The skipper just was an observer.

Q: And Dornin put Beach on the periscope.**

Captain Cutter: That's right, a good decision, although Dusty was very good himself. Dusty was also very good on the TDC.*** He was a TDC operator. I was a TDC operator, and so was O'Kane. And we could get more out of an attack watching the torpedo data computer than we would at the periscope. Although when I did get to be skipper, I stayed on the periscope, because I could look at the TDC right there. For a fellow like McGregor, the TDC was a mystery to him---the solution of the fire control problem. Boy, we were good in training period. God, we went out there---the people who rode us were highly complimentary of the state of the readiness of the ship and complimented the captain for the job he

---

*Commander Dudley W. Morton, USN, who commanded the USS Wahoo (SS-238) with Lieutenant Commander Richard H. O'Kane, USN, as executive officer.
**Lieutenant Commander Robert E. Dornin, USN, who commanded the USS Trigger (SS-237) with Lieutenant Edward L. Beach, USN, as executive officer.
***TDC---torpedo data computer.

had done. He had done a good job. But then we got out in the war zone, and he left me at the periscope, but with no decisions to make. I mean, how much periscope I had up, what depth to run so I had enough scope up to see what I was doing, etc. Well, I'll give you an example. One Sunday morning--I'll never forget--off Palau and we were way out; it was one of the times we were returning to Toagel Mlungui Pass after the convoy had gotten away, and we ran into an unescorted tanker coming out of Palau. He was 150 to 200 miles off the coast, no escorts, no planes--an overcast, rainy day. We picked it up at about 10,000 yards, and it was very significant, the officer of the deck--this same guy, Les Lessard, was at the periscope. He sighted this thing coming, and he sent for me instead of the captain. So I came up to the conning tower and took a look and said, "Right full rudder, all ahead two-thirds." I took another look, and we were about 2,500 yards off the track, range 10,000 yards. Boy, we were in a beautiful spot. All we had to do was keep coming around, get ourselves on a 90 track, go dead slow speed and wait for him to come on, and we were going to fire at about 800 yards range--like shooting fish in a barrel. This guy wasn't zigging, a big ship. So I sent for the captain. He came up, and I told him the situation.

After we had steadied down on course for a 90-degree track shot, he said, "Right full rudder, all ahead two-thirds."

I said, "Captain, what are you doing?"

"I'm coming around for a stern tube shot."

"Why?"

"I want to give the after room some practice."

We hadn't given the forward room any practice yet. I couldn't believe it. By God, we opened out, and we fired four stern torpedoes at a range of 4,500 yards.

Q: Instead of 800 yards?

Captain Cutter: Yes. They were steam torpedoes. The guy saw the wakes, and he maneuvered to avoid. Then I couldn't believe my ears again. He said, "Make ready the bow tubes, set all torpedoes on low power." Which gave you about a 9,000-yard torpedo run at 27 knots, as opposed to 47 knots at 6,500 yards. By God, he came around again, and here is this tanker going with a 180 angle on the bow--in other words, we were looking up his rear end--and we fired six torpedoes. And they were smoking along, beyond the torpedo run. This guy was making about 15 knots, and the torpedoes could never catch him before he got out of range. Of course, there were six more torpedoes down the tube. God Almighty, I couldn't believe it. Why would a man do that? We wasted ten precious torpedoes.

Q: Had he not had any previous war patrols?

Captain Cutter: Sure, he made four in the Gar, and he sank one 1,500-ton ship, unescorted. He was a very close friend of Admiral Christie.* He was an excellent golfer, and so was Christie, and they were big buddies down there in Brisbane where he was based in the Gar. They decided to give him one more chance, so they ordered him to the Seahorse, and with it I was ordered. I had had three war patrols. Currie was ordered, he was class of '37 at the Naval Academy, and I was '35.** Currie had been with Gilmore, the guy who said, "Take her down."***

Q: Howard Gilmore?

Captain Cutter: That's right, and Currie was his diving officer. He was very experienced, and he had been through it, because Gilmore was good. He just didn't last long enough to prove it, but he was excellent. Then the other guy was off the Saury, and he had made eight war patrols. Of course, a lot of them were short, but he had been through it. That was Spud Lindon, out of

---

*In August 1942, Captain Ralph W. Christie, USN, had taken over as Commander Task Force 42 (Eastern Australia Submarine Group), based at Brisbane.
**Lieutenant John P. Currie, USN.
***On 7 February 1943, Lieutenant Commander Howard W. Gilmore, USN, was in command of the USS Growler (SS-215) when she rammed a Japanese gunboat and suffered a heavy machine gun attack. Gilmore ordered his executive officer to "Take her down," thus sacrificing his own life in order to ensure the safety of the submarine and the remainder of her crew. He was posthumously awarded the Medal of Honor.

'39, and an excellent officer.* Then we had Bill Budding, a fourth Naval Academy man—everything was judged in those days by Naval Academy, you know—and no other submarine had the luxury of that.** They would have a couple of Naval Academy officers, and the rest were reserves. So we were really loaded, and they did that purposely for their pal McGregor. That's right. And he blew it.

Q: You didn't have the disadvantage you spoke about earlier of Naval Academy people fresh out?

Captain Cutter: Oh, no, except Budding. The rest of us were war tested. Oh, hell, yes, we were trained. With Parks you took the initiative. As long as it was within your sphere of influence, he let you go free. I mean, you did what you thought you should do.

Q: Who would have been the guy that loaded up the ship with these good people? Was it Babe Brown?***

Captain Cutter: No, this was done by BuPers, but the force commanders had a lot to do with it.**** But at BuPers the

---

*Lieutenant Elbert C. Lindon, USN.
**Ensign William A. Budding, Jr., USN.
***Captain John H. Brown, USN, submarine force training officer.
****BuPers—Bureau of Naval Personnel.

Cutter #2 - 264

submarine detail officer, who was an ex-submarine skipper and a pretty senior guy—they all knew each other. And he ordered all experienced people to give McGregor a chance—"He hasn't had any talent. He's a good man, but he hasn't had a chance." Because he would always blame his people. Like I told you about the fitness report I got from him. So they gave him a chance.

Q: So you made one patrol with him. Then Brown came in, and what was his technique really for finding out what had happened?

Captain Cutter: Because we were never in the area; we were always pursuing and weren't getting anything. We returned to the area and hadn't sunk a thing. Brown knew me; he knew Parks; he knew I had been with Parks; he knew what we had done in the Pompano. And he knew damn well that I was not going to be quiet and that there was going to be friction. He just intuitively knew it. It was arranged that that dispatch where I was ordered to relieve McGregor was delivered as the first piece of paper that came aboard when we reached port.

Q: So Brown hadn't even had a chance to talk to the crew before he did that.

Captain Cutter: No, of course not. No, no, no, he was in Pearl Harbor. It was all in the dispatches. Well, I am sure it was

Brown. I doubt if Voge would do that, because Voge was a kind, gentle sort of a man, and I don't think he would say, "Return to Toagel Mlungui best speed and remain there for remainder of patrol."

That was really a slap in the face, telling him what to do out in an area, giving him an order. Unheard of. They would give you suggestions: "There is a task force coming through," or "We suggest that you cover this area." Something like that but not a direct order. "You shall stay there." In other words, you couldn't even chase a convoy going out. To me, it was a slap in the face.

Q: Where did the relief take place?

Captain Cutter: At Midway; there was no relief. He just left and I took command; that was all; I just fleeted up. McGrievy, who was then chief of the boat---he was the guy who became commander and became kind of a problem until he matured and became a real gung-ho naval officer. McGrievy was the chief of the boat, who is the most important man on the submarine except the skipper and the exec. You know about the chief of the boat.

Q: Senior enlisted man.

Captain Cutter: Yes, and they are unique in the service. I

don't think any enlisted man in the service has more responsibility than the chief of the boat in submarines; they are sort of assistant executive officers. McGrievy told me afterward that if they had been any place but Midway, half of the crew would have gone over the hill when I got command. But there was no place to go, so they stayed. They didn't want to go out because of what McGregor had told them about me up in the conning tower. They had absolutely no confidence in me at all.

Q: What did he say, that you were foolhardy, reckless, or what?

Captain Cutter: Well, in the first place he didn't believe that the <u>Pompano</u> had done the things that I said they did. And he said words like, "He just isn't in his right mind" and stuff like that, that I was nuts. I never found that out until much later. Those kids were loyal; they didn't say anything about the captain. And it wasn't until quite a bit later--I don't even think on the first patrol did I know it. It was after they got to know me and we had a little success, why, they came in and told me. I later saw McGregor again. One time we were going to the Navy-USC football game in '49.* The Navy played USC out there, and I had been at the ticket office. And, by golly, McGregor came to the ticket office. We didn't speak, ignored each other. And his wife was there, Grace, a lovely person and,

---

*USC--University of Southern California.

by golly, she came up to me and congratulated me on what the Seahorse had done. Now that was pretty big.

Q: She had a lot of class.

Captain Cutter: You bet. She had a lot of class; she was a great gal. I never saw her again either.

Q: How did he take it when he got the dispatch ordering him removed?

Captain Cutter: I never knew. He didn't say anything. He left. Pleatman went back to new construction.* Bob Rice, my first skipper in the S-30, became submarine detail officer.** So when I got back from that first patrol, I wrote to Bob and told him to for God's sake send Pleatman to a government boat—those built in either Portsmouth or Mare Island. Because for those boats your time in new construction was five months. They were commissioned earlier, before they were completed. In a private yard, they were aboard only three months, because the crew was not given a boat until it was commissioned. They were not permitted aboard until it was commissioned, except to check the systems and get to

---

*Lieutenant (junior grade) Ralph Pleatman, USNR.
**Lieutenant Robert H. Rice, USN, was commanding officer of the USS S-30 when Cutter had temporary duty in that boat following completion of submarine school. Rice held the rank of commander while serving as detail officer in the Bureau of Naval Personnel in World War II.

know the boat and get the crew together and get trained on shore-based facilities and so forth, but they had nothing to do with the submarine. You did in the government yard; you stood watches aboard in the boat for security purposes and things like that. So I wrote to Bob. Ralph was going back to an EB boat when I got him out to Midway, so then he got the _Devilfish_ up in Portsmouth.* Bob did it; he sent him to a government boat. So he spent five months there with his bride. Of course, he wasn't mad with me at all after the run anyway, but on his way up there he stopped off in New London and this guy McGregor was assistant chief of staff to ComSubLant in New London, so Ralph went in to see him. I had never confided to Ralph about all this problem stuff. He knew a little bit about it but not all the details. He went in to see Mac, and McGregor didn't believe that we had done what was on the patrol reports, after that first run. Isn't that something?

Q: He was hard to convince.

Captain Cutter: And he told Pleatman that. Pleatman said, "Well, Commander, I was there, I saw it. We were on the surface."

---

*EB refers to submarines built by the Electric Boat Company of Groton, Connecticut.

Q: Well, your first run then as skipper of the Seahorse—where did you go on that one?*

Captain Cutter: East China Sea. That's where I ran into Dornin in the waiting area and we sank the two boats. We made it to the East China Sea and then back to Pearl Harbor. Then to Palau.

Q: You told me something last night, I think when we weren't recording, about how you got to pick your patrol area. Would you discuss that?

Captain Cutter: All skippers did. If you happened to go out on a first patrol and make a good run—well, if you got a good submarine for whatever reason—either the crew was good, or you were good, or whatever, then Dick Voge would call you up and said, "Where do you want to go?" Because you had proved yourself, and he would send you to a productive area. So it was a cumulative thing. The guys who were lucky, we will say, in the first patrol were given things, handed to them then. You went into areas where there were targets, because they wanted to send you there rather than somebody that was not likely to do anything. Just think what a terrible thing it was to send the Seahorse to Palau on its first patrol. We had only 50-some

---
*Cutter assumed command of the Seahorse at Midway on 30 September 1943 and began his first war patrol as skipper on 20 October. For a discussion of the patrol, see Clay Blair, Jr., Silent Victory (J.B. Lippincott Company, 1975), pages 518-520.

submarines. With that well-trained crew and all those torpedoes and nothing happened. Terrible. I felt a very grave responsibility. We had to get results when we went out there, because we were the only offensive thing we had at that time. We were the only ones out in the Far Pacific; that was before the fleet got out there.

Q: This was mid-1943?

Captain Cutter: Yes, and early 1944. Things didn't get hot out there until after we took Saipan.

Captain Cutter: What kind of briefing would you get before you would go out on patrol?

Captain Cutter: We would get a description of the area, and Admiral Lockwood generally would talk to you--just more of a social thing than anything else and express confidence in you and wish you well and all that sort of stuff.*

Q: Sort of a father figure?

Captain Cutter: Yes, a father figure, and I don't recall too

---

*Charles A. Lockwood, Jr., promoted from rear admiral to vice admiral in October 1943, was Commander Submarines Pacific Fleet.

much. The intelligence people would give us what data they had on their ASW activity out there and what the traffic situation was and where the best places were to go in the area.* It's a long time ago, and I don't remember exactly. The only one I remember was the time Admiral Lockwood told me I couldn't be a prisoner, which I was not intending to do anyway.

Q: Were your charts better then than they had been before?

Captain Cutter: No, they were better at Saipan than they were down in the Marshalls. I don't think we had any good charts at any time during the war in the Marshall Islands. We never got a chance to send any hydrographic ships down there. In Saipan they weren't too bad.

The way I got this Japanese submarine—I was told to, whenever feasible, find out the 600-fathom curve, because outside of 600 fathoms you couldn't mine. And they were afraid that Saipan was going to be mined inside the 600-fathom curve, so where is it? On this Sunday morning, the 20th of April—Easter Sunday 1944—we were doing that. And we were close enough to see the breakwater in Saipan Harbor. We had a lot of periscope up, we were submerged, and I had a very meticulous executive officer, Spud Lindon; this guy out of '39 was still aboard and he had to do everything to a tenth of a yard, which was beyond the accuracy

---

*ASW—antisubmarine warfare.

Cutter #2 - 272

of the equipment that we had. So he was taking three bearings; every time he would take an observation he would get the smokestack of the sugar mill and a lighthouse and the left tangent of the island, which was a sheer cliff. That was plainly marked on the chart, and he would use those three bearings to plot our accurate position. And this was what he was doing. We had the other periscope up and they were supposed to look out for anybody coming out, because we had a lot of periscope up to be able to see, you know---probably 12 feet. So I had breakfast, and I came up and just casually, without thinking about anything at all, took the number one periscope, which had more light through it than the attack periscope, and just took a slow turn. And something caught my eye. I came back on it, saw something white, and, hell, there was a rising sun on the side of a submarine conning tower. I took a couple looks at him, and he was constant helming. When I first saw him, there was no chance of getting in, because we were almost broad on his beam. My God, I took another look and we are on his bow, port. He had come around; he was zigzagging 60 degrees either side of base course. It is impossible to get very far doing that, but it does make it tough if there is a submarine there, and this is what he was doing--- making it tough. It just so happened that he was zigging about, he would be 30 degrees on his port bow and we would end up about 80 or 90 degrees on his starboard bow as he was coming up. Hoffman was on there---the sonarman I was telling you about who became a commander—and he had his chart there and identified it as an R-class submarine at 10.3 knots and 120 turns, I don't actually know what it was, but anyway Hoffman said, "He is making 10.3 knots." So we set that in the TDC, and then when he got in close enough we fired a torpedo to run at 1,600 yards. We fired electric torpedoes, and as he was swinging—it was a very slow change of course—and as he was on his starboard swing, I fired and led him about 30 degrees. I gave him a course about 30 degrees to the right of his true course. We fired electric torpedoes, and he never saw them coming. Hell, that was in a flat, calm sea with just a light swell—a greasy sea, you know. And I was just seeing through the top of the waves; the periscope was just breaking the top of the waves, and I could see they must have had 20 guys up there in whites, all lookouts. Because they knew we were there. We had been in there and had sunk some ships there, and they knew we were there. They were coming into port. I fired one inside the bow and one inside the stern; I fired two torpedoes and either the first or second, I don't know which one hit, but there was a tremendous explosion. The reason I couldn't fire three, which I wanted to do, was that I told them to hold the poppets open for eight seconds, because that was what we were supposed to do. The poppet valve swallows the bubble. You fire a torpedo out with water slug, with air, and then if you don't do something about it, it's going to make a big bubble up on the surface. So we had what they call poppet valves which automatically open—big valves—that would let the air come into the boat. It would swallow the bubble, and there would be very little disturbance on the surface. Our instructions were to hold them open eight seconds—way too much, but we had never done it before. Before, you would hold them open until you got water in the boat; then you would close them by hand. This time I said, "Hold them open for eight seconds," because I didn't want any bubble. It was too long; we got a hell of a lot of water in the forward torpedo room, so we got a down angle and I couldn't fire the last torpedo because we went under. See, we had an eight-second interval between torpedoes. He was gone, nothing there. So I had no evidence of any sinking, except this tremendous explosion. So, being a submarine, he could have dived. In fact, we didn't get credit for that doggoned thing until after the war. What had happened was that that night, we had the exact position of firing because we had been doing this accurate navigation, so I knew exactly where it was. That night we came back there to see if there was any diesel oil. Hell, we followed the diesel slick for ten miles. He was down there, so we knew we had sunk him and we claimed him. But we didn't get credit for it until after the war was over.*

Q: That was pretty unusual for one submarine to sink another, wasn't it?

---
*On 20 April 1944, while patrolling submerged off Saipan, the Seahorse sank the Japanese submarine RO-45.

Cutter #2 - 275

Captain Cutter: It didn't happen very often. There weren't many chances. You didn't get many chances at it.

Q: When you were doing this precise navigation, did you have the fathometer then to record the depth?

Captain Cutter: Oh, yes, but there were no patrol boats out. It was a beautiful Sunday morning. There were no patrol boats around and that's why we were doing it. We thought it was a perfectly safe thing to do. And this guy was coming in from patrol apparently; he had to be.

Q: How good were your recognition manuals to be able to recognize enemy ships and airplanes?

Captain Cutter: They weren't good at all. You look through that book---I was at one time embarrassed, but am not anymore, because everybody did the same thing. All submarines carried recognition books containing the silhouettes of all Japanese ships. After an attack, the officers would come and show you the recognition book. So you and they picked the biggest ship that looked like that silhouette---just human nature. So most of us about doubled our real tonnage. Some of them were a lot worse; Dick O'Kane was way over. That's not being dishonest. What the heck? That's why I was glad to see that Blair judged things not by tonnage but

Cutter #2 - 276

on number of ships sunk.* That's what counted. That's what they did for award purposes, awarding skippers. If you got four ships, you got a Navy Cross. I told Admiral Lockwood one time, "I'm tired of these Navy Crosses. What you should have is an award for superior ability. We're good, and the Legion of Merit isn't good enough. You ought to have a special award for somebody who is particularly good." Kind of an egotistical thing to say, but that's the way I felt, and that's what I said.

Q: Did you have any other means of measuring tonnage besides the recognition books?

Captain Cutter: That's all we had. Of course, later on--after the war was over--the Army and Navy Assessment Committee got the exact dope. It was amazing how they acquired that information and how accurate it was as to where the ships were sunk and everything; the Japs kept good records. I think I sank a couple of ships we didn't get credit for. Maybe they weren't registered, and other skippers had the same thing, but there was only two. And they may not have, but I thought the evidence was conclusive. We weren't too bad; we claimed two more ships than we actually sank, which wasn't too bad. Tonnage, we were off by

---

*See Clay Blair, Jr., Silent Victory (Philadelphia: J.B. Lippincott Company, 1975), page 984. In the final postwar accounting, O'Kane finished with 24 confirmed sinkings, and Cutter tied with Mush Morton for second place with 19 apiece.

about 100%, I guess. Anyway, we got credit for 72,000 tons, and I think we claimed 140,000 tons.

Q: The tonnage champion for one target is Joe Enright in the Archerfish.* Did you ever have any contact with him?

Captain Cutter: Yes, I knew Joe. Joe was in my submarine school class. Joe is a fine man, and that was the only ship he sank.

Q: What was the procedure on writing patrol reports? How soon did you do that?

Captain Cutter: We kept a log every day. Of course, we kept a log, but then I guess everybody did it differently. I had my exec, every day, write a diary of what had happened. Then, when we were coming back from patrol we generally had two weeks, plenty of time to type it up. He would write it, and I would approve what he said. We made it in chronological order of events. It was no elaborate thing at all—just what happened and then what we observed. Most of our comments would come on ASW activity and any changes that we thought we needed in our equipment. One of the things that—oh, I don't go into detail—we made a dive once and our pit log came out. It wasn't supposed

---

*On 29 November 1944, the USS Archerfish (SS-311), commanded by Commander Joseph F. Enright, USN, sank the unfinished Japanese aircraft carrier Shinano. He was credited with 59,000 tons, the most tonnage sunk on a single submarine war patrol.

to, but it came out and hit the overhead, and we flooded the forward torpedo room. Thank goodness, it was during a training exercise, so we were able to come back to the surface and they were able to plug it. We didn't do any real damage, but it could have been serious. So we advised or recommended that they put a positive stop. All it involved was putting something down from the overhead that would meet the sword arm if that happened again and stop it from coming out of the hole in the hull. The pit log sword arm was about three feet long, so it wouldn't be able to come out of its gland down there where it went through the hull. That was one of several things that we recommended.

Q: What would be the procedure for debriefing at the end of a patrol?

Captain Cutter: Most of the time, the first debriefing you would get would be from the division commander and the squadron commander. They would generally have you to dinner and give you a few drinks. However, in Pearl Harbor the first debriefing came when Admiral Lockwood met every ship that came in, and there would be a debrief down in the wardroom, in your wardroom. You would go over the patrol report with him and just skim through the thing, because they were pretty thick, pretty voluminous. He would comment and ask questions on why you did this, why did you do that, and what happened. He was always very kind in his questioning. Voge was always with him, and Grenfell was generally along, and then they would later ask specific questions.* The debriefing wasn't particularly extensive. Then you would have to go before the division commander and the squadron commander, but that was always quite informal, and they would get just enough information to write up an endorsement which wouldn't mean anything. Endorsements didn't mean anything. SubPac's endorsements did, because they would comment on particular things and what corrective action should be taken. And they would be sort of guides for other submarines. Because everybody read these patrol reports. I think we wrote patrol reports with that in mind---to be as helpful as we could to other people. Others did, too.

Q: Did you do much periscope photography?

Captain Cutter: I didn't; I wish I had.

Q: Parks was sort of a pioneer in that.

Captain Cutter: He sure was, the first one. Parks was first in a lot of things. This was before the war that he did this periscope photography bit.

---

*Commander Richard G. Voge, USN, operations officer for Commander Submarines Pacific Fleet; Commander Elton W. Grenfell, USN, war plans officer on the SubPac staff.

Q: Did you work with him on that?

Captain Cutter: He did it all. I will say when Parks zeroed in on something, boy, he pursued it to the bitter end. He learned an awful lot about photography and learned a lot about periscope photography. And he was the first one to have one installed that you could look through the camera and through the periscope at the same time. Others had tried it, and they would look through the periscope to see what they were seeing and then put the camera on. Well, by that time, the situation would change perhaps. But he would look through there and he would snap pictures when he was seeing what was happening, which later on they all did.

Q: You mentioned this one very long, sleepless period. What was the general routine, keeping in mind that this is an exception?

Captain Cutter: The general routine was—in the daytime in enemy-controlled waters we stayed submerged, and that's when we slept. Because contact was not that often. I could sleep in the daytime, not very much, but some—at night, never. I just couldn't sleep at night, and I don't think others did either. I was never able—when I got to be division commander and a squadron commander, I could never sleep in a submarine at night. I could sleep in the daytime fine but not at night. Funny.

Q: How much sleep would you average during a 24-hour period, let's say, on a patrol?

Captain Cutter: A couple of hours.

Q: During the day?

Captain Cutter: Yes. Those patrols were rough, and that's why you had this reaction. That's what I think anyway. You've heard a lot of stories, I suppose, about stuff that went on---the relaxing got pretty violent. Not violent but ...

Q: Exuberant?

Captain Cutter: Exuberant, that's the word, yes, and we drank far too much. We were out in Midway, and there was a guy by the name of Dick Harlow. Dick Harlow was coach at Harvard, and was coach at Western Maryland College when I was on the boxing team at the Academy, and he was the boxing coach at Western Maryland and football coach, too.* He offered me a scholarship to Western Maryland if I didn't get in the Naval Academy, so that was my connection with Dick Harlow. A wonderful man. By golly, he had

---

*Lieutenant Commander Richard C. Harlow, USNR, who was football coach at Western Maryland College from 1925 to 1934 and at Harvard University from 1935 to 1949 (except for his Navy stint from 1942 to 1944).

gotten into the Tunney program, which was made up of athletes—Frank Leahy was in it, Gene Tunney.* And they would be out in charge of recreation in these areas and Harlow was an ornithologist.

Q: George Halas was in that, too, wasn't he?**

Captain Cutter: Yes, he was, that's right. Harlow was a world-famous ornithologist; it was his hobby and he was recognized in it. Midway was just heaven to Dick, because there were so many birds there, and that's why he got on Midway. He came out and he was a marvelous man, I mean a perfect gentleman. They called him the Squire of Harvard Square when he was coaching at Harvard—that's what the other coaches referred to him as. Dick was out there and he just couldn't understand how these submariners would drink like they did. And he would say, "Slade, you are destroying yourself. This is terrible—all this booze. What you should do is rest and exercise and get your health back rather than tearing it down."

Well, I don't know what I said, but I know what I would say now: "There is such a thing as mental health," and that is much more important than physical health. We were all young; we were all healthy. As soon as our two weeks' rest was up, we got all

---
*Frank Leahy was Notre Dame's football coach; Gene Tunney was former world heavyweight boxing champion.
**George Halas was for many years coach and owner of the Chicago Bears professional football team.

healthy again and went back to work. I took him out on our training exercise and showed him how serious this business was and how seriously they took their training--all of them, enlisted and officers, and he was very much impressed with it. But he sure felt that we were destroying ourselves physically.

Q: Did you catch up on any sleep then during the rest periods?

Captain Cutter: No, didn't sleep much. No, we just got along without it.

Q: I think that was sort of a natural selection process. The good skippers were the ones that did have a lot of stamina.

Captain Cutter: We had to, oh, yes. I had a lot of trouble with my stomach. I got in there one time and told the doctor about it, and he gave me aluminum hydroxide--these white pills, I think it is aluminum hydroxide--that they take for ulcers, chalk-like stuff. And I would just chew those when I would get this burning sensation. What the hell, you are drinking 25 or 30 cups of coffee a day and smoking two packs or three packs of cigarettes, just to keep going.

Q: I can see where a health nut would not approve.

Captain Cutter: And you would come in way overweight; we were eating all the time.

Q: Was the food good?

Captain Cutter: Oh, yes, always, always. My god, we always were sure we had a good cook; they all were good. All of our meat was boned, and we had a freezer. We would get the choice cuts of beef, and even our turkey was boned turkey, fresh. Everything was boned for space. We had wonderful food.

Q: What kind of meal arrangements did you have? Probably pretty much catch as catch can.

Captain Cutter: Not normally. If we weren't in contact, the officers would sit down to a regular meal. The officer of the deck was up on the bridge, and we would eat. Same way with the crew. The crew mess was small, and it took three shifts to feed them. So that was sort of catch as catch can back there. One time off Saipan when we were in contact with enemy antisubmarine forces for four nights and three days, they were never really in contact with us, but they were always there. And we never did get a battery charge in on the surface, because the damn airplanes were up there. We were able to keep away from the destroyers by sonar. We could avoid; whenever they came toward us, we would head off 90 degrees from their direction. And we were able to avoid detection, but it was constant surveillance of us on them. I'll never forget this fellow Roy Hoffman, who, as I told you, was so good. He was up there one daytime on the sonar and the enemy would ping, ping, ping. Did you ever hear it? The sonar ping.

Q: On TV I have.

Captain Cutter: Well, it's a musical tone, out it goes and then you wait for the echo coming back. But this was the enemy's; there was no echo coming back, and we were listening to it. He got damn tired of it and we are all crapped out. We are asleep, or resting at least, the off-watch people. In the conning tower the periscope went down a periscope well, and to keep the periscope from fogging the ventilation system went into it--to keep the moisture content down. With that ventilation duct going into it, of course, all sound could go out, all through the ship from forward to aft. So Hoffman got sick and tired of listening to this damn ping, and he thought that others should share it with him. So he turned the gain up maximum and dropped his earphones into the periscope well. And I'll tell you, he got everybody up, including the captain, in one hell of a hurry. It sounded like it was right outside the hull. Some sense of humor. I didn't say anything to him. I didn't blame him; he had been taking it all afternoon. But that time—you talked about eating—nobody ate. I'll never forget that the dining table set up there, and nobody ever sat down. I guess they had to eat something, I don't know what they ate. I guess they grabbed something. I was in the conning tower all the time and the steward sent me sandwiches, nobody was hungry, too uptight.

Q: The stomach is all knotted up, no room for food.

Captain Cutter: You're right, you're not interested. All you want is coffee—coffee and cigarettes.

Q: How much contact could you keep with the wider world and the total war picture in that kind of situation?

Captain Cutter: Well, it was pretty good. We had KGEI in San Francisco—short wave—and we were able to get it almost every night. And that was news; KGEI was almost all news, very little music on it. That's where we would hear—we were off Saipan and we heard the Eighth Air Force had bombed Saipan, and we knew damn well they hadn't, because we were there. So I was ordered three times to go to the east of the island, 30 miles, to be there when the airplanes were shot down if they were, and to rescue the pilots of the Air Force. I went over there twice. In order to do that, we had to go between Saipan and a small island just north of Saipan. There was a narrow pass through which we had to go, and they had patrol ships there so we had to get through there at night to go to this point east of the island. And we would be there all day long, and if any targets came in we would miss them. Or if any ships would go out, we would miss them. We did it twice and no bombs; no planes came over. The third time, I didn't go. This was terrible, really; we were violating a direct order. But I knew more than they did back in Pearl Harbor; I knew the Air Force wasn't coming over. So we dove and we stayed right off the Tanapag Harbor, sighted the airfield. Not a plane except routine patrols took off. If there had been a bombing raid, they would have scrambled the fighters, and they didn't. No bombs at all. We could hear bombs 50 miles away, in a submarine you can---through the water, you know. There were no bombs dropped and no activity whatever. That night again, KGEI reported that the Eighth Air Force had bombed Saipan, and they had never come anywhere near it. I know that. But I can't blame the kids for doing it; they weren't trained thoroughly. They didn't have any traditions of the service like the Navy did, going back to John Paul Jones and the rest of them, you know. They had no traditions like that--29-year-old colonels more interested in getting promoted, really, than in what they were doing. They weren't efficient; they weren't good navigators. It was not their fault; it was the system. I'm not condemning them. I'm just reporting the facts as I saw them at that time.

Q: How much of a help was Ultra to you?

Captain Cutter: Oh, tremendous. That's how I never got into Palau. That second patrol we never really got into the area because of Ultras. I picked up an Ultra before I got there and then picked up another one; the convoy had left that afternoon, and we intercepted it east of the island. They were heading down towards New Guinea.

Q: How much at the time were you told about the source of information, and how much did you have to guess?

Captain Cutter: None. That was a well-kept secret, but we knew it was coming from somewhere. We didn't know about the Black Chamber or anything like that. I didn't know anything about it. All I knew was that the dope we got was good. I didn't know where it came from, and I didn't care, as long as they kept giving it to us.

Q: Was that part of the reason, do you think, that Admiral Lockwood told you not to be taken prisoner off Saipan?

Captain Cutter: No, he told me the reason was that we were going to invade it and he gave a date in May, which actually it wasn't. It turned out to be the 15th of June; for some reason, it was delayed. Cromwell, you know, decided to go down with the Sculpin rather than---because he knew about the Marshall Islands operation coming up.* I told my wife I would never be taken prisoner, because she didn't want me to be. We heard terrible stories, and I guess it was just about as bad as we heard---what the Japs were doing. But that didn't bother me any.

Q: In his book Double-Edged Secrets, Jasper Holmes says really it was the knowledge of Ultra, more than the Marshalls, that he thinks Cromwell sacrificed himself for.** Because that would have had a long-term effect.

Captain Cutter: I think the Marshalls were already in the process of invading. Didn't we have our own surface ships there at the time?

Q: I am not sure of the timing.

Captain Cutter: It must have been Ultra; I think he is right. Anyway, he knew too much. He made that statement before, and

---

*Captain John P. Cromwell, USN, Commander Submarine Division 43, was embarked in the USS Sculpin (SS-191) on 18 November 1943 when she lost a gun duel with the Japanese destroyer Yamagumo. After the skipper had been killed, the senior surviving officer ordered the boat scuttled. Captain Cromwell elected to go down with the submarine rather than reveal what he knew about Ultra and upcoming operations. He was awarded a posthumous Medal of Honor.

**See W.J. Holmes, Double-Edged Secrets (Annapolis: Naval Institute Press, 1979), pages 148-149.

that ensign stayed there with him.*

Q: But this was a specific thing with Saipan that couldn't be compromised.

Captain Cutter: That's right, that was Saipan. It was not Ultra; it was the Saipan operation.

Q: Anything of note about the rest of that patrol?

Captain Cutter: That's the patrol when we went down to Brisbane. Then the last patrol I made we came up from Brisbane and ran into that task force, and I went on up the Straits between Luzon and Formosa and we rendezvoused at night with Tony Gallaher and I went over in a rubber boat. We had a conference, and he gave me an operation order. That's where I got my op order, from him.**

Q: Was he wolf pack commander?

Captain Cutter: Yes, he was senior to me. He laid out the plan

---

*Ensign W.M. Fielder, USNR, pumped too much water out of the Sculpin, causing her to surface in the presence of the enemy destroyer. Perhaps because of his mistake, he elected to stay with the boat rather than be captured.

**Commander Antone R. Gallaher, USN, commanding officer of the USS Bang (SS-385). The wolf pack, which formed on 25 June 1944, comprised the Bang, Seahorse, and Growler. See Clay Blair, Jr., Silent Victory, pages 674-675.

of what we were going to do, and I agreed to it. It looked okay to me, so we just did it. It was really covering more area that way than one submarine could do. And in case it had been feasible, we would have gone in and attacked independently. But it was better notifying the other guy, "Hey, I've got a contact over here."

That's why Tony got whizzed off at us, because we didn't tell him about this convoy we had.

Q: Did you have short-range communication for that?

Captain Cutter: We did it by radar. We would key the radar to Morse Code, and it was a two-letter code: AR, MB. Each pair of letters meant something. There was no way they could RDF that, so it was very effective.*

Q: That's what Admiral Loughlin said he used.** I think it was the SJ radar.

Captain Cutter: Yes, it was SJ.

Q: And he was in the same wolf pack with Gene Fluckey. He did

---

*RDF—radio direction finding.
**Lieutenant Commander C.E. Loughlin, USN, commanding officer of the Queenfish (SS-393) operated in a wolf pack with Lieutenant Commander Eugene B. Fluckey, USN, skipper of the USS Barb (SS-220). Loughlin's oral history discusses communication by radar.

very well, of course.

Captain Cutter: Yes. Well, Gene was good. There was no getting around that. He is the one who went up and put demolition charges on the railroad trestle up on Hokkaido and watched it blow up. And I think they said they saw the horse races or some damn silly thing. It made good reading.

Q: Did you have much encounter with mines other than what you have already expressed from following in a surface ship?

Captain Cutter: In the Pompano we had mine cable cutters. They were mounted on the bow. They were electric, and they fanned out above your bow planes---forward of the bow planes, I guess it was. And two contacts ran the whole length of them. If a wire made contact, it made a dead short across the battery, and it would sever it. In the Formosa Strait they said possible mines, you know. One day while we were submerged, it functioned, so we assumed it was a mine cable that was cut. That's the only evidence I had of ever being in a mine field. I really don't believe that where we were in the Strait of Tsushima that there were any mines. Later on, there were, but farther in. You had to get right in the straits, and we never got that far. We were a few miles east of the straits.

Cutter #2 - 293

Q: So then you wound up that patrol and headed back and thought you were getting temporarily relieved for one patrol.

Captain Cutter: I think Blair said that I was relieved for cause or something. I don't know what it was about.*

Q: I think he said it was a chance to get some leave and go back to see your family.

Captain Cutter: That's what Brown said, but then they ordered me to new construction after I got back.** They cancelled my return to the ship. At the time, I was very unhappy, but shortly after I got back to New London, I was very happy with it. I was back with my family, which meant a lot more.

Q: How long had it been since you had seen them?

Captain Cutter: Thirteen months. It was kind of bad, you know, because we would go to sea, and the wives wouldn't hear from us for 60 days. At first, they didn't know, but my wife finally got sources of information. So whenever we reported in a sinking—that went to Mare Island. See, we had a submarine administrative office there at Mare Island, the communication department. She

---
*See Clay Blair, Jr., Silent Victory, pages 676-677.
**Rear Admiral John H. Brown, USN.

Cutter #2 - 294

got to know the communication officer, and he would say, "We have heard from the Seahorse." That's all she wanted to know—that we were still all right. And when we sank ships, he would say, "The Seahorse is doing pretty good." So she was able to keep track; she knew. And then we reported returning from patrol, she knew that. So she never went more than a couple of weeks without information, so it wasn't so hard on her. She was living in Vallejo.

Q: Did you get any chances to write to her?

Captain Cutter: Oh, sure, oh, yes, my goodness, I wrote voluminously. I had a box so long and so high, full of envelopes and all serialized. I started out with number one and went right on through. I've never read them.

Q: Did you censor each other's mail on the submarine?

Captain Cutter: Yes, it was censored pretty broadly. We never censored the skipper's mail. My mail was never censored. But I never divulged anything; everything was human interest.

Q: It was a self-censorship on your part?

Captain Cutter: Oh, sure. It was all human interest, not where we were but what we were doing. If we sank a ship, I would tell about that, but she didn't know where it was. We weren't giving any information that would comfort the enemy in any way or that he could use.

Q: Especially because there would be a time lag between when you had done something and when it was mailed.

Captain Cutter: Oh, yes, I would mail 20 letters or more to her every time we got in from patrol, and I would get that many back from her.

Q: I'm sure that helped morale.

Captain Cutter: Yes, it sure did. That mail and ice cream that would come aboard, and the fresh fruit and lettuce and vegetables.

Q: Where did you get the ice cream?

Captain Cutter: Actually, the ice cream wasn't such a big deal, because we could make it aboard. I shouldn't have mentioned ice cream, as a matter of fact, although we always got it. I went alongside a cruiser once, and what we wanted was coffee, this was at Satawan Island. They were bombarding it, and so the skipper sent a message to come alongside and, "Is there anything you want?"

I said, "Yes, we want some coffee. We've run out of coffee." The coffee we got during the war came in five-gallon tins. The sugar we got came in the same size tin and so did the flour. They all looked alike. The base up there—we think it was a torpedo gang. Coffee was getting kind of short, and they substituted sugar or flour for coffee. We got the right number of cans, but we had a lot more sugar and flour than we needed and not enough coffee. We ran out of coffee, and that was a tragedy. And hell, the patrol wasn't over yet.

Q: What base was that, Pearl?

Captain Cutter: Yes. We think it was the sub base at Pearl—that's what my torpedomen thought. We left Saipan and were at Satawan Island for this bombardment—this was before we went to Brisbane—and we still had two weeks to go before we would be in port, before we could get any coffee. So we asked for coffee. We went alongside and they gave us lots of coffee, and also lots of ice cream and some fresh vegetables, which were very welcome. Coming in from patrol, the thing the boys really went for was the fresh vegetables and lettuce.

Q: Fresh milk was also something that was hard to get.

Captain Cutter: Well, we had powdered milk, and we got used to it. We could make it cold; we had refrigeration. Also powdered eggs; we got to like them. If you eat anything long enough, you like it. We never were lacking for anything that we needed, and we always had a clean bunk if you weren't otherwise occupied. It was a pretty good life, really, considering.

Q: If you don't mind a few depth charging attacks now and then.

Captain Cutter: Yes, yes.

Q: You told what it was like when you underwent the first one. How was it later as you got more used to them?

Captain Cutter: You're awfully busy, and I always felt awfully sorry for the guys below who didn't know what was going on. We knew what was going on in the conning tower. We knew where they were; we knew when they were making a run; and we knew when to expect them. We knew when they passed overhead up there across our bow, we knew the charges were coming down. And we would take evasive action before they had a chance to get down there. We also knew that in a depth charge there are two waves. One is the shock wave which travels at the speed of light; that's instantaneous. And the other is the sound wave, which goes at the speed of sound in water, which is something around 4,000 feet per second. If a depth charge was far enough away so that you had a click and a bang, the click would be the shock wave. That sounded like a hammer hitting the hull. And the tremendous noise came from the sound wave. The shock wave was not loud, but that was the one that would rip you open, compared with the sound wave. If we heard a click and a boom, to hell with them. It was only when we heard nothing but the boom that we got worried, because they were close then. In other words, they are close enough so that you can't differentiate in the time between the two; they are all one. If we heard the click, boom, we didn't worry.

Q: What was your most harrowing experience from that?

Captain Cutter: The most harrowing experience I had in the war was in the Pompano with Thomas.* We were in Sagami Wan, which is south of the entrance into Tokyo Bay. A lot of people say you are in Tokyo Bay, but we weren't in Tokyo Bay. You couldn't get in there, but we were in the Sagami Wan, which is south of Tokyo Bay, and between O-Shima, which is an island in the middle of the bay and Mikomoto Light, which was on the port side, the eastern side going into Tokyo Harbor---the entrance to Tokyo Harbor. We had surfaced. We got an Ultra that ships were coming through there, and that's why we were there. It was after sunset. I

---

*The incident described here took place on 9 August 1942.

thought it was dark; we looked through the periscope and it looked dark. You can't tell, because you don't get much light transmission through a periscope, not as much as through binoculars. Well, we got on the bridge. It was overcast, and there was a haze and the visibility wasn't too good. We got on the surface, and, my God, we thought we were naked; it was daylight. Well, we were on the surface and nobody was around so we would wait it out, because it was going to be dark in a little while. Boy, all of a sudden on the starboard quarter searchlights illuminated us and six shells came out from two 8-inch gun turrets. It was a cruiser that fired at us. Well, they went over, and we heard them hit the water as we went down. We didn't stay to see the next salvo. We got under, and then the destroyers came over, and, boy, they worked us over. There is a big current, five or six knots, that goes into Sagami Wan and sweeps around and goes out--part of the Japanese Current. It goes out on up the coast of Japan. We were in that current. We had been submerged all day long. We dove about 3:00 o'clock in the morning---this is summertime---and Tokyo is quite a ways north in latitude, so we had to dive real early in the morning because it was getting light. We had been down for 16 hours, and the air was bad. The battery was down, because we had been bucking that current, so all we could do was dive, just go down there and hope to God they weren't lucky. We couldn't take much evasive action; we didn't have enough battery for it. The *Pompano* was 252 feet

Cutter #2 - 300

test depth. We couldn't run our pumps for fear the Japanese would hear them, because they made a hell of a noise. As I said, there was a lot of things wrong with the Pompano. Her trim pump was loud; so was the drain pump. So we couldn't run them, and water was coming in aft through the inboard exhaust valve, leaking from the engine room, and that was flooding the engine room bilges. And the main generators were attached to the engines, so the water got up into the generators, which is another story for later on. We finally got down to 407 feet, and there were all these crackling sounds. And the cork started to buckle loose on the bulkheads. That ship had 5/8-inch steel plating, which was mild steel. The Seahorse was made of 7/8-inch high tensile steel, which was a lot of difference. Well, all of a sudden they left us. They lost contact, I guess, and they were gone. So I was navigator. I had no idea where we were; I had no idea at all. So the captain blew all main ballast in order to come to the surface. I was the first one out; I was navigator. I don't know what I was looking for, but anyway, I was first one out of the hatch, looked up and Jesus, here was what I thought was a searchlight right on us. I said, "Oh, shit," which is a good expression under the circumstances. I thought it was a cruiser with that searchlight up there, high above us. It was Mikomoto Light. That was really something.

Q: It solved your navigation problem in a hurry.

Captain Cutter: It solved the navigation problem, but I knew there was only one way to go, and that was to the south, because there was nothing but Japland to the north. We blew them, but fortunately we didn't go aground. It must have been far enough out from the base of it. Anyway, it was further than I thought; maybe it was 150 yards away. I forgot to say that we hit the bottom; that was why we surfaced. We were hand steering in the control room, and two men were on that and they were just flipped, because the rudder hit something and spun the wheel, being in hand operation. That's when we surfaced, because we knew we were on the ground somewhere. We were very close to Japan, because this is very deep water out there at the entrance to the bay, where all that current had been running. So we came around, and we got two of four engines started. And as soon as we got them started and we got heading out there, the engine room said, "For God's sake, don't have to dive, because we are done." The fuel pumps had grounded out. They were electric, and they had been grounded out by this water that had gone in the engine room. They lasted long enough to get fuel to the engines to start them, and once the engines started the attached fuel pumps, like they have on a truck diesel engine, take over. So you had fuel going to your injectors, but to start them you have these separate electric fuel pumps, and they were gone. That was two engines we were on, because the after engines they couldn't start at all, because they were too deep. We had this big up angle,

Cutter #2 - 302

and the after engines were flooded and both generators. So we had to get the hell out of there, and we did, no sweat. And we got a partial battery charge; we couldn't run full speed on propulsion. We had to put some into the battery to get the battery up in case we had to dive. We had to be able to stay down a while. Anyway, we got out of there and spent the next day submerged. We took the train motor for the sonar, the only electric motor that would fit, and put that in the fuel pumps. We only had one pump, but you could cross connect them. If you had one, you were all right, because after you get one started you could cross connect it and it would start the other engine. It was good that somebody had the foresight. I think it would start the after ones, too. In the *Pompano* we had one engine room; all four engines were in the one room. In the *Seahorse* and the later boats they had two engine rooms, forward room and after room.

Q: So you had some good mechanical ingenuity in your crew to come up with this.

Captain Cutter: Yes, that was the original crew. Yes, they did and they were motivated, plenty. I think that was the worst experience we had in the war. I thought school was out. I didn't know how we were going to get out of there. As a matter of fact, the captain finally told Connole, who was the third officer--I was exec, he was third--to get all of our records together.* And he went into his room and stayed in there for a while. I guess he had given up, Tommy had, but then he came out and when whatever it was hit the rudder and flipped the helmsman, he came out and told us to surface.

Q: After you came back from your last Seahorse patrol you reported to the East Coast, then you moved into the Requin. How long before she was commissioned did you take over?

Captain Cutter: I went up there the 1st of January, New Year's Day. They were going to set a record that year. This was before they knew the war was going to be over, and they planned to start the 1st of January to launch a submarine and then the government yard was going to set a record building submarines. Well, before that happened, they pushed everything back. They realized the war was coming to an end and they cut back on the submarine building program. So the Requin was actually delayed four months, and that's when I went to the new construction training school rather than to the Requin, because there was no need to be there. I had to kill those four months. When I went to the Requin, my wife was sponsor for it when it was christened.** A great crew was assembled for it, and we were there from January

---
*Lieutenant David R. Connole, USN.
**The Requin (SS-481) was christened by Mrs. Cutter on 1 January 1945 and went into commission 28 April 1945.

Cutter #2 - 304

to June. Then we left Portsmouth in June.

Q: It was a great crew because you had hand-picked them.

Captain Cutter: You bet, 26 off the Seahorse and the rest of them came from the Trigger, the Gudgeon, and the Snook, who were skippered by guys that I really admired. And I knew that these guys had the records, and if they got good marks from those guys, they would be good, and they were. Then I got the cream of the crop out of the submarine school through Mrs. Tolman who was a good friend of my wife's and she was secretary to the skipper of the school and I had told her, "Give me the names of all those who stand top of the class." Which she did, and they came across my desk, and I had them put on the Requin. One of them was from my home town, Aurora, Illinois. And when I was a kid, that year I didn't go to school, before I went to Elmhurst, I worked at the All-Steel Equipment Company as timekeeper, and his father was foreman in my department. Isn't that interesting? He stood at the top of his class in submarine school, really a top-flight person.

Q: By 1945 there wasn't much to shoot at for submarines, though. You really had command during the best time for a submarine skipper.

Captain Cutter: Sure, I did. O'Kane did. Fluckey did. And the fellows who got the most ships sunk were lucky to be there at the right time. Morton wasn't, as a matter of fact. Morton was there before the hunting got real good, and so was Dealey. But they went out, and they found their targets. They went into harm's way---as one of the old timers said. They were great.

Q: Most of those guys you named all got Medals of Honor; what separated you from them, or do you know?

Captain Cutter: Well, I think I got my results. As I told Admiral Lockwood, I got my results by skill. I didn't have to go beyond the call of duty, which you have to get for a Medal of Honor. And how you write up your patrol report. Nobody thought of that; nobody worried about it. Dealey got one. Morton didn't get one. O'Kane did. Fluckey did. Of the top five, O'Kane, Fluckey, Morton---Morton didn't, I didn't---and Dealey did. So three of the five did. But I'm alive, and Morton isn't, and neither is Dealey. O'Kane was taken prisoner and took a tremendous beating. He never has recovered physically, I don't think. He lost a kidney, I believe. They beat the hell out of him. Gene, of course, came through with flying colors and made flag rank, as he should have done. Still hale and hearty and still living in Portugal, I believe.

Q: I have heard that he moved to this area recently.

Captain Cutter: You ought to get hold of him; he'd be a real good subject.

Q: I'd like to.

Captain Cutter: He'll do it, too.

Q: A couple of other Medal of Honor men were Red Ramage and George Street.* Did you have any contact with them?

Captain Cutter: Well, Ramage later was chief of staff to SubLant when I was assistant chief of staff, so I got to know Red pretty well. He was with Parks, and he and Parks did not see eye to eye at all. Did he go into that?

Q: I don't remember that part of his oral history.

Captain Cutter: Well, you see, Parks was aboard the _Parche_ as the wolf pack commander, and he was butting in all the time on Ramage, and they had words. They didn't like each other at all. Ramage really went berserk that night on the surface; well, he

---

*Commander Lawson P. Ramage, USN; Lieutenant Commander George L. Street III, USN.

really didn't. I mean, he was on the surface, and I guess he went under the stern of one ship so close that they couldn't depress the guns low enough to hit him. Some people, at the time, thought that Ramage did it to show Parks. Ramage is a very brave man and a very good man. He was excellent, excellent, but they were two pretty strong characters, and they didn't get along very well.

Q: I'm surprised that Parks would interfere, since you said that he was such a stickler for following the normal protocol.

Captain Cutter: He was needling him all the time. He wouldn't tell him how to do it, but they weren't getting contacts. They were out on patrol for quite a while, and it was in the South China Sea, where we had been. They were the next ones after we were there, and Parks couldn't understand why he couldn't find any ships. I guess they weren't running through there. I think he gave Red a bad time.

Q: I guess Ramage did show him then.

Captain Cutter: He sure did; he sure did. And Parks, to his credit, wrote that patrol report up. He wrote it up honestly, but he could have written it in other ways that Ramage wouldn't have gotten a Medal of Honor. That's a pretty hard thing to get.

You've got to do something above and beyond the call of duty. So what is above and beyond the call of duty? What Street was doing I don't know, but he had Beach with him.* And I don't know anything about that.

Q: You are talking really about only half a dozen people, so that was a very select group.

Captain Cutter: You bet it was, and I am sure they were all deserving.

Q: What kind of a contrast was it then for you to adjust to the shipyard life or the training program after this frenetic activity?

Captain Cutter: Well, I didn't have too good a reputation with certain quarters. One of them was the commanding officer of the shipyard, Stoney Roper, who was an ex-submariner.** He was skipper of the New Orleans, the cruiser that was damaged off Guadalcanal. And Stoney got to be captain of the yard. He was really a real good guy, but I had a reputation of being a meddler or something, a complainer about the shipyard. I don't know what

---

*Lieutenant Edward L. Beach, USN, was Street's executive officer in the Tirante (SS-420) for the patrol in early 1945 during which Street earned the Medal of Honor.
**Captain Clifford H. Roper, USN.

he thought, but he said, when I got up there, "Slade, your ship will be commissioned [at whatever the date it was going to be], and I don't want to see you until that ship is commissioned. You stay out of the yard. We'll build the ship, and you take it away. And you stay the hell out of it."

"Aye, aye, Sir."

So that suited me fine. I followed his advice. I would get in there about 10:00 o'clock and look over my personal mail. I had a marvelous exec, Don Young, who was a reserve officer. (I visited him in Pittsburgh on my way east this time.) He is a wonderful guy; he owns his own company out there and is doing very, very well. Anyway, he was extremely competent and I let him run the show. So I met up with Frank Walker and Madley and Tom Kimmel, although Tom was too serious; he wouldn't go up there and do what we did.* They would open the bar for beer, and we would go up there and drink beer and eat lunch and then get all sleepy and go home at 2:00 o'clock. On the way home, pick up two-and-a-half pound lobsters to have at night. I got up to 265 pounds.

Q: Kind of hard to fit down through a hatch.

---

*Lieutenant Commander Francis D. Walker, Jr., USN, who had commanded the Crevalle; Lieutenant Commander Edward P. Madley, USN; Lieutenant Commander Thomas K. Kimmel, USN, who had served in the S-40 and the Balao (SS-285) before being pulled out of submarines upon the death of his brother Manning.

Captain Cutter: It sure was and hard to get clothes on, too, but we had a good time. It was really fine. My poor daughter was then about six years old, and she would get up in the morning and make her own breakfast and get herself off to school. And poor Frannie, I had kept her up all night. We were leading kind of a harum-scarum life. We had a good time. You know there was rationing in those days—food was very serious—but not in the commissary. We had all the meat we wanted and everything. They kind of pampered us up there, you know. Frank Walker was back there for rehabilitation, I think, and I sort of felt I was—we had a good time.

Q: Did you get to travel to Boston and New York?

Captain Cutter: Oh, sure, we went to baseball games and went to New York. I remember Ted Williams playing with the Boston Red Sox. We had a darn good time. We could get plenty of gasoline, too. I don't know how we got that, but we did. People took care of us.

Q: They were probably very grateful for what you had been doing.

Captain Cutter: I guess they were. The ship was an outstanding submarine. Training was done off Panama, and Johnny Johns was the training officer; he was a classmate of Lew Parks, and a good friend of Lew's.* When we got done down there, he said he had trained 53 submarines, and <u>Requin</u> was by far the best submarine he trained.

Q: Was he attached to ComSubLant?

Captain Cutter: SubPac. He was on the Pacific side. Then we went from there out to Pearl, and our training out there was very perfunctory. We got not much, because we had already had it. Boy, I'll tell you one of the things of the war--we were at sea when V-J Day came along.** We were at sea; we wanted to come in that night, but they wouldn't let us enter. They had the boom across or something like that. They could have given us permission to come in, and they wouldn't do it. So we were off the entrance buoy to Pearl Harbor all night long with all these things going on, fireworks and the lights on, and we wanted to be there. That was bad enough, but when I got in and had somebody tell me that they had deliberately kept us out there--to teach us a lesson or something--boy, that burned me up plenty.

Q: So you were at Pearl both at the very beginning and at the very end.

---

*Captain John G. Johns, USN.
**V-J Day---victory over Japan, 14 August 1945.

Captain Cutter: That's right.

Q: You mentioned last night sort of a fleeting contact you had with Admiral Nimitz about being married early. Did you have any other dealings with him?

Captain Cutter: No, I went up there, I believe, three times I had interviews with him. The others were just routine things. They were very interesting--these noon hour things. That's why Admiral Lockwood would send skippers who had had a good patrol up there, because Admiral Nimitz was interested. His son Chester was then a submarine skipper in the Southwest Pacific.*

One time I went up there, and Admiral Nimitz had just gotten back from Kwajalein. And he was waiting for the pictures to be processed and delivered to him. And while I was talking to him, it was just before his lunch that he would do this, the pictures arrived. He was anxious to see them, and he said, "Cutter, would you like to see pictures of Kwajalein?" And, boy, they were gruesome. It was just after the island was secured, and the dead were still lying around. Boy, it was startling to me, because I had never seen that side of war, except what I saw in *Life* Magazine. But these were some pictures. He was in a lot of them, so he showed them to me. He was a very warm person. He

---

*Lieutenant Commander Chester W. Nimitz, Jr., USN, commanded the USS *Haddo* (SS-255).

was a great man. Did you read his biography by Potter?*

Q: Yes. He is portrayed as a great storyteller, always a story to fit the occasion.

Captain Cutter: Yes. Of course, I didn't know that part of him. I just knew him as a very kindly, warm person. He surrounded himself with good people, and he made the right decisions. This country always seems to bring them out when we need them, the right man in the right place.

Q: We haven't done so well recently as we did back then.

Captain Cutter: No, I guess we haven't. Take Halsey for instance. I mean, what would have happened to him in peacetime? He was a man for the times, and he did a magnificent job.

Q: Most people had a sea/shore rotation through the war. You had no shore duty. Why was that?

Captain Cutter: I don't think anybody did that I knew, none of the submariners. Some of them but not many; they kept us going. Well, I had new construction on the Seahorse and new construction

---

*E.B. Potter, Nimitz (Annapolis: Naval Institute Press, 1976).

in the Requin, so there were two breaks in it.

Q: But there had to be people in staff jobs and in the school and that sort of thing.

Captain Cutter: Oh, yes, there were, lots of them. But the ones that I know like Bub Ward, Chuck Triebel, and Bill Post and, of course, O'Kane became a prisoner. Fluckey spent most of the war ashore. He got out there, I think, in '44. He took command after I did, and he really went at it right from the start. I think he had one PCO run, and then he was on his own.

Q: What happened with the Requin after the war then?

Captain Cutter: I was relieved by George Street in Portsmouth, and they converted it into a radar picket. They didn't know what else to do with it. They put a snorkel on it, and it just faded into oblivion. It is now down in Tampa, Florida, as a relic--a museum, I guess.

Q: How long did you have command of her?

Captain Cutter: I took command, I guess, in April up at Portsmouth. That was in '45, and it was May or June of '46. We were in Key West and went up to Portsmouth shipyard for overhaul, and there I was relieved and went to the Bureau of Personnel, running the all-Navy sports program.

Q: What sort of operations did you have during the time after you got back from the Pacific?

Captain Cutter: The only thing we did down in Key West was to provide services for ASW destroyers.* The ASW school was there, and we had very little pro-sub. I don't think I fired a torpedo down there, as I recall. We were providing services for the sonar school.

Q: As a target?

Captain Cutter: As a target, right.

Q: Did you have the problem that a good many ships did after the war, that the crew was disappearing en masse?

Captain Cutter: Oh, sure. They sure did. We had a nucleus, and they held things together; the ships didn't suffer. We had no need for a lot of training to go out on a war patrol, but we had a full crew. Honestly, I don't know where they came from; we were way overstaffed with chief petty officers, way over. But

---
*ASW--antisubmarine warfare.

chiefs were doing first and second class jobs, so they were experienced. They stayed in, the chiefs did. They had a pretty good thing going, so they weren't the ones that were separated.

Q: It was the people who enlisted for the duration and didn't have that seniority.

Captain Cutter: Yes, and a lot of chiefs were in there for the duration. They made chief in two or three years, but they did have a lot of experience. And chief petty officers were making a fairly decent salary, and they had security. They had time towards retirement, and they were married, and they liked the life, so they stayed. They were getting pay and a half, so we had more chiefs than non-chiefs. This lasted for quite a while.

Q: Did that cause problems in running the ship?

Captain Cutter: No, not at all. The chief who was low man on the totem pole did the second class job. Instead of a supervisor, he would be a controllerman or an engineman or whatever had to be done.

Q: They recognized the realities of the situation.

Captain Cutter: Oh, sure, they were good men, and those ahead of

Cutter #2 - 317

them had been there first. They recognized and accepted the seniority system. No problem.

Q: How did the BuPers job come about then?

Captain Cutter: A guy named Whitey Taylor, a destroyer man—he had been my ordnance prof at the Naval Academy.* And he was a fine football player in his own day, and Whitey recommended me to run this Navy sports program, which they considered very important at the time. This was during the demobilization, and in those days we had the battle force, the air stations around, and we had teams in everything: football, basketball, boxing, wrestling, and so forth. So we set up an all-Navy sports program which ended up in a championship each year in each sport. It was a good idea, but the Navy deteriorated in numbers. We had less people and the forces—we went into task forces rather than having all the battleships together, all the aircraft carriers. You'd mix them all up, and there wasn't any cohesive force there. The Marines were the only ones, and they went off on their own and had their own programs. I stayed in there for three years, and I took the Armed Forces Olympic team over to London, so I got to participate in the Olympics.

Q: This was in 1948?

---
*Captain Edmund B. Taylor, USN.

Cutter #2 - 318

Captain Cutter: Yes, in 1948. I was the boxing referee in the Olympics. We had boxing referees in the United States who were very competent, but they had all received pay. And if you had ever been paid to referee a boxing bout, you couldn't referee at the Olympics. Silly, you know. I had never received pay. I had a lot of refereeing in the Navy, so I became an Olympic referee.

Q: Do you remember any incidents from the Olympics that stand out?

Captain Cutter: Yes, I remember one. It was an Egyptian against an Italian. I was refereeing the bout, and we had been given instructions--any low blows or anything like that you say, "Stop." Everybody knew the word "Stop," and they knew the word "Box." So if they had committed a foul you said, "Stop" and then by pantomine you told them what they had done wrong and then "Box." And then you motion to the judges whether to take off points. This Italian, who was coached by an American, I mean a U.S. citizen--I guess he was in the Army or something over there, but he was of Italian descent and he was coaching the Italian boxing team. He must have come from Brooklyn (from his dialect), and the Egyptian was coached by an Egyptian. Anyway, they said if they did it three times to disqualify them. So I disqualified the guy. My God, I was jumped all over by the Italian coach, this American. I didn't have any clothes over there, so I was in uniform, khaki. I didn't have my insignia on, but it was a khaki uniform; the rest of them had whites. You couldn't get anything in England to fit me. There was no such thing as going out and buying white ducks and a white shirt, so I wore my khakis. It was all I had.

The boxing coach of the Italian team threw a glove at me. They had the boxing ring in the center of a swimming pool, so nobody could get in it, you know, and charge it, I guess. Feelings ran very high in that boxing business. As soon as the glove whizzed over my head and landed in the water, I disqualified them. And, my God, the Egyptian coach later gave me a bottle of wine, and the other coach gave me one hell of a bad time, and I got disqualified. And that was the last bout I ever refereed. So they just fired me, threw me out. That was fun, though. We completely dominated the Olympics, the U.S. Armed Forces team did. We had the two great sprinters—previously at Penn State. They finished one-two in the 100 meter and the 200 meter. One won the 200 meter and the other won the 100 meter.

Q: And Bob Mathias won the decathlon.

Captain Cutter: He did, but he wasn't in the armed forces team. That was really an experience.

Q: This in a sense was a resurrection of the prewar sports

program, wasn't it?

Captain Cutter: Yes, they tried to, but it didn't work out, because as I say, there wasn't the---we used to have a Battle Force and a Scouting Force and a Carrier Force; each carrier had a football team. And Quantico had a team, and Lejeune had a team, and so on. Of course, the Marines kept it up, but you couldn't do it in the Navy. So we went to all-star teams, like SubPac had a team. That didn't work out, because they came from different ships, and there is no real esprit de corps there. The loyalty of a person is to his ship, not to the force.

Q: Well, there wasn't a chance to practice together much either, was there?

Captain Cutter: Yes, there was. The SubPac football team was assembled on the Sperry. I was director of athletics when I was exec of the Sperry in 1949 and 1950. And Don Whitmire was an all-American at Alabama before he came to the Naval Academy.[*] He was in the football Hall of Fame. And Bo Coppedge, who is now director of athletics, he was there.[**] He was one of the coaches. And a guy named Bones Thomas, who was another football player at the Academy.[***] They were coaching this all-star team.

---

[*]Lieutenant (junior grade) Donald B. Whitmire, USN.
[**]Lieutenant (junior grade) John O. Coppedge, USN.
[***]Lieutenant (junior grade) Homer Bohn Thomas, Jr., USN.

Q: Would they get TAD orders away from their ships?*

Captain Cutter: That's right. And then we would practice ashore every day. It was purely a football team; that's all they did. We played the University of Mexico in Mexico City. We played Brigham Young University. We played University of California B squad; we didn't play their varsity. And we played Naval Training Center at San Diego and the Marines at the Marine Corps Recruit Depot in San Diego. And then recruit training had their team that was drawn from the various activities within the training center.

Q: What were your personal duties in connection with the program? Were they mostly administrative?

Captain Cutter: Yes, arranging all the tournaments, putting out the rules and regulations for eligibility and the schedules for them. It was quite a job; I didn't like it.

Q: Why not?

Captain Cutter: It wasn't the Navy. And that's how I got to be director of athletics, which I didn't want. I was at SubLant in

---

*TAD—temporary additional duty.

New London for a meeting in 1956, and Joe Grenfell was there.* Joe was a friend of mine, and we met at a cocktail party at the submarine base. I don't know how Joe got mixed up with the athletic program at the Academy, but he wanted to know if I wanted to be director of athletics. Right after the idea hit me, I said, "Well, I'll think it over." I got talking to my wife about it. I was going to go to shore duty. She didn't want to go back to Washington, and I didn't know where I was going to go, so I said, "Okay." Then he told me my job would be to fire Erdelatz.** That became one of the most miserable damn jobs I ever had in my life. Now Loughlin should have fired him.***

Q: What an interesting contrast, because Loughlin says in his oral history that he campaigned very actively to get the job. And you didn't want it.

Captain Cutter: Yes. Well, I don't know why he did, but he did and I guess Elliott did a fine job overall. He did a very fine

---

*Rear Admiral Elton W. Grenfell, USN, a submariner who was then on duty in the Bureau of Naval Personnel.
**Edward J. Erdelatz, head football coach at the Naval Academy for the seasons of 1950 through 1959, during which time his teams had a record of 50-26-8.
***Captain C. Elliott Loughlin, USN, served as the Naval Academy's director of athletics from 1954 to 1957. Loughlin, who was graduated from the Academy in 1933, was an All-America basketball player ("roundballer") as a midshipman. On the occasion of Loughlin's relief as director of athletics by Cutter, Sports Illustrated published a brief tribute to both men. See "Pat on the Back," 3 June 1957, page 80.

job public relations-wise for the Navy. He did a good job in that respect, but he couldn't handle Erdelatz, which I think he will acknowledge. The main reason was that Erdelatz would say to him, "You are a roundballer. You don't understand the problems of football." And, therefore, he had no way of controlling him. Erdelatz couldn't tell me that. I was All-America, you know, and I had coached football and at least knew enough about it that I could tell him, "Well, blocking and tackling wins football games still. I don't care how much the game has changed." It had changed a lot, but the fundamentals hadn't. And he was impossible but he was psychotic according to the psychologist there at the Academy. He was all right except during football season. Then, Jesus, he was just impossible. I think Elliott would admit that---he couldn't handle him.

Then we had Admiral Smedberg, a delightful guy and so forth, but a great sports fan.* And I told him, "We've got to fire this guy. He is disloyal to you. He is disloyal to the Academy. He is turning the midshipmen against the Navy."

As a matter of fact, the first year I was there---of the graduating class, there were 21 lettermen that graduated that year. Only one went into the line of the Navy---only one. All the rest of them either tendered their resignations or went into the Supply Corps. They couldn't care less about the Navy. And

---

*Rear Admiral William R. Smedberg III, USN, Superintendent of the Naval Academy from March 1956 to June 1958.

to hear the coach say they were a bunch of--he referred to Smedberg as a fool. I told Smedberg that, because it came back to me from the equipment manager, a guy by the name of Rasmussen, who was a very loyal Navy man; he couldn't stand it.* So finally Erdelatz took the whole coaching staff down to Texas A&M; he thought he had a job down there. He had been offered a lot of money--television money and all this sort of stuff. Well, he got down there, and they had failed to check it out with the president of the university, this was just one of the Texas boosters, not even a graduate. He had a lot of oil money and was very active in the boosters' club down there. They thought they would get this great Erdelatz to coach Texas A&M and do the same things there that he had done at the Naval Academy. He was a good football coach, and he was so sure he was going to get the job that he took his whole crew down there and he was turned down. He came skulking back. I said, "Now is the time to get rid of him, because he did not get my permission."

I didn't even know it; I read about it in the papers. Well, I went over to see Smeddy, and Smedberg said, "Oh, no, you can't do that, Slade. He beat Army this year. Look at his record. The graduates wouldn't take it."

I said, "They would if you let the word out on the reason for it. They certainly would."

Well, we had the football banquet, which was held in those

---

*George Rasmussen.

days always in the Superintendent's quarters. They had their girls there and there was a banquet, and there would be punch for the midshipmen. The director of athletics, and Rip Miller, and the head coach would be the guests of the Smedbergs up in their private quarters.* The first year we were there, that was the program. But the next year we weren't invited to Smedberg's private quarters, and I wondered what the heck was going on? I wasn't invited up, and neither was Rip. By golly, when it came time for dinner down the stairway from their quarters came the Superintendent and Mrs. Smedberg and Erdelatz and Agnes. He had had Erdelatz up there and not Rip and me. This was really bad, because this gave Erdelatz—he became absolutely arrogant after that. I couldn't control him at all. Then Melson came.** One day I got a report from the Lions' Club. They used to have 7:00 o'clock breakfasts out in town. Johnny Cox, who was the director of information for the athletic association—a good, loyal, solid man, came to me and he said, "Slade, Erdelatz was out there bad naming the Naval Academy and the admiral at this breakfast, how he was getting no support and this sort of stuff."***

So I called Eddie on the phone and said, "Come on up to the office. There is something I want to talk to you about."

---

*Edgar E. Miller, who was football coach when Cutter was a midshipman, had by the 1950s become assistant director of athletics.
**Rear Admiral Charles L. Melson, USN, Superintendent of the Naval Academy from June 1958 to June 1960.
***John T. Cox, director of public relations, Naval Academy Athletic Association.

He came up, and I confronted him with this. He categorically denied it. Okay, I accepted it. Well, I got another report from another source; this was from a man who had been there, one of the Lions people, and he wanted me to know what this guy had said out there. He was really shocked by it, so he told me. This time I called Eddie on the phone, and I said, "Eddie, I know you told me you didn't do it, but I got another report from another source, a member of the club there. It is the very same thing, and I have to believe it."

He said, "I am sick and tired of this bullshit," and he hung up.

Well, I sat there for two or three minutes and cooled off, I guess, a little bit. I called back to have him come up to the office, and his secretary, Joyce, said, "Mr. Erdelatz has gone to Baltimore."[*]

So I said, "I'll talk to Wayne Hardin."[**]

I wanted to ask him something about this, and he said, "Oh, I know. I was there."

I said, "You were there and heard that?!"

He said, "Yes."

I said, "Who else was there?"

---

[*]Joyce Purdy has been secretary for Naval Academy football coaches since 1951.
[**]Wayne Hardin, offensive backfield coach, an assistant under Erdelatz.

He said, "Ernie Jorge and Steve Belichick."*

Steve was still here, so I called Steve and said, "Steve?"

"Yes, I was there." That's all he said.

I called Jorge, and he wanted to get out of it. He was a personal friend of Eddie. Eddie had brought him from St. Mary's with him, and poor Ernie didn't want to tell me, but I said, "Look, Wayne says so; so does Steve. You were there, weren't you?"

"Yes."

"You heard it, didn't you?"

"Yes."

I said, "Okay."

So I went over to see Melson right then. I said, "Admiral, I want to fire Erdelatz."

He didn't even ask me why. He said, "It's your decision. Call a meeting of the board and see if they approve."

So I called a meeting of the athletic control board. On the board were Bush Bringle, Ned Dougherty, K.G. Schacht, and a guy by the name of Vic Smith.** They were the members of the board, and Bringle being the commandant, although he was junior to all

---

*Ernest J. Jorge, offensive line coach; Stephen N. Belichick, defensive backfield coach.

**Captain William F. Bringle, USN, Commandant of Midshipmen; Captain Joseph E. Dougherty, USN, head of the Department of Foreign Languages; Captain Kenneth G. Schacht, head of the Department of Seamanship and Navigation; Captain John Victor Smith, USN, academic aide to the Superintendent and secretary to the Academic Board.

of us—he was outstanding; he became a vice admiral—he was sitting at the head of the table, because he was the head man. He was president of the board of the athletic association. So he presided. He called in the witnesses and asked them just one question, "Do you consider Mr. Erdelatz a good influence on the midshipmen?"

And everyone said, "No."

"Why?" was the next question.

"Because he talks against the Navy and against the Superintendent and so forth."

And so with that, they voted immediately. It was all done in a couple of hours. They voted to fire him, and so they called Eddie in and sat him down and told him what had happened and that he was dismissed. And this was after spring football practice, which is one heck of a time to fire a coach. But they fired him, and they got in Wayne Hardin. And the board didn't want to hire him, because they thought he was too young, and then on top of that they wanted to pay him $12,000 a year, and Eddie was getting $17,000. I said, "By God, if you are hiring a guy to replace somebody you have fired, you pay him as much as you paid the guy you are firing." They didn't do that, but they paid him a little more than $12,000. Wayne was a good coach and still is a good coach, a fine coach.

Q: I think he just retired from Temple.

Captain Cutter: He did. He got out for some reason or other, and I read in the <u>Philadelphia Inquirer</u> a letter to the editor from Red Coward who relieved me as director of athletics, a testimonial to Wayne Hardin, what a fine coach he was and how he wished him the best.* And here was a guy living down in North Carolina, heard about it, and wrote to the Pennsylvania paper to support Wayne. He was a fine coach. He got cross-threaded somehow at the Academy. I don't know the details of that; he was here five years with a very fine record. But he ran the offense under Erdelatz. He was the architect of our offense and a good leader. Well, he proved it, a good man.

Q: I heard Hardin tried to usurp Rip Miller.

Captain Cutter: I know Rip. Rip is one of my dearest friends, and Rip was very, very sensitive about anyone he thought was trying to get his job. As he approached retirement, he was really paranoid about people taking his job away from him. That's not a criticism, but that's the way he felt. I don't blame him too much, because Wayne was very aggressive, and Wayne wanted to take over that job and wanted to be relieved as head coach, when Rip retired. He wanted that commitment. Well, Rip thought he was easing him out. So that's why they fired him. Then Wayne got in touch with me, "Can't you do something?"

---

*Captain Asbury Coward III, USN.

I couldn't do anything. He told me the story, and he said, "Hell, I don't want that. Rip can stay here until he dies. I don't care, but I just want something to look for in the future; I want some security."

That's what happened.

Q: Erdelatz's departure was portrayed publicly as a resignation.*

Captain Cutter: Oh, sure.

Q: Why was that when if it had been indicated as a firing, that would have helped to explain it to the people who would get angry about it?

Captain Cutter: Well, they wouldn't be angry at us in the Navy if we didn't fire him. I guess that's what they thought--the people who made that decision. I didn't make it. I wanted to say we fired him and why. All those details were taken out of my hands; it was handled at the level of the Secretary of the Navy. It had to be approved by the Secretary of the Navy. There was no problem. It went through the Superintendent to the SecNav, and he approved it. I don't know whether they even told him why, but

---

*"Sinking the Navy?" Newsweek, 20 April 1959, page 106; Tex Maule, "A Naval Disengagement," Sports Illustrated, 20 April 1959, page 75.

the decision was made that it would appear as a resignation. It was decided that it was better that way. Perhaps it was. He left and he got paid up through August, I think. He got his $17,000 a year for several months. He called me one morning and wanted us to pay for transporting his furniture from his house out to the West Coast. We never did that. I said no, we wouldn't do it. He accepted it. But this was no longer football season. He was an entirely different man outside of football season.

Q: I think he caught on with the Oakland team in the American Football League for a few years.

Captain Cutter: One year, and he was fired.* In fact, do you know how they fired him?

Q: No.

Captain Cutter: The owner called him in for a press conference. He brought Eddie in and told the reporters that Erdelatz was fired and walked out and left Eddie there to explain. Now that is about as cruel as you can get. We didn't do that at all to Eddie, he was handled--as I say, we didn't have to pay him that

---

*Erdelatz coached the Oakland Raiders to a record of 6-6 in 1960, the first year of play in the American Football League. He was fired 18 September 1961 after his team lost the first two games of the new season by scores of 50-0 and 44-0.

much, but the idea was to avoid any bad public relations for the Navy. I think that having it appear that he resigned--none of the alumni would blame us or blame the Academy.

Q: I think the fact that Hardin did so well so soon helped out, too.

Captain Cutter: Yes, it helped a lot. You bet it did. He beat Army four out of five years.

Q: And had two Heisman Trophy winners.*

Captain Cutter: Wayne was good.

Q: How did that resolve itself, since it was not going too well and you didn't like it? Did you then ask for a transfer?

Captain Cutter: No, I got fired, which nobody ever told me and nobody has ever brought it out since then. But I'll tell anybody, because I only had two years. Admiral Smith, Chief of Naval Personnel, Page Smith, a heck of a nice guy, and he was Chief of Information prior to Lew Parks.** Lew Parks took over Chief of Information, and Parks was the one who got me into that

---

*Joe Bellino won the Heisman Trophy, given to the player voted top player in college football in a given year, in 1960; Roger Staubach won the award in 1963.
**Vice Admiral Harold P. Smith, USN.

miserable job, for which I was not qualified either from the standpoint of training or aptitude. I just wasn't fit for it. They never should have ordered me there. Anyway, he called me over. In fact, I was down at a school in Norfolk, at the Armed Forces Staff College, and I got a call out of the lecture we were having, "The Chief of Naval Personnel wants to talk to you." He said, "Slade, if you don't care for your career, I do. You are due for a sea command, and you should figure on leaving this summer."

That seemed strange to me, with everybody else having been there three years. Although Loughlin was two years ahead of me and from the standpoint of rotation I should go to sea, but nobody had been transferred after less than three years in that job. So when I got back, I went over to see Admiral Smith. Because I could talk to him; I knew him personally as well as officially and I said, "Admiral, this is fine except for one thing." And I told him the story about Erdelatz. This was before Erdelatz was fired. I told him what Erdelatz was doing and said, "He will be absolutely unmanageable if I get out of here. He will say he got me fired, which I think is true. I strongly recommend that you do not transfer me until Erdelatz is gone---or let me finish out my three years."

But as soon as Erdelatz was fired, I got my orders, within a couple of months. There was a lot of controversy. Eddie had a marvelous contact with sportswriters; he was a very personable individual. As a matter of fact, before I ever went down there to the Academy as director of athletics or even thought about it—when I was on duty in Washington—Eddie Erdelatz invited me over to his home to be a weekend guest, and we went fishing together. And I wondered, "What the hell is he doing this for?" I guess he figured I was a candidate for director of athletics one of these days, and this was just in case. I can't think of any other reason. I didn't even know him, except casually. I thought it was very strange to be invited to his home, but he did it in a very gracious way and I accepted. And his wife was a swell gal. Agnes Erdelatz was lovely, a very nice hostess. Everything was fine—til I got down there. The first thing that happened when I took that job over—within a few days, Eddie called me up. He never called me Slade again. He always called me Slade before; now I'm "Captain." He said, "Captain, do you know that you are authorized to have the admiral's barge on Sundays if he doesn't want it?"

I said, "No, I didn't know that."

"Well, you are." And he said, "The football season is starting in two or three weeks and the coaches—I would like to have one nice Sunday with them before we get into the grind of the football season. And I would like to take them and their wives out on the barge. And you and Frannie go along. We would like to have you with us. It is reserved for heads of departments only." (And we took turns doing it.)

Nobody senior to me wanted it that particular weekend, so I got it. I told Eddie it was all set.

A couple of days later he called and acted very embarrassed and said, "Do you mind if you don't go? Because I think the coaches would feel more at ease, and I want them to relax and have a good time."

So I said, "That's fine, Eddie. I don't care."

I didn't know anything was wrong then, because Elliott just said he was difficult. He didn't give me any specifics when I relieved him. The next thing I knew, about the next day or two, he called me again and invited me. Uh-oh, this is manipulation, I am back on the list again! So I said, "Thank you very much, I have made other plans." And I let it go at that. So they went out on the boat and had their Sunday outing. But that's the way he worked, trying to get me in line. Then it came time to go to our second football game with Boston College, and we chartered a Constellation—you know, the old three-tailed thing—to fly up there. And there were about three or four extra seats, Rip went along and some of the official party but not very many. Ben Carnevale wanted to go along to do some recruiting in the Boston area. Well, this was saving us money, and I said, "Fine, come along." So I put him on the list.

I got a call from Erdelatz, "He can't go. You can't mix football and basketball."

I said, "What the hell. He isn't coaching anybody on that."

So Eddie, at 2:00 o'clock in the morning, called Rip Miller. Rip is asleep at home. This thing became an obsession with him. Well, Carnevale was going, and Carnevale went, and it was a very distasteful thing. We all sat in the forward cabin there; the team sat aft. Everything was downhill from there on. I suppose I handled things wrong, I don't know, but, anyway, it just ended up very bad. But the point remains, I was told when I went down there that I was to fire Erdelatz. That came from Grenfell, not from the Superintendent.

Q: Why Grenfell?

Captain Cutter: They had heard about his influence on the midshipmen---the way they put it, "He is too big for his britches. And this is reflected in the midshipmen that are coming out for the football team; they don't feel as loyal to the Naval Academy." If anybody played in the game for one minute, Erdelatz had it worked out so that they were excused from classes on Monday. On Wednesday they had a scouting report, and they would have it at the boathouse and they would have a steak dinner, and they would get back about 11:00 o'clock at night---this was a Tuesday night. They never went to class on Friday before a game. What the hell---they are gone Monday. Thursday they are no good, because they hadn't had a chance to study the night before. And Friday they are gone. How in the world are you going to carry on an academic program like that without someone feeding them stuff they shouldn't have? In other words, we were heading for a West Point scandal. Midshipmen have got to be students. You can't have that sort of thing going on.

So when I started taking away some of these outrageous perks, he bucked. And he would report to his pals in the various media what a son of a bitch I was, and that I was trying to destroy the football program and all this sort of stuff. And finally old Shirley Povich, whom we never liked at the Naval Academy when I was a midshipman, because he'd write it as it was. Do you know the name?*

Q: Sure, he was there for 50 years.

Captain Cutter: Shirley Povich called me up one day and said, "What are you doing this evening?"

It was late afternoon, and I said, "Nothing."

"Are you going to be home around 5:00 o'clock?"

And I said, "Yes."

So Shirley Povich came to my quarters, and we had a couple of scotch and sodas there. And he wanted me to know that he knew what was going on down here and that he was behind me, and he would let the other people know.

---

*Shirley Povich—a man, despite the name—was sports editor and columnist for The Washington Post from the 1920s to the 1970s.

And I said, "Well, how about Jimmy Cannon up there on that New York rag?"*

"Well," he said, "I can't do much about him; nobody can."

I'll tell you, I never had any more trouble from The Washington Post, the Evening Star and the Baltimore Sun--the people who knew. It was all the wire services that Erdelatz used; they didn't know the details. A fellow by the name of Thompson was the AP stringer down here, and he knew what was going on.** He was very fair and honest.

Q: I'm surprised that the order to fire Erdelatz didn't go to the Superintendent rather than to you, if this was a BuPers action.

Captain Cutter: It wasn't a BuPers action. BuPers does not tell officers how to do their jobs. Joe Grenfell carried a lot of weight with the Chief of BuPers. He was a very rabid Navy sports fan. He was all blue and gold, old Joe was. He was a submariner and a submarine skipper but before I got command, and by this time he was a rear admiral. He and other interested people wanted somebody in there that had been a football player, that was recognized as having some ability, who could talk to

---

*Jimmy Cannon was a nationally known sports columnist for the New York Post.
**Herbert Thompson of the Associated Press bureau in Annapolis.

Cutter #2 - 339

Erdelatz. That was so he couldn't say, "He is a roundballer and he doesn't know what the hell is going on, doesn't understand the problem."

We're spending a lot of time on a lot of nonsense.

Q: Well, how did you leave the job in athletics in the late Forties? You say that was not working out as you had hoped?

Captain Cutter: That was all right. I finished that job and went from there to Sperry as executive officer and got a division command. That was routine. You would be an exec one year and then you'd get a division. Then you went back to shore duty, and I went to BuPers again. I went into special services, which I shouldn't have gone into. I didn't like it; we had the officers' clubs—nothing really to do with the Navy. Then Parks called me over to public information, gave me a big buildup on the job, and it was very interesting. But I didn't have any training for that. You really should have some journalism training and understand the thing a little better. I didn't understand it.

Q: Well, if we could spend some time on the job in the Sperry, what was the condition of the submarine force at that point?

Captain Cutter: Bad. The submarines were still in good shape, but the surface personnel in the tenders was terrible. My God, we were getting boys in there that couldn't even see; we even received one in the Sperry who was legally blind. Recruiting was very difficult then. All the services were having a bad time getting enough good men. It was a challenge to get the ship running and to keep serving the submarines properly. I liked that job. I really enjoyed it; we got the Battle Efficiency Pennant, which was a very competitive thing.

Q: Who was the skipper?

Captain Cutter: Dave Whelchel, who was a very good friend of mine.* He was submarine skipper during World War II, the same time I was. He was class of '30 at Annapolis and top-flight. He died here in May. Dave was a very fine person and a real good skipper.

Q: You really had a lot of background just from serving in the submarines and knowing the mechanical things that needed to be done, so I would think that would help in that kind of job.

Captain Cutter: It did. We had very fine, outstanding people in the repair department, and these guys were good. No, it was a good job, pleasant, and I enjoyed it. And it was good having a

---
*Captain David L. Whelchel, USN. Later a rear admiral, he died 29 May 1982.

lot of these kids running around there that were very marginal. They never would be enlisted today, but the Navy took them in, and I think we did them a lot of good. We turned back to society a lot better people than we had gotten in.

Q: One of the key men in a tender, of course, is the repair officer. How good a relationship did you have with him?

Captain Cutter: He was a very dear friend of mine; he was the chief electrician's mate in the Pompano when I went to the Pompano. Fay Wadhams was his name, a real gentleman and a very, very capable man.* We were good personal friends, which developed back when I was a lieutenant (junior grade) in the Pompano. And he made the war patrols with me.

Q: That was one of the great things about the Navy when it was smaller, that people knew each other and you could develop a long-lasting relationship which would continue.

Captain Cutter: Yes.

Q: Where was the Sperry home ported?

Captain Cutter: San Diego. And the Nereus was there, and there

---
*Lieutenant Fay W. Wadhams, USN.

was Submarine Squadron Three and Submarine Squadron Five. The *Sperry* was in Submarine Squadron Three. It had 12 or 15 submarines in it and was very competitive with SubRon Five. We in SubRon Three were fighting them in competition all the time, and it was fun.

Q: What are the bases for judging tenders? You don't have the operations that most combatants have.

Captain Cutter: Well, we had to go out on operations once a month. We would go out there, and they would give us damage control problems. And also the effectiveness of your repair party carried a big factor. Then your communications, how you stood in the communications competition, and the engineering competition. We in SubRon Three didn't get much opportunity to show it when we went out once a month; SubRon Five did, too. And shiphandling and the operational readiness inspection that the squadron commander gave you, and the administrative inspection that you got from the other people. Of course, they would come and tear you apart if they could, and you would try to hide all your things under the rug.

Q: You weren't being as open as you had been right after the war?

Cutter #2 - 343

Captain Cutter: Oh, no! I had learned; I had gotten over that. And we went over them and they tried to cover everything, and we tried to get to the root of it. It was fun.

Q: Was that an adjustment in going to a much bigger ship than anything you had served in since the Idaho?

Captain Cutter: Not long. It was at first. Those tenders weren't too big. The Sperry wasn't, and Dave gave me a lot of opportunity for shiphandling, which helped me later on when I got a capital ship. I think all submariners were good shiphandlers. You get an awful lot of experience, because you start right out as a junior officer and the captain lets you do it. Everybody takes pride in their seamanship, and they are generally pretty good.

Q: Is that intended as, the executive officer's job in a tender, as a training ground for working with multiple groups of submarines as you will as a division commander?

Captain Cutter: No, I don't think so. It is just a stepping-stone up; you are there observing the tender and repair crew and watching all these submarines alongside and dealing with the commanding officer and the executive officer and engineering officer. You get to learn a lot about the force and the people, and then the next year you take command of one of the divisions. So you know them already and they know you; it was a good system. The captain of the tender would generally take command of the squadron alongside, same thing. They would know you, and you would know them. They had a good system going.

Index to

Series of Taped Interviews

with

Captain Slade D. Cutter, USN(Ret.)

Air Forces
    See Army Air Forces

Albacore, USS (AGSS-569)
    Aggressive commanding officer puts this innovative submarine through her paces in the mid-1950s, pp. 398-399

Anderson, Robert H.
    Favorable assessment as Secretary of the Navy in the mid-1950s, p. 575

Anti-Semitism
    Jewish submarine officer manages to mediate his commanding officer's negative attitudes in the early 1940s, pp. 68, 74

Antisubmarine Warfare (ASW)
    Japanese capabilities in World War II, pp. 160, 215-216; Requin (SS-481) used as target for ASW school in Key West in 1946, p. 315; Nautilus (SSN-571) able to confound U.S. destroyer during exercise in mid-1950s, p. 395; ASW exercise in 1950s marred by destroyer skipper in hurry to reach port, pp. 402-404; Seahorse (SS-304) draws ASW attention so Saipan beaches can be surveyed for 1944 invasion, p. 531

Archerfish, USS (SS-311)
    Credited with most Japanese tonnage sunk in a single patrol for hit on Japanese carrier in November 1944, p. 277

Army Air Forces
    Mistakenly pursue USS Seahorse (SS-304) with B-24s during World War II, pp. 216-218, 550-551; angers Navy commander of Midway Island with allegations after June 1942 action, p. 248; search planes needed Navy navigators to get back to Midway, pp. 248-249; mistakenly report having bombed Saipan, pp. 286-287

Army-Navy Football Game
    1926, p. 19; 1934, pp. 12, 78-82; 1981, pp. 82, 481-482; importance to coach's stature, pp. 324, 332

"Articles for the Government of the Navy"
    Dilemma for older submarine skippers familiar with this governing set of rules, p. 208

Athletics
    Cutter's father forbids him to play football in high school, pp. 2, 4, 12; Cutter plays football at Severn School and makes All-State team in 1930, pp. 5, 12, 30; thoughts on children playing football, pp. 12-13; Cutter offered professional

boxing contract after graduation from Naval Academy in 1935, p. 33; battleship <u>Idaho</u> (BB-42)'s team in mid-1930s, pp. 48-50, 112, 119-121; Cutter golfs with Babe Brown in late 1940s, pp. 57-59; relative simplicity of football in late 1930s, pp. 118-119; Cutter's criticism of basketball rules is misinterpreted by press in late 1950s, p. 183; Cutter attends professional baseball games during World War II, p. 310; service-wide Navy football teams in late 1940s, pp. 319-321; submarine force football teams after World War II do little to improve morale, p. 352; Cutter becomes director of athletics at small Arizona boys' school in mid-1960s, p. 466; <u>See</u> Olympics; Henry R. Sanders; Paul Brown

Athletics, U.S. Naval Academy
Cutter boxes at academy in early 1930s, pp. 6, 31-34; Cutter on football team in early 1930s, pp. 6, 12, 61-64, 78-82, 89-92; Cutter as assistant football coach in late 1930s, p. 112; drawbacks of using active duty military as athletic coaches, p. 118; Cutter fires difficult football coach in 1959, pp. 322-339; Cutter pressured to allow admiral's plebe son, a lackluster athlete, to attend costly national meet, pp. 462-464; coaching problems caused by strict academic standards, pp. 521-522, 592-593; Cutter selects new wrestling coach in late 1950s, pp. 578-579; Cutter promotes lacrosse coach from plebe to varsity, pp. 579-580; Californian crew coach blackballed by eastern fraternity of coaches, pp. 580-582; "revolt" on lacrosse team in late 1950s, pp. 583-585; swimming program in late 1950s, p. 585; phys. ed. program, pp. 585-587; finances, pp. 588-590, 598; basketball program, p. 599; dissension over location of Air Force game in late 1950s, pp. 600-601; Navy-Marine Corps Memorial Stadium built in late 1950s, pp. 601-602; <u>See</u> Army-Navy Game; Wayne Hardin; Edgar E. Miller; RADM Thomas J. Hamilton; Benjamin Carnevale; Edward J. Erdelatz; Anthony J. Rubino; Edwin C. Peery; Raymond H. Swartz; Willis P. Bilderback; Hamilton W. Webb; ENS Francis D. Crinkley

Austin, Captain Marshall, H., USN   (USNA, 1935)
Assessed as an outstanding officer who, incredibly, was asked to retire after 26 years, pp. 519-520

Australia
American submarine crews on liberty in Australia during World War II, pp. 219-225, 235-236, 245-246; messages from U.S. ships to Pearl Harbor sometimes were received here, p. 226; <u>See</u> "Rats of Tobruk"

Aviation
   Training of Navy pilots versus Army Air Forces in World War II, p. 97; correlation between people who play contact sports and aviators, p. 47; weight standard for student pilots in mid-1930s, p. 105; in battleship Idaho (BB-42) in mid-1930s, p. 509; jealousy over flight pay from non-aviators, p. 510

Awa Maru
   Breakdown in communications causes Queenfish (SS-393) to sink this Japanese passenger cargo ship given safe passage in April 1945, pp. 548-549

Axene, Lieutenant Commander Dean L., USN (USNA, 1945)
   As quiet, competent executive officer of the Nautilus (SSN-571) in the mid-1950s, pp. 396-397, 399

Badger, Commander Oscar C., USN (USNA, 1911)
   Impressive to Cutter as Naval Academy executive officer in the mid-1930s, pp. 93-94

Baldwin, Hanson W. (USNA, 1924)
   Assessed as pro-Navy newsman in the early 1950s, pp. 386, 573

Barracks, Lieutenant Commander Robert A., USNR
   Reserve newsman aids Cutter during his duty in Navy Information in the early 1950s, pp. 364-365

Basketball
   Cutter's criticism of basketball rules is misinterpreted by press in late 1950s, p. 183; Naval Academy basketball program in the late 1950s, p. 599; See Benjamin Carnevale

Battle Efficiency Pennants
   Engineer in New Mexico (BB-40) severely conserves fuel to win battle efficiency pennant in mid-1930s, pp. 121-122, 522; competition within Atlantic submarine squadrons in 1950s, pp. 391-393; how competition between tenders judged, p. 342

Bay of Pigs
   Northampton (CLC-1) called on short notice to Cuba in 1961, but only used for rescue of anti-Castro troops after failed attempt, p. 424; ADM McDonald's thoughts on U.S. position in situation, pp. 424-425

Beach, Captain Edward L., USN (USNA, 1939)
   Asset to skippers as executive officer, pp. 67-68, 308; possible explanation for his not making flag rank, pp. 104-105; used by Trigger (SS-237) skipper Dornin for approaches, p. 259

Beckett, Captain John W., USMC
   Philosophies on quality of Marine recruits in the late 1930s, pp. 48-49

Bendix Corporation
   Strike during World War II prevents some submarines from having radar capability, pp. 232-233

Bennett, Captain Fred G., USN (USNA, 1936)
   Selected to flag rank by board that passed over Cutter in the early 1960s, p. 461

Bennington, USS (CVS-20)
   Cutter describes scene aboard this carrier after catapult fire in May 1954, p. 576

Benson, Captain Roy S., USN (USNA, 1929)
   Cutter's predecessor at Navy Information advises him on position assumed in July 1952, p. 364

Bermuda
   Great golf course lures RADM Frank Watkins to island in mid-1950s, p. 391; Commander Second Fleet, VADM Ricketts, hosts dry party aboard Northampton (CLC-1) in the early 1960s, pp. 430, 606-607

Bilderback, Willis P.
   Cutter promotes plebe lacrosse coach to varsity and improves the team's standings in the late 1950s, pp. 579-580

Blair, Clay, Jr.
   As Time's Pentagon correspondent in the mid-1950s, obtains classified information, pp. 367-368; prints story on Navy's supposed dislike of RADM Rickover in 1954, pp. 369-370; role in Saturday Evening Post's demise in 1959, p. 370; assumes Cutter's dislike of Rickover, pp. 371, 373; Blair's writings on Rickover influence article by Finney implying that the Navy was against the development and testing of nuclear power, pp. 374-377; received information from inside source at Department of Defense, pp. 378-379

Blandy, Rear Admiral William H.P., USN (USNA, 1913)
   As chief of the Bureau of Ordnance during the first part of World War II, seen by some as responsible for faulty torpedoes, p. 174

Borries, Midshipman Fred, Jr., USN (USNA, 1935)
　　Connection between aggressive football player and aggressive pilot, p. 47; as All-American back on Navy football team, pp. 64, 79

Boxing
　　Cutter boxes at the Naval Academy in the early 1930s, pp. 6, 31-34; Cutter offered professional contract after graduation in 1935, p. 33; Cutter referees boxing matches at the 1948 London Olympics, pp. 318-319; See Hamilton W. Webb

Bringle, Captain William F., USN (USNA, 1937)
　　Involvement in decision to fire football coach Erdelatz while Commandant of Midshipmen in 1959, pp. 327-328; Superintendent Melson includes Bringle in decision on Air Force football game in late 1950s, pp. 600-601

Britain
　　Participation in Strike Force South in early 1960s, pp. 433, 440, 442

Brown, Rear Admiral John H., Jr., USN (USNA, 1914)
　　Relieves Cutter from command of Seahorse (SS-304) at Pearl Harbor in August 1944 so he can go back to the States for rest, pp. 55-56; qualities assessed, pp. 57, 59-61; as golf player, pp. 57-59; orders Cutter to relieve Commander Donald McGregor as skipper of the Seahorse in September 1943, pp. 69, 152, 264-265

Brown, Paul
　　Future pro football coach notable as assistant football coach at Severn School in the early 1930s, pp. 5, 30-31

Buckbee, Representative John T. (Republican-Illinois)
　　Appoints Cutter to the Naval Academy in 1931, pp. 3-5

Budding, Ensign William A., USN (USNA, 1943)
　　Young Seahorse (SS-304) officer, whose father was in charge of sub's construction, ensures top quality and safety, pp. 209-211; rudeness to Budding by Trigger (SS-237) crew leads to brawl at a luau during World War II, pp. 537-538

Bureau of Personnel
　　Cutter looks up fitness reports in 1951 and finds an unsatisfactory one from 1943, p. 153; See Special Services; Naval Personnel

Burke, Admiral Arleigh A., USN   (USNA, 1923)
    Discovers lead when *Time*'s Pentagon correspondent mentions classified project in the early 1950s, p. 368; briefs *Baltimore Sun* newsman on Polaris, p. 385; aptitude for flag rank, p. 459

"The Caine Mutiny"
    Movie held up for two years in the early 1950s because Chinfo Lew Parks was overly concerned with Navy image, pp. 365-366, 574

Calcaterra, Motor Machinist's Mate First Class Herbert A., USN
    Large *Pompano* (SS-181) sailor helps Cutter saw through pipe under tense wartime conditions, p. 230; killed by Japanese gun in September 1942, pp. 241-243; drunken, furniture-throwing spree at Royal Hawaiian Hotel, pp. 243-244

Caldwell, Captain Henry H., USN   (USNA, 1927)
    Takes Cutter on a precarious plane ride from Texas to California in September 1945, p. 568

California, USS   (BB-44)
    Use of radar during exercise at Pearl Harbor in early 1941 surprises submarines, p. 179; surviving officer from Japanese attack recruited by *Pompano* (SS-181), pp. 185-187

Captain's Mast
    Commanding officer Lew Parks dismisses case of USS *Pompano* (SS-181) crewmember late for curfew when logical excuse is offered, pp. 180-181; *Pompano* sailor busted for being absent in early 1940s, pp. 198-199

Carnevale, Benjamin
    Head basketball coach at the Naval Academy in the late 1950s invites Cutter to sportswriters' luncheon where Cutter is misquoted, p. 183; presence on football trip to Boston angers football coach, pp. 335-336; left unobstructed to run basketball program, p. 599

Carney, Admiral Robert D., USN   (USNA, 1916)
    As Chief of Naval Operations in January 1954, angered by Clay Blair's *Time* article on Navy's supposed dislike of RADM Rickover, pp. 369-370, 380-381; finesse at speechmaking as an example of his aptitude for flag rank, pp. 458-459, 575

Carpender, Vice Admiral Arthur S., USN   (USNA, 1908)
    Commander Naval Forces Southwest Pacific's relationship with General MacArthur in 1944, p. 219

Casualties
   Cutter's reaction to the losses of fellow Naval Academy graduates and former submariners, pp. 97-101; loss of USS Dorado (SS-248) in October 1943, pp. 126-127; loss of USS Tang (SS-306) in October 1944, p. 161

Cavalla, USS (SS-244)
   Sinks Japanese ship in June 1944 in preliminary action during invasion of Saipan, p. 228

Censorship
   Of letters in USS Seahorse (SS-302) during World War II, pp. 294-295

Central Intelligence Agency
   Involvement in 1961 Bay of Pigs incident, pp. 424, 426

Chapple, Commander Wreford G., USN (USNA, 1930)
   Favorable assessment of skill as World War II submarine skipper, pp. 502-503

Chief of the Boat
   Responsibility in submarines, pp. 265-266

Christie, Lieutenant Ralph W., USN (USNA, 1915)
   Insisted that the magnetic exploder torpedo was effective in the 1920s, but it was later inactivated, p. 173

CinCSouth (Commander in Chief Allied Forces, Southern Europe)
   Scope of responsibility for command in the early 1960s, pp. 437-438, 440-441; status in the early 1980s, pp. 441-442; See ADM James S. Russell, USN

Claggett, Lieutenant Commander Bladen D., USN (USNA, 1935)
   Commanding officer of USS Dace (SS-247) spends liberty in Brisbane with Cutter in mid-1944, pp. 220-222

Clark, Midshipman William L., USN (USNA, 1935)
   Cutter's classmate and punter on the Navy football team, pp. 79-80; has punting foot blessed by the Pope during a midshipmen cruise in 1934, p. 83

Classified Information
   Sharing among NATO countries in the early 1960s, p. 440; See LOFAR

Close, Lieutenant (junior grade) Robert H., USN (USNA, 1934)
   Mixed assessment by shipmate Cutter from duty on S-30 in 1938, p. 115

Commander in Chief Allied Forces, Southern Europe
See CinCSouth

Communications
Poor status during Pearl Harbor attack, p. 195; sometime circuitous route from Pacific ships to Pearl Harbor, pp. 225-226; San Francisco radio station picked up by USS Seahorse (SS-304), pp. 286-287; Mrs. Cutter gets information on Seahorse's safety from communications officer at Mare Island, pp. 293-294; top secret communications in Northampton (CLC-1) with mission of intercepting Soviet messages, p. 429; communications breakdown causes sinking of Japanese ship given safe conduct in April 1945, pp. 548-549; messages between submarines kept to a minimum, p. 550; See Radio Operation; Censorship; Message Traffic

Comstock, Commander Merrill, USN (USNA, 1917)
As Commander Submarine Division 13 in the early 1940s, goes along to observe Cutter's submarine qualification, pp. 125, 128

Connole, Commander David R., USN (USNA, 1936)
Cutter's reaction to the death of his friend in the USS Trigger (SS-237) in March 1945, pp. 99-100; submarine qualifications held up by USS Pompano (SS-181) skipper to keep experienced officers aboard as the war approached, p. 123; sub qualifications, pp. 127-128; incident with shore patrol in Honolulu after war patrol in June 1942, pp. 132-136; skill at keeping sub in diving trim, p. 257; told to gather Pompano papers during depth charge attack in August 1942, pp. 302-303

Coote, Commander John, RN
Impression of first ride in Albacore (AGSS-569) in the mid-1950s, p. 398

Crawford, Rear Admiral George C., USN (USNA, 1921B)
As Commander Submarine Force Atlantic Fleet in the early 1950s, remembered by Cutter as an old-timer with peculiar ideas, pp. 389-390

Crew
Cutter hires new Naval Academy crew coach from California in the late 1950s, and the coach is blackballed by the eastern fraternity of coaches, pp. 580-582

Crinkley, Ensign Francis D., USN (USNA, 1931)
Cutter used as a sparring partner when Crinkley trained for the 1932 Olympics, p. 32

Cromwell, Captain John P., USN (USNA, 1924)
   As Commander Submarine Division 32, sacrifices life to keep
   information about Japanese codebreaking and upcoming U.S. sub
   operations from Japanese in November 1943, pp. 289-290

Currie, Lieutenant John P., USN (USNA, 1937)
   Experienced diving officer in USS Seahorse (SS-304) in 1943,
   p. 262

Cushman, Midshipman Robert E., Jr., USN (USNA, 1935)
   Future Marine Corps Commandant's encounter with a prostitute
   on a midshipman cruise in 1932, pp. 490-491

Cutter, Frances Leffler
   Marries Cutter in 1936 despite Navy regulations, pp. 36-38,
   106-107, 472-473; meets Cutter at Christmas party in 1930, pp.
   38-39; support of Cutter's career, pp. 140-141, 143, 405, 476,
   604; visited by RADM Kidd in November 1941, who subtly offered
   help during imminent war, p. 193; christens USS Requin
   (SS-481) in January 1945, p. 303; entertains at Great Lakes in
   the mid-1960s, pp. 421, 447, 476; health, pp. 424, 445, 470,
   479-481; accompanies Cutter for NATO duty in Naples in early
   1960s, pp. 432-436, 461; enjoyment of Cutter's job at private
   boys school in Arizona after retirement, p. 468; children, pp.
   474-475, 480-487; dated Cutter at Naval Academy in early
   1930s, p. 476; death in October 1981, pp. 479-480; accompanies
   Cutter to submarine veterans' meeting in Arizona, p. 496;
   Cutters entertain K.G. Schacht in September 1945, p. 569

Cutter, Ruth Buek
   Long-standing friendship with Cutter leads to marriage in
   January 1982, pp. 470, 481-485; accompanies Cutter to
   USS Seahorse (SS-304) reunions, pp. 471, 493; relationship
   with Cutter, p. 486

Cutter, Captain Slade D., USN (USNA, 1935)
   Birth in 1911 and early years, pp. 1-2, 6, 10-11, 13-16, 20-
   29, 110-111, 304; parents, siblings, and ancestry, pp. 1-2, 4,
   6-12, 16-17, 20-21, 23, 25-26, 33, 464, 481, 487-488; interest
   in music, pp. 2, 25-29, 139-140; music scholarship to Elmhurst
   College in late 1920s, pp. 139-140; prep school at Severn,
   1930-1931, pp. 3-5, 17-18, 30-32, 35, 39-40; Naval Academy
   years, 1931-1935, pp. 5-6, 32-36, 40-46, 61-64, 78-81, 83-85,
   88-96, 103-105, 193-194, 476, 488-492, 515; resigns from Navy
   in 1936 to get married, but request is denied, pp. 36-38, 473-
   474; wife and children, pp. 36-40, 96, 99, 106-107, 140-141,
   143, 193, 199, 293, 303-304, 405, 421, 424, 432-436, 445, 447,
   461, 468, 470-476, 479-487, 493, 496, 504, 521, 567, 569, 595-
   597, 604, 612; duty in battleship USS Idaho (BB-42), 1935-
   1937, pp. 48-50, 85, 105-110, 112, 119-121, 147, 504-511;

assistant football coach at the Naval Academy in 1937 and 1938, pp. 112-113; submarine school in 1938, pp. 112, 144, 147, 154-158, 161, 512; duty in USS S-30 in 1938, pp. 113-116; duty in USS Pompano (SS-181), 1938-1942, pp. 68, 70, 106, 123-138, 155, 160-162, 165-167, 171-182, 184-188, 192-208, 215, 225-226, 229-233, 238-249, 252-253, 256-258, 279-280, 298-303, 494-495; service in USS Seahorse (SS-304), 1942-1944, pp. 37-38, 53-57, 66-78, 141-143, 145-154, 162-165, 168-171, 189-192, 209-213, 216-228, 233-237, 245-246, 249-251, 258-293, 493-494, 516-517, 523-554; in charge of the construction training school in 1944 and 1945, pp. 65-66, 308-310; commanding officer of USS Requin (SS-481) from 1945 to 1946, pp. 65-67, 213-214, 293, 303-304, 310-311, 314-417, 546, 554, 565-572; in charge of All-Navy sports program at BuPers, 1946-1949, pp. 315, 317-321, 339; executive officer, USS Sperry (AS-12) from 1949-1950, pp. 320, 339-346, 350, 423, 443; Commander Submarine Division 32 from 1950 to 1951, pp. 346-355, 498-499; director of Special Services, 1951-1952, pp. 339, 355-364; director of Navy Information from 1952-1954, pp. 81, 182-183, 332-333, 339, 364-389, 457, 565, 573-577; assistant chief of staff to Commander Submarine Force Atlantic Fleet and training officer from 1954-1956, pp. 306, 389-401, 562-564; Commander Submarine Squadron Six from 1956-1957, pp. 401-406, 555-562; director of athletics at the Naval Academy from 1957-1959, pp. 183, 321-339, 406-407, 462-464, 577-602; commanding officer of USS Neosho (AO-143) from 1959-1960, pp. 406-418, 603; commanding officer, USS Northampton (CLC-1) from 1960-1961, pp. 412, 419-432, 603-611; assistant chief of staff, Strike Force South (NATO) from 1961-1963, pp. 425-426, 432-440, 611; commanding officer, Naval Training Center Great Lakes from 1963-1964, pp. 421-422, 437, 442-453, 476-477, 611-612; director, Navy Museum from 1964-1965, pp. 444-445, 453-456, 545, 612-615; post-retirement jobs, pp. 464-469

Daley, Richard J.
Chicago's long-time mayor reviews graduation parades at Great Lakes in the early 1960s, pp. 422, 477

Davis, Midshipman Joseph B., USN   (USNA, 1932)
Ends up with Cutter's date at a Christmas party in the early 1930s, pp. 39-40

Dealey, Commander Sanuel D., USN   (USNA, 1930)
Assessed as topflight submarine skipper who stressed teamwork, but was a little too daring as World War II commanding officer of the USS Harder (SS-257), pp. 65, 76-77, 100; as Medal of Honor winner, p. 305

Debell, Wilmot T.
   Severn School math teacher interests Cutter in boxing in the early 1930s, p. 32; teaches Cutter about fractions, which his Illinois education neglected, pp. 35-36

Diesel Engines
   See Engines---Diesel

Delano, Captain Harvey, USN (USNA, 1906)
   Assessed as commanding officer of the USS Idaho (BB-42) in the mid-1930s, p. 107

Depth Charge Indicator
   Explanation of warning system in World War II submarines, p. 211

Depth Charges
   Cutter felt safe staying close to his target after hit because he figured they wouldn't launch depth charges with survivors in the water, p. 169; attack after Seahorse (SS-304) use of pillen werfers, pp. 170-171; Seahorse stays under for 16 hours during persistent attack, pp. 247-248; two stages of attack, pp. 297-298; Cutter's reaction to attacks, p. 546

Desegregation
   Within Navy in 1950s from Navy Information perspective, pp. 386-388, 497-498

Deutermann, Vice Admiral Harold T., USN (USNA, 1927)
   Favorably assessed by Cutter as Commander Second Fleet in the early 1960s, p. 421; reviews Great Lakes graduation at Cutter's request in the mid-1960s, pp. 422, 476

DF (Direction-finding)
   Use of radio DF during World War II, pp. 216, 233-234

Donaho, Captain Glynn R., USN (USNA, 1928)
   Assessed as stern submarine squadron commander in the late 1940s, pp. 349-351

Doolittle Raid
   April 1942 U.S. attack on Tokyo results in beefed up Japanese patrols in 600-mile radius of Japan, p. 241

Dorado, USS (SS-248)
   Sunk by American patrol planes with loss of Cutter's friend Penrod Schneider in October 1943, pp. 126-127

Dornin, Commander Robert E., USN (USNA, 1935)
    Offers to come down to Honolulu jail to spring Pompano
    (SS-181) officers in June 1942, but is threatened with
    incarceration, pp. 135, 137-138; as commanding officer of
    USS Trigger (SS-237) in early November 1943, presence off
    Kobe with Seahorse and Halibut, pp. 145-146; rumor of trouble
    between Cutter and Dornin, pp. 146-147; gets one of few loads
    of good torpedoes from Midway in October 1943, p. 168; though
    skilled at the procedure, used executive officer Ned Beach for
    approaching in Trigger, p. 259; drags future Mrs. Cutter while
    a midshipman in the 1930s, p. 493; top quality at Naval
    Academy, sub school, and in sub duty, p. 514; luau with
    Cutter's Seahorse crew leads to brawl, pp. 536-539

Drugs
    Benzedrine given to submarine skippers during World War II,
    pp. 53-55; aluminum hydroxide given to Cutter for stomach
    troubles during World War II submarine patrols, p. 283

Education
    Public school education in rural Illinois in the late 1910s,
    pp. 1-2, 5-6, 14-15, 25, 34-35; Cutter as teacher, director of
    athletics and headmaster at private school in Arizona in the
    mid-1960s, pp. 464-469; See U.S. Naval Academy; Naval War
    College; Elmhurst College; Notre Dame University; Navy
    Postgraduate School; Severn School; Submarine School

Eisenhower, General Dwight D., USA (USMA, 1915)
    President Eisenhower angered at the idea that the submarine
    Nautilus (SSN-571), sponsored by his wife in 1954, was only a
    test vehicle, pp. 374, 377-378

Electrical Systems
    Electric fuel pumps on USS Pompano (SS-181) shorted by leak in
    engine room during World War II depth charge attack, and
    repaired with ingenuity, pp. 300-302

Eller, Rear Admiral Ernest M., USN (USNA, 1925)
    Recommends Cutter as director of the Navy Museum in 1964, pp.
    444-445, 613; as an asset to museum, p. 612

Elmhurst College, Elmhurst, Illinois
    Cutter spends a year on a music scholarship at this small,
    Evangelical-affiliated school in late 1920s, pp. 139-140

Engines--Diesel
    Discussion of inferior Hooven-Owens-Rentschler engines used in
    submarines in the 1930s, pp. 165-166; precarious situation in

USS Pompano (SS-181) during World War II patrol caused by flooded generators, pp. 301-302

Enright, Commander Joseph F., USN (USNA, 1933)
Credited with most Japanese tonnage sunk on a single patrol for November 1944 hit on a Japanese carrier as commander of USS Archerfish (SS-311), p. 277

Enterprise, USS (CV-6)
Planes from this carrier mistake USS Pompano (SS-181) for enemy in December 1941 and drop three bombs, pp. 200, 215

Erdelatz, Edward J.
Cutter stuck with firing erratic Naval Academy football coach in 1959, pp. 322-339, 591, 597-599

Farming
Discussion of correct practices versus those in 1920s, pp. 23-24

Fatigue
During World War II, extended general quarters status while on submarine patrols, pp. 53-54

Fechteler, Admiral William M., USN (USNA, 1916)
Rough and ready Chief of Naval Operations in the early 1950s gave his okay for production assistance to the movie "The Caine Mutiny," pp. 366, 574

Fenno, Lieutenant Commander Frank W., Jr., USN (USNA, 1925)
As commanding officer of the USS Trout (SS-202), returned to Pearl Harbor after Midway action with Japanese prisoners and was made to wait until Marine guards came aboard to remove them, p. 129

Fife, Rear Admiral James, Jr., USN (USNA, 1918)
Tombstone promotion to four stars based on combat awards, p. 254; service in British submarines early in World War II, p. 254

Finney, John
New York Times writer puts forth wire service story in mid-1950s suggesting that the nuclear-powered submarine Nautilus (SSN-571) didn't have the combat capabilities of World War II diesel boats, pp. 374-377, 573

Fitness Reports
   In 1951, Cutter fights an unsatisfactory report from 1943, pp. 153-154; bearing of good reports on selection for sub school, pp. 147, 513

Flag Officers
   Discussion of desirable qualities necessary to attain flag rank, pp. 458-464, 499

Flagships
   Inconvenience for ship commanding officer, pp. 427, 606-608

Fluckey, Captain Eugene B., USN (USNA, 1935)
   Assessed by Cutter as good submarine skipper who learned from others' experiences and wrote dramatic war reports, pp. 144, 255, 292, 314, 456, 534; as Medal of Honor winner, p. 305; sample of patrol report on display at Navy Museum in Washington in the mid-1960s, p. 456; takes on fund-raising for the Naval Academy's football stadium in the late 1950s, pp. 601-602

Food
   Quality of food aboard World War II submarines, pp. 284, 295-297; eating conditions in tense wartime situations, p. 286; pig roasted in Honolulu for luau between war patrols for two submarines, p. 537

Football
   Cutter's father forbids him to play in high school, pp. 2, 4, 12; Cutter plays at Severn School and makes All-State team in 1930, pp. 5, 12, 30; Cutter's thoughts on children playing football, pp. 12-13; Cutter on Naval Academy football team in early 1930s, pp. 6, 12, 61-64, 78-82, 89-92; battleship Idaho (BB-42)'s team in the mid-1930s, pp. 48-50, 112, 119-121; Cutter as assistant football coach at the Naval Academy in the late 1930s, p. 112; relative simplicity of football in late 1930s, pp. 118-119; service-wide Navy football teams in late 1940s, pp. 319-321; Cutter fires difficult Naval Academy football coach in 1959, pp. 322-329; submarine force football teams do little to improve morale after World War II, p. 352; dissension over location of Navy-Air Force game in late 1950s, pp. 600-601; Navy-Marine Corps Memorial Stadium built in Annapolis in late 1950s, pp. 601-602; See also Paul Brown; Henry R. Sanders; Edward J. Erdelatz; Wayne Hardin; Edgar E. Miller; Army-Navy Football Game

Foreign Ports
    USS Neosho (AO-143) crew well-behaved after indoctrination on foreign port visits during Mediterranean cruise in the late 1950s, p. 416; See Australia

France
    Participation in Strike Force South in early 1960s, p. 433

Galantin, Commander Ignatius J., USN (USNA, 1933)
    As commanding officer of the USS Halibut (SS-232), present off Kobe in early November 1943 with USS Seahorse (SS-304) and USS Trigger (SS-237) waiting to sink Japanese vessels entering South China Sea, pp. 144-145

Gallaher, Commander Antone R., USN (USNA, 1933)
    Cutter uses their differing experiences on sub patrols as an example of the role luck can play in wartime success, pp. 77-78, 164-165; initially angry at Cutter for not advising him of a target when they were in wolf pack together in June 1944, pp. 163-164, 291; as commander of wolf pack, gives Cutter operational orders in June 1944, pp. 290-291, 533-534

German Navy
    Difficulty with psychological adjustment for submariners in World War II, p. 160; sub force criticized for over-communicating, p. 550; primitive nature of sub duty, p. 553

Golf
    Cutter improves golf game after lopsided match with Babe Brown in the late 1940s, pp. 57-59

Greenman, Lieutenant Commander William G., USN (USNA, 1912)
    As battalion officer in the early 1930s, feud with another officer results in Cutter's punishment for trivial matter, pp. 89-91

Grenfell, Rear Admiral Elton W., USN (USNA, 1926)
    Responsible for Cutter's selection as Naval Academy director of athletics in 1957, pp. 321-322, 338

Gummerson, Lieutenant Commander Kenneth C., USN
    Competent and aggressive as the first commanding officer of the USS Albacore (AGSS-569) in the mid-1950s, p. 398

Haiti
    USS Northampton (CLC-1) sent to show flag in early 1960s, p. 424

Halibut, USS (SS-232)
   Present off Kobe in early November 1943 with USS Seahorse (SS-304) and USS Trigger (SS-237) waiting to sink Japanese vessels entering South China Sea, pp. 144-145

Halsey, Admiral William F., Jr., USN (USNA, 1904)
   Assessed by Cutter as great wartime leader who might not have been as good in peacetime, pp. 313, 501-502

Hamilton, Captain Thomas J., USN (USNA, 1927)
   Cutter's assessment of Naval Academy football coach in the mid-1930s, pp. 63-64, 80, 118; post-World War II director of athletics credited with setting up Naval Academy phys. ed. program, pp. 585-586; relations with Naval Academy Superintendent Holloway in the mid-1940s, p. 586

Hanson, Lieutenant Commander Ralph E., USN (USNA, 1921)
   First commanding officer of the USS Pompano (SS-181) in 1937, assessed as fine officer but too old for submarine command, p. 165

Harbold, Midshipman Robert P., USN (USNA, 1934)
   First-string Navy football player and boxer who was troubled by susceptibility to concussion, p. 61

Hardhead, USS (SS-365)
   Aft torpedo hatch creased during periscope approach practice in the mid-1950s, pp. 389-390

Hardin, Wayne
   As assistant football coach under Eddie Erdelatz in the late 1950s, confirms his boss's rude behavior at a public function, pp. 326-327; chosen as head coach in 1959 despite age, p. 328; assessed as coach, pp. 328-329, 332

Hardwick, Henry
   As titular head football coach at the Naval Academy in the late 1930s, p. 118

Harlow, Lieutenant Commander Richard C., USNR
   Athletic coach on wartime duty concerned with health of submarine officers during World War II, pp. 281-283

Hart, Rear Admiral Thomas C., USN (USNA, 1896)
   Naval Academy Superintendent in the early 1930s assessed from midshipman vantage point and compared to his successor, pp. 93, 95-96

Hoffman, Chief Radioman Roy L., USN
   Skilled radio operator in USS Seahorse (SS-304) could recognize message senders by their key touch, pp. 234-235; considered indispensable by Cutter, pp. 245, 548; identifies Japanese submarine off Saipan in April 1944 that Seahorse sinks, pp. 272-273; broadcasts sonar ping throughout Seahorse during tense period to keep crew abreast of situation, pp. 285-286; dealings with Cutter during depth charge situation, p. 546

Holloway, Rear Admiral James L., Jr., USN (USNA, 1919)
   His assessment of the mission of the Naval Academy, pp. 44-45, 96; relations with his director of athletics in the mid-1940s, p. 586

Holman, Lieutenant Commander William G., USN (USNA, 1936)
   Cutter and another officer pull a prank on USS Dace (SS-247) executive officer Holman while he was passed-out drunk on liberty in mid-1944, pp. 221-222

Homosexuals
   At Great lakes in the mid-1960s, p. 444; director of boys' school where Cutter works post-retirement is gay, p. 467

Hooven-Owens-Rentschler Company
   Submarine engines built by this company in Ohio in the 1930s later judged inferior, pp. 165-166

Hurricanes
   USS Requin (SS-481) goes through center of storm transiting from Panama to New York in September 1945, pp. 565-566

Idaho, USS (BB-42)
   Cutter coaches ship football team with a proliferation of Marines in the mid-1930s, pp. 48-50, 112, 119-121; discussion of skippers and officers in the mid-1930s, pp. 105-110, 505-506; former submarine officers in crew, pp. 108-110, 505; operations in the mid-1930s, pp. 120-121

Illinois, University of
   Cutter's interest in football team as child in 1920s, p. 16

Infidelity
   Submariners' unfaithfulness to wives during World War II liberties, pp. 223-225

Information, Office of
   See Navy Information

Inspections--Personnel
   Spit and polish inspections in USS Northampton (CLC-1) necessitated by her status as a flagship in the early 1960s, pp. 427-428

Intelligence
   Given to submarines before World War II war patrols, p. 271; See Ultra

Italy
   Participation in Strike Force South in early 1960s, p. 433; living conditions for Cutters during NATO assignment, pp. 435-436

Ives, Commander Norman S., USN (USNA, 1920)
   As Commander Submarine Division 43 on 7 December 1941, refrains from sending message of attack on his division to Pearl Harbor because they already had enough trouble, p. 195

Jackson, Senator Henry M. (Democrat--Washington)
   Backs promotion of Captain Rickover to flag rank in the early 1950s, p. 371

Jacobs, Midshipman John F., Jr., USN (USNA, 1932)
   Harasses Cutter as a plebe, but spoons him several months before graduation, pp. 41-42

Japan
   Fanaticism made Japanese prone to sabotage when taken aboard U.S. submarines after ship sinkings, pp. 75-76; Cutter assesses their World War II antisubmarine warfare capabilities as mediocre, pp. 160, 215-216; Japanese tanker sunk in June 1944, pp. 162-164; superior night glasses aboard subs, pp. 179-180; submarine sunk off Saipan in April 1944, pp. 271-275; current around Tokyo Bay, p. 299

Johns, Captain John G., USN (USNA, 1925)
   Commends USS Requin (SS-481) as best submarine during training in Panama in 1945, pp. 66, 310-311

Johnson, Lyndon B.
   Cutter embarrassed by his visit to NATO command in Naples in the early 1960s, pp. 438-440

Junior Officers (JOs)
   Rotation of ensigns through various departments, in ships for experience in the mid-1930s, p. 109; camaraderie among JOs in the mid-1930s, p. 511

Kane, Midshipman William R., USN (USNA, 1933)
   Connection between aggressive football player and aggressive flyer, p. 47; Cutter replaces Killer Kane as tackle on Navy football team when Kane graduated, p. 62

Kennedy, John F.
   Served by USS Northampton (CLC-1) as national command post in the 1960s, pp. 419-420; speculation on medical conditions, pp. 420-421; Cutter impressed by his visit to NATO command in Naples in the early 1960s, pp. 439-440

Kennedy, Robert F.
   Involvement in Bay of Pigs incident in 1961, p. 425

Key West, Florida
   Relations between city and Navy in the mid-1950s, pp. 519-520

Kidd, Rear Admiral Isaac C., USN (USNA, 1906)
   As Commander Battleship Division One in late 1941, offers assistance to Cutter's wife right before U.S. entry into World War II, p. 193; Cutter got to know the Kidds while boxing at the Naval Academy in the early 1930s, pp. 193-194

Kimball, Dan A.
   Secretary of the Navy in the early 1950s assessed as a political hack, p. 575

Kimmel, Lieutenant Commander Manning M., USN (USNA, 1935)
   Cutter recalls the death of his classmate and son of the former Commander in Chief U.S. Pacific Fleet in July 1944, p. 101

Kimmel, Lieutenant Commander Thomas K., USN (USNA, 1936)
   Cutter's friendship with son of former Commander in Chief U.S. Pacific Fleet, pp. 101-102, 309, 511; reaction to his father's treatment after the Pearl Harbor attack and to the loss of his brother in July 1944, pp. 102-103

Kwajalein
   Admiral Nimitz shows Cutter gruesome photos of island soon after it was secured in early 1944, p. 312; Cutter had disciplinary problems from USS Seahorse (SS-304) reassigned to LST scheduled for amphibious landing here, pp. 543-544

Lacrosse
   Cutter promotes lacrosse coach from plebe to varsity in late 1950s, pp. 579-580; "revolt" on Naval Academy lacrosse team over uniforms, pp. 583-585; See Willis P. Bilderback

LaGuardia, Fiorello H.
　New York City mayor was responsible for raise in submariners' pay to pay-and-a-quarter before World War II, pp. 566-567

Lake, Private Arthur, USMC
　World War I enlistee and cousin of Cutter influences him to aspire toward the Marine Corps for service selection, p. 11

Leadership
　Lack of billets between world wars causes some officers who had been skippers to be relegated to lowly jobs, and only the very best were able to command, pp. 107-108; behavior of skipper under attack, p. 209; qualities of leadership, pp. 492-494; war brings out the best in leaders, pp. 313, 501-502

Lee, Midshipman Holman, Jr., USN (USNA, 1935)
　Cutter receives demerits after being accused by an officer of grimacing at classmate Lee during grace, pp. 89-92

Liberty
　Cutter and other USS Pompano (SS-181) officers jailed temporarily after joy ride in "borrowed" car upon return from war patrol in June 1942, pp. 132-133; sub crews in Australia in mid-1944, pp. 219-225, 235-236, 245-246; well-behaved USS Neosho (AO-143) crew in Mediterranean ports in the late 1950s, p. 416; in France on midshipmen cruise in 1932, pp. 490-491; Hawaiian luau ends in fight during World War II, pp. 536-539

Lindon, Lieutenant Elbert C., USN (USNA, 1939)
　Relieves Cutter as OOD in USS Seahorse (SS-304) and wakes him when the commanding officer changes course, losing a Japanese target they had been trailing during a 1942 war patrol, p. 151; skipper McGregor replaces Cutter as executive officer with Lindon in 1942, pp. 152, 271-272; too meticulous as Seahorse navigator, p. 542

Liquor
　Special Services gets complaints from civilian merchants and temperance groups about selling liquor on bases in the early 1950s, pp. 361-362; used as incentive for crew proficiency in the USS Pompano (SS-181) during World War II, p. 494

Litchfield, USS (DD-336)
　Old destroyer used as target for submarine qualification for officers in USS Pompano (SS-181) in the early 1940s, pp. 124-128

Little, Lieutenant Marion N., USN (USNA, 1922)
Former submarine commander relegated to being a battleship turret officer in the mid-1930s because of lack of billets, pp. 108-109, 505.

LOFAR (Low-Frequency Acquisition and Ranging)
Classified information on LOFAR leaked to Pentagon media correspondent in the early 1950s, pp. 367-368.

Lockwood, Vice Admiral Charles A., USN (USNA, 1912)
As Commander Submarines Pacific Fleet in October 1943, assists Cutter in selecting crew to improve morale in USS Seahorse (SS-304), pp. 70-71; leaves decision on one-sided destruction of Japanese trawlers to Cutter, p. 73; predicts absence of Japanese target for Cutter off Pearl Harbor, p. 77; tells Cutter he should not allow himself to be taken prisoner before war patrol around time of Saipan invasion in Spring of 1943, pp. 142, 271, 288-289; defends Cutter in effort to correct unsatisfactory fitness report in 1951, pp. 153-154; demanded to know what was wrong with torpedoes, pp. 168-169; intercepts letter calling for court-martial of Admiral Blandy, p. 174; chides Cutter for assuming blame after Army error, pp. 217, 551; recalls USS Pompano (SS-181) to Pearl Harbor after close call in South China Sea, p. 239; send-off to subs, pp. 270-271; debriefed every sub returning from Pacific patrol, p. 278; sends USS Seahorse (SS-304) to draw off Japanese antisubmarine warfare forces so Saipan beaches can be surveyed for invasion, p. 531

Loomis, Captain Sam C. Jr., USN (USNA, 1935)
Academic difficulties at the Naval Academy and at sub school, p. 515; as submarine commander during World War II, pp. 516-517, 549-550; health problems, pp. 518-519

Loomis, Mrs. Sam C.
Influence on Cutter's decision to attend the Naval Academy in the late 1920s, pp. 2-4, 15, 140

Loughlin, Captain C. Elliott, USN (USNA, 1933)
As director of athletics in the mid-1950s, Cutter feels that Loughlin should have fired the difficult head football coach at the Naval Academy, pp. 322-333, 335, 339; as commanding officer of the USS Queenfish (SS-393) that sunk Japanese ship given safe conduct in April 1945, pp. 548-549

MacArthur, General Douglas, USA (USMA, 1903)
MacArthur's staff sends message restraining USS Seahorse (SS-304) on race to R&R in Australia in 1944, pp. 218-219

McCain, Captain John S., Jr., USN (USNA, 1931)
   In 1951, encourages Cutter to look up his fitness reports and fight an unsatisfactory one, p. 153

McCall, Lieutenant Francis B., USN (USNA, 1925)
   B Division officer in Idaho (BB-42) influences Cutter to choose submarine duty, pp. 108-109, 505

McDonald, Rear Admiral David L., USN (USNA, 1928)
   As Commander Carrier Division Six in 1961, involvement and thoughts on Bay of Pigs, pp. 424-426

McFarland, USS (DD-237)
   Escorted Submarine Division 43 into Pearl Harbor shortly after Japanese attack, p. 196

McGrath, Lieutenant Thomas P., USN (USNA, 1940)
   Cutter discusses his friend, lost in the USS Pompano (SS-181) in September 1943, p. 98; vehemence against Japanese after Pearl Harbor attack on his ship (USS California) gets him assigned to sub duty without benefit of training, pp. 185-188

McGregor, Commander Donald, USN (USNA, 1926)
   As commanding officer of the USS Seahorse (SS-304) in mid-1943 recommends Cutter for disqualification from submarine duty, but is soon relieved by him, pp. 68-70, 152, 264-267; attitude towards sonar, pp. 69-70, 154-155; unsuccessful first patrol in Seahorse (SS-304), pp. 149-152, 260-261; Cutter fights unsatisfactory fitness report given him by McGregor in 1943, pp. 153-154, 264; commended as training officer in Seahorse (SS-304), pp. 258-260; prior submarine experience, p. 262; given good submarine with seasoned crew as personal favor, pp. 262-264; disbelief of Pompano (SS-181)'s successes, pp. 266-268

McGrievy, Ensign Joseph L., USN
   Former enlisted man whose great eyesight facilitated night attacks for USS Seahorse (SS-304), pp. 235-237, 245-246, 524; as chief of the boat, advises Cutter that Seahorse (SS-304) crew mistakenly had no faith in him, pp. 265-266

Magnetic Exploder
   Commanding officer Lew Parks didn't trust theoretical testing he had seen done on this device that is finally made inactive, pp. 173-174; See Torpedoes

Mare Island Naval Shipyard, Vallejo, California
   Quality of construction of USS Seahorse (SS-304) doubly guaranteed by presence of shipbuilding superintendent's son in crew in 1943, pp. 209-210

"Marianas Turkey Shoot"
   USS Seahorse (SS-304)'s contribution to preliminaries to this June 1944 action during invasion of Saipan, pp. 226-228, 234-235

Marine Corps, U.S.
   Fitness of Marine recruits in World War II manifests itself on battleship Idaho (BB-42)'s football team, pp. 48-49; small quota of Naval Academy graduates allowed to enter Corps prevents Cutter from getting the service of his choice in 1935, pp. 105, 432; military police at Honolulu chase Cutter and shipmates in appropriated Army car, and they wind up in jail, pp. 134-136; Cutter impressed by Marine detachment in USS Northampton (CLC-1) in early 1960s, pp. 431-432

Married Officers
   When his request to resign is turned down in 1936, Ensign Cutter marries anyway, pp. 36-38, 106-107, 472-473

Martin, Ensign William I., USN   (USNA, 1934)
   Popular flyer in Idaho (BB-42) in the mid-1930s, pp. 509-510

Mason, USS (DE-529)
   Cutter's classmate Norman Meyer commands all-black crewed ship in mid-1945, p. 497

Medal of Honor
   Discussion of receipt by several top World War II submarine commanders, pp. 305-308

Media
   Cutter discusses newsmen he came to admire through Navy Information duty in the mid-1950s, pp. 384-386; See Time; Saturday Evening Post; New York Times; Clay Blair, Jr.

Melson, Rear Admiral Charles L., USN   (USNA, 1927)
   As Superintendent of the Naval Academy in the late 1950s, supports Cutter's decision to fire football coach Eddie Erdelatz, pp. 325, 327; bypasses Cutter in discussion of Navy-Air Force football game location, pp. 600-601

Merchant Marine
   Difficulties with Merchant Marine-trained officers serving mandatory active duty stint with the Navy in late 1950s, pp. 408-409, 411, 416, 605

Message Traffic
   For U.S. submarines during World War II, p. 146

Meyer, Lieutenant Commander Norman H., USN (USNA, 1935)
   Obvious leader even as a midshipman in the mid-1930s, p. 492; commands all-black crew in USS Mason (DE-529) in mid-1945, p. 497

Midway Island
   Japanese prisoners taken after June 1942 battle to Pearl Harbor, pp. 128-130; commanding officer of atoll demoralized by problems after action, pp. 248-249, 251; description of Midway two days after battle, pp. 249, 252

Military Police (MPs)
   Marine MPs in Honolulu chase Cutter and USS Pompano (SS-181) shipmates, and eventually they end up in jail, pp. 133-136

Miller, Edgar E. "Rip"
   Cutter's assessment of Naval Academy head football coach in the early 1930s, pp. 63, 80; accompanies midshipmen on summer cruise to Europe in 1934, p. 83; snubbed by Superintendent Smedberg in favor of coach Erdelatz in the late 1950s, p. 325; relations with football coach Wayne Hardin, pp. 329-330; relationship with Eddie Erdelatz, p. 336; entertained by Commandant Ninth Naval District instead of Cutter when visiting Great Lakes in mid-1960s, p. 448; Cutter implements some of Miller's suggestions as director of athletics in the late 1950s, p. 578

Millis, Walter
   Briefed by Chief of Naval Operations Burke on the Polaris program in the 1950s, pp. 385, 573

Mine Warfare
   Danger for submarines in Strait of Tsushima during World War II, pp. 148-149, 292; USS Pompano (SS-181) equipped with mine cable cutters, p. 292

Minorities
   In submarines during World War II, pp. 495-497; See Desegregation

Mississippi, USS (BB-41)
   Overly cautious ex-reserve officer in gun turret during short-range battle practice bottlenecks drill in mid-1930s, p. 85

Momsen Lung
   Used by USS Tang (SS-306) survivors after sinking of this submarine in October 1944, p. 161

Monroe, Captain Henry S., USN (USNA, 1933)
   As Commander Service Force Sixth Fleet, interfaced with fleet commander VADM George Anderson in the late 1950s, pp. 410-411

Morton, Commander Dudley W., USN (USNA, 1930)
   Submarine skipper lost in the USS Wahoo (SS-238) in October 1943, assessed as a bit too daring, but a good submariner, pp. 77, 100, 147-148, 305, 502; assigned as relief skipper for USS Pompano (SS-181) in 1942, but is kept there for only two days, pp. 240, 246; Cutter feels Morton was better off with Wahoo than Pompano, p. 247

Morale
   Poor morale aboard USS Seahorse (SS-304) when Cutter assumed command in September 1943, pp. 70, 74; Cutter's wife's contribution to his peace of mind during war patrols, pp. 141, 143; mail, pp. 294-295; among service force personnel in late 1950s, p. 418; strong ship loyalty leads to fight among crews at Hawaiian luau in early 1940s, pp. 536-539

Music
   Cutter's interest in music and accomplishment on the flute, pp. 2, 25-29, 139-140

NATO
   Greek, Turkish, British, and French contributions to Strike Force South in early 1960s, p. 433; role in smooth Greek-Turkish relations, pp. 433-434; sharing of classified information, p. 440; multinationally-crewed ship, p. 608; See Strike Force South

Nautilus, USS (SSN-571)
   Navy reported to undermine importance of first nuclear submarine by Time author in 1954, pp. 369, 373-378, 563; exercises in mid-1950s, pp. 394-395; Cutter writes article in 1955 from experiences as training officer, pp. 562-564; See CDR Eugene P. Wilkinson, USN

Naval Academy, U.S.
   Cutter offered catch-up geometry class during plebe summer in 1931, pp. 5-6; Cutter's plebe year, pp. 40-42; program in 1930s versus 1980s, pp. 44-46, 96; summer cruises in early 1930s, pp. 83, 488-491; graduates compared to reservists, pp. 85-87, 489; assessment of various officers stationed at

academy in early 1930s, pp. 89-94; quality of instructors in early 1930s, pp. 94-95; uniform standards in early 1930s, pp. 95-96; service selection in mid-1930s, p. 105; indoctrination in submarines for midshipmen in late 1930s, p. 113; Cutter's sub school class consisted of many Naval Academy stripers from mid-1930s, p. 157; desirability of graduates in fleet during World War II, p. 263; athletic coaches had to be hired in an instructor's billet in late 1950s, p. 579; academic board, pp. 593-594; Cutter punished for trivial infraction he didn't feel he'd committed in early 1930s, pp. 89-92; See RADM Thomas C. Hart; RADM David F. Sellers; VADM William R. Smedberg III; RADM Charles L. Melson; CAPT William F. Bringle; CAPT Oscar C. Badger; LTJG Eugene E. Paro; CDR Mahlon S. Tisdale; LT Robert H. Smith; MIDN Holman Lee, Jr.

Naval Reserves
Glut of reservists after World War I caused resentment among Naval Academy graduates who had promotions held up, pp. 84-85; reservists compared to Naval Academy graduates, pp. 85-87; reservist-manned ship makes excellent approach on USS Neosho (AO-143) in the late 1950s, pp. 415-416; reserve officer on staff in USS Northampton (CLC-1) unhappy with inspection by Cutter, pp. 427-428; control over reserves by commandant of the Ninth Naval District in the mid-1960s, p. 453

Navy Information
Cutter discusses responsibilities of his billet as director of public information assumed in July 1952, pp. 365-367, 383-384; value of line officer versus public affairs specialist as chief of information, pp. 382-383

Naval Training Center, Great Lakes, Illinois
Graduation parades, pp. 421-422, 442, 476-477; importance of training to Navy and individuals, pp. 442-444; poor image of officers assigned to dead-end jobs by local civilians, p. 449; duties of commanding officer in mid-1960s, pp. 452, 611-612

Naval War College, Newport, Rhode Island
Potential importance for selection to flag rank, pp. 457, 461-462, 499

Navy Postgraduate School, Monterey, California
Special Services gives non-appropriated funds for starting activities in Monterey in the early 1950s, p. 363

Navy Museum, Washington, D.C.
Cutter's contributions as director in the mid-1960s, pp. 453-455, 612; Cutter's staff in the mid-1960s, p. 613; funding

for, p. 614; security, pp. 614-615; See Rear Admiral Ernest M. Eller

Neosho, USS (AO-143)
Condition of ship and crew in late 1950s, pp. 407-409, 411-414, 603; four-month Mediterranean deployment in late 1950s, pp. 409-417; evaporator troubles, p. 413; Cutter monitors encyclopedia sales pitch aboard, pp. 416-417

New Mexico, USS (BB-40)
Engineer Rickover severely conserves fuel oil to win efficiency pennant for this battleship in the mid-1930s, pp. 121-122

New York Times
Writer does story on nuclear submarines being unsatisfactory that is picked up by the wire services in mid-1950s, pp. 375-376

Nichols, Commander Stanley G., USN (USNA, 1926)
Prank pulled on Nichols while passed-out drunk on liberty in Brisbane in mid-1944, pp. 221-222

Nimitz, Fleet Admiral Chester W., USN (USNA, 1905)
When greeting Cutter after a World War II sub patrol, brings up his non-regulation marriage in 1936, pp. 37-38, 473; characterized as warm and friendly during three post-patrol meetings, pp. 312-313; as great wartime or peacetime leader, pp. 501-502; as chief of naval operations in post-war period asks Navy secretary to disapprove his son's request to resign, p. 556

Nimitz, Captain Chester W., Jr., USN (USNA, 1936)
Reaction when arrested for speeding, pp. 555-556; relationship with father, pp. 556, 560; post-retirement employment in the mid-1950s, pp. 556-559; as a leader, pp. 560-561

Ninth Naval District
Superfluous nature of commandant's billet in the mid-1960s, p. 446

Northampton, USS (CLC-1)
Likelihood of commanding officers to attain flag rank, p. 419; used as national command post for President Kennedy in the early 1960s, pp. 419-421; changes necessitated for command post service, p. 420; smoothness of ceremonies aboard, p. 423; social events aboard, pp. 429-430; command of, compared to submarine command, pp. 603-604; tug thumps ship while under pilot's command, pp. 609-610

Notre Dame University, South Bend, Indiana
    Handling of athletes with respect to academics in the 1960s, pp. 590-591

Nuclear Power
    Cutter feels civilian nuclear power program could have benefited from the leadership of Admiral Rickover, p. 122

Nuclear-powered Submarines
    Navy mistakenly reputed to be fighting advent of nuclear power in the mid-1950s, pp. 375-376; misunderstanding of submarines by other fleet components, p. 394; showed its value by confounding U.S. antisubmarine warfare forces during exercise in the mid-1950s, p. 395; potential if available during World War II, p. 397; makes conventional submarines obsolete, pp. 397-398, 561-562; Cutter assesses value, pp. 564-565; See Albacore, USS (AGSS-569); Nautilus, USS (SSN-571)

O'Kane, Lieutenant Commander Richard H., USN (USNA, 1934)
    Used as an example of how the best submarine skippers are not too smart, pp. 77, 144, 147; escaped sinking of USS Tang (SS-306) in October 1944 with Momsen lung, p. 151; example of fastidiousness, pp. 249-251, 351; used by USS Wahoo (SS-238) skipper as approach officer, p. 259; optimistic estimator of tonnage sunk, p. 275; Medal of Honor winner, p. 305; Cutter concedes that O'Kane was superior sub skipper, p. 458; at sub school in the late 1930s, pp. 512-513; difficulties at Saipan during World War II, pp. 530-531

Olympics
    Cutter used as a sparring partner to help ENS Crinkley train for 1932 Olympics, p. 32; Cutter takes armed forces team to 1948 London Olympics and referees boxing, pp. 317-319

Outlaw, Lieutenant (junior grade) Edward C., USN (USNA, 1935)
    While pilot assigned to USS Enterprise (CV-6) in mid-December 1941, mistakenly drops bombs on USS Pompano (SS-181), pp. 200, 205

Parche, USS (SS-384)
    Fiery relationship between commanding officer Ramage and submarine division commander Parks during World War II, pp. 306-307

Parks, Rear Admiral Lewis S., USN (USNA, 1925)
    As commanding officer of USS Pompano (SS-181) from 1939 to 1942, initially rejects services of his new executive officer, but eventually they become friends, pp. 68, 84; Cutter's

advocation of Parks's methods of submarine command misinterpreted by USS Seahorse (SS-304) commander McGregor, pp. 68-69, 151; dislike of naval reserves, pp. 68, 84-85; in order to keep experienced officers in USS Pompano (SS-304) as war neared, held up their sub qualifications, pp. 123-124; insisted that his officers do preliminaries to torpedo launches in their heads, pp. 124-125, 162; qualifies three officers for command at same time as their initial sub qualificiations, p. 128; influence on Cutter, pp. 128, 212; though friendly with Cutter off-duty, insisted on adherence to rank aboard ship, pp. 128-131; hell-raising incident with shore patrol in Honolulu after war patrol in June 1942, pp. 131-138; contempt for Japanese antisubmarine warfare capabilities, p. 160; fearlessly runs Pompano (SS-181) on surface in December 1941 to make better time on trip from Pearl Harbor to Wake, pp. 160-161, 199; not overly popular due to competitiveness, pp. 162, 171; sent to Pompano (SS-181) with re-worked engines from manufacturer in the late 1930s, pp. 165-166; great knowledge of engines, p. 168; accused of cowardice when he surfaced during a fleet exercise when he was supposed to be using sonar, pp. 172-173; skeptical of usefulness of magnetic exploder, pp. 173-174; as leader, pp. 177, 180-181, 185, 253, 259; recruits crew member from Pearl Harbor survivors, pp. 185-187; as wartime skipper, pp. 199-201, 204-207, 256; behavior under attack, pp. 206-207; pioneer in periscope photography prior to World War II, pp. 279-280; relationship with Red Ramage, pp. 306-307, 535-536; pulls Cutter into public information job in the early 1950s, overly concerned with putting Navy in a good light, pp. 365-366, 381-382; accused of undermining the nuclear power program in a January 1954 Time article, pp. 374, 377, 380; concern with Cutter's career, p. 436; attitude towards patrol report style, pp. 456-457; Cutter concedes Parks's superiority as sub skipper, p. 458

Paro, Lieutenant (junior grade) Eugene E., USN (USNA, 1925)
Cutter credits his company officer Paro as a great influence on him, p. 93

Parsons, Captain William S., USN (USNA, 1922)
Selected to flag rank in the early 1950s by a board that was supposed to select Captain Rickover, p. 371

Pearl Harbor
USS Pompano (SS-181) returns to Pearl Harbor on 9 December 1941 and recruits new crew member from survivors, pp. 185-187, 197; description of Pompano's approach after Japanese attack, p. 196

Peery, Edwin C.
   Cutter selects Peery as head wrestling coach at the Naval Academy in the late 1950s for his well known name in wrestling circles and for his ability to recruit, pp. 578-579

Periscope Approaches
   Training comes under scrutiny in mid-1950s, pp. 389-390

Personnel, Naval
   Demobilization at end of World War II leaves lack of chiefs in submarine duty, pp. 315-317; recruiting difficulties result in deficient personnel in late 1940s, pp. 339-341; questionable quality of personnel assigned to service forces, pp. 407-408, 412-414, 417-418; difficulties with merchant marine officers doing mandatory Navy service, pp. 408-409, 411, 418, 605; importance of training, as well as retention efforts, pp. 442-443; captain weeded out in mid-1950s when it appeared there were too many, pp. 518-519; See Minorities; Desegregation; Junior Officers; Naval Reserves; Flag Officers; Selection Boards

Pillen Werfers
   Released by USS Seahorse (SS-304) to confuse Japanese sonar with almost disastrous effect, pp. 169-171

Pleatman, Lieutenant (junior grade) Ralph F., USNR
   As new officer in USS Pompano (SS-181) in the early 1940s, is initially rejected by his skipper, but they eventually become friends, pp. 68, 84; as weapons officer, pp. 68, 72; Cutter requests Pleatman for his USS Seahorse (SS-304) crew immediately after his marriage in October 1943, pp. 70-71, 141; as morale builder in Seahorse (SS-304), pp. 74, 86; defends Pompano (SS-181) successes to disbelieving officer, p. 268

"Plucking"
   Examples of captains who were asked to retire after 26 years instead of the normal 30, pp. 518-520

Pompano, USS (SS-181)
   Class of submarines assessed by Cutter, p. 60; initially poor relationship between commanding and executive officers in early part of World War II, p. 68; Cutter's reaction to his former sub's loss in September 1943, p. 98; commanding officer Parks holds up sub qualifications for three officers to keep experienced men in crew, pp. 123-124; Parks insists that officers do preparations for torpedo launches without gadgetry, pp. 124-125; sub and command qualifications aboard,

pp. 125-128; picks up Japanese prisoner at Midway for delivery to Pearl Harbor in mid-1942, pp. 128-130; crew member's inability to cope with sub duty stress, p. 160; engines sent back to factory after commissioning, and eventually judged as no good, pp. 164-165; discussion of officers in the late 1930s, pp. 166-167; participation in fleet exercise using sonar, pp. 172-173; torpedoes aboard, p. 175; morale aboard in 1941, pp. 181-182, 185; gets new crewmembers in December 1941 from Pearl Harbor survivors, pp. 185-188, 197; conning tower doors removed at Mare Island in late 1941, pp. 192-193; misses Japanese attack at Pearl Harbor because of engine trouble, but is strafed on the surface 135 miles away, pp. 194-196; approaches Pearl Harbor after attack, pp. 196-197; captain's mast aboard, pp. 180-181, 198-199; World War II operations, pp. 199-207, 227-233, 238-243, 298-303; sinks Japanese fishing boat with .50-caliber machine gun, pp. 230-232; crewman killed by Japanese gun, pp. 241-242; poor quality of submarine, pp. 247, 299-300; close brush with depth charges, pp. 298-303; rewards of liquor used to motivate lookouts, pp. 494-495; See LCDR Ralph E. Hanson; RADM Lewis S. Parks

Portsmouth Naval Shipyard, Portsmouth, New Hampshire
Cutter has former shipmate stationed to new construction in Portsmouth in 1943 so he can spend more time with his new bride and be available for transfer to USS Seahorse (SS-304), pp. 267-268; easy pace of shipyard duty in 1944-1945, pp. 308-310

Povich, Shirley
Washington Post sports columnist supports Cutter's position on firing football coach Erdelatz in 1959, pp. 337-338

Pratt, Midshipman Richard R., USN (USNA, 1936)
Navy quarterback calls for Cutter to kick winning points in 1934 Army-Navy game, pp. 79-80

Prina, Lieutenant L. Edgar, USNR
Reserve newsman aids Cutter during his Navy Information tour in the early 1950s, especially concerning the Nautilus (SSN-571) flap in 1954, pp. 364-365, 379-380, 573

Prisoners of War
USS Pompano (SS-181) picks up Japanese prisoner at Midway shortly after June 1942 battle and takes him to Pearl Harbor, pp. 128-129, 249; Cutter told not to be taken prisoner during his Pacific war patrols because of his prior knowledge of the planned invasion of Saipan, pp. 142, 271, 288-289; Pompano (SS-181) rescues Japanese from ship sunk in September 1942, pp. 241-242; Cutter's friend K.G. Schacht earns Navy-

wide respect for his honorable disposition as Japanese prisoner, pp. 522-523

Professional Jealousy
Cutter's belief in Navy system precludes bitterness about career, pp. 457-461, 499-501; over flight pay from non-aviators, p. 510

Propulsion
Engines on USS Seahorse (SS-304)-class submarines produced more power than generators and motors designed to handle, pp. 227-228

Prostitution
Future Marine Corps leader's brush with a prostitute during a midshipmen cruise in 1932, pp. 490-491

Protocol
Social amenities adhered to in Navy prior to World War II, pp. 477-479

Public Relations
Importance to Naval Training Center, Great Lakes in the mid-1960s, pp. 449-452; See Navy Information

Raborn, Captain William F., USN (USNA, 1928)
Open dealings with the media during his involvement with Polaris in the 1950s, pp. 576-577

Radar
Aboard the USS California (BB-44) at Pearl Harbor in early 1941, p. 179; Bendix Corporation strike during World War II prevents some submarines from having radar capability, pp. 232-233; used for communications, p. 291; value to World War II submarines, p. 526; jury-rigged repair in USS Seahorse (SS-304), p. 552

Radio Operation
Proficient radio operators could recognize message-senders by their key touch, pp. 234-235

Ramage, Commander Lawson P., USN (USNA, 1931)
Relationship with Lew Parks, pp. 306-307, 535-536; as Medal of Honor winner, pp. 306-307

Recognition Manuals
Poor quality during World War II, p. 275

Reed, Torpedoman's Mate Second Class G. Russell, USN
    Put off of USS Pompano (SS-181) for disciplinary reasons in 1941, rejoins crew after Pearl Harbor attack, p. 197; tried at captain's mast for going UA, pp. 198-199

Reina Mercedes, USS (IX-25)
    Midshipmen charged with Class A offenses interned in this ship in the early 1930s, p. 91

Replenishment Underway
    Responsibility of oiler commanding officer, pp. 412, 415

Requin, USS (SS-481)
    Cutter handpicks crew while at construction training school in 1944, pp. 65-66, 304; commended by training officer in Panama as best he'd dealt with, pp. 66, 310-311, 554; loaded with ammunition at Pearl Harbor, but war ends before first patrol, pp. 66-67; inspection at Key West in 1946, pp. 213-215; building delayed by slowdown near war's end, p. 303; off Pearl Harbor entrance on V-J Day, p. 311; converted to radar picket ship after war, p. 314; use as a target for antisubmarine warfare school in Key West in mid-1940s, p. 315; commissioning party in Boston in 1945, pp. 545-546; goes through eye of hurricane during transit from Panama to New York in September 1945, pp. 565-566

Rest and Recreation (R&R)
    See Liberty

Reuther, Chief Yeoman Roland A., USN
    Maneuvers his way into service in the USS Seahorse (SS-304), and later retires as a captain, pp. 539-541

Rice, Eunice Willson
    Wife of Cutter's commanding officer in S-30 in the late 1930s, and a Japanese codebreaker during World War II, p. 117

Rice, Commander Robert H., USN (USNA, 1927)
    Advises Cutter on sinking civilian Japanese ships during World War II, p. 73; Cutter's favorable assessment of Rice as commanding officer of S-30 in the late 1930s, pp. 113-117; helps Cutter get an officer he wanted assigned to USS Seahorse (SS-304) in 1943, pp. 267-268

Ricketts, Vice Admiral Claude V., USN (USNA, 1929)
    Hard worker and closed-mouthed as Commander Second Fleet in the early 1960s, pp. 422, 427-430, 459, 605-607, 609-611; promotes multinationally-crewed ship, p. 608; example of human side, p. 609

Rickover, Admiral Hyman G., USN (USNA, 1922)
Severely conserves fuel as engineer in the USS New Mexico (BB-40) in the mid-1930s to win battle efficiency pennant, pp. 121-122, 522; praised for his handling of the Navy's nuclear power program, pp. 122, 371, 564; attitude towards bureaucracy, p. 123; Time writer Clay Blair reports Navy's opposition to Rickover in mid-1950s, pp. 369-370, 373; circumstances of flag rank promotions, pp. 371-373, 460; hypocritical in promoting disarmament in the early 1980s, p. 373; uses obnoxiousness as a tool to get listeners' attention, pp. 399-401; defended by Cutter's friend, K.G. Schacht, p. 522; puts in request for Naval Academy athletic tickets for someone else in late 1950s, but is scrupulously honest about it, pp. 588-589

Roper, Captain Clifford H., USN (USNA, 1916)
Relationship with Cutter as commander of the shipyard working on USS Requin (SS-481) in 1944-1945, pp. 308-309

Rubino, Anthony J.
Success with sports program at Florida air station brings him to Cutter's attention in the late 1950s, pp. 585-586

Russell, Admiral James S., USN (USNA, 1926)
Assessed as Commander in Chief Allied Forces Southern Europe in the early 1960s, p. 438; on flag selection board when Cutter was passed over, pp. 460-462

Russia
Cutter's relief at news of the end of World War II coupled with apprehension about Russians, pp. 554-555

Ryan, Cornelius
Newsman visiting in San Diego overhears disparaging comments about Cutter in the early 1950s, pp. 498-499

S-30, USS (SS-135)
Incident while diving midshipmen in mid-1938, pp. 113-115; controls accidentally rigged backwards during Cavite overhaul, pp. 114-115; Cutter briefly runs submarine aground and is helped by his unperturbed commanding officer, p. 116

S-51, USS (SS-162)
Collision and sinking of this submarine off Block Island in September 1925 left Cutter, as a child, disenchanted with submarine duty, pp. 110-111, 161

Sabotage
  Peril for U.S. submarines taking on Japanese survivors of ship sinkings during World War II, p. 75

Saipan
  USS Seahorse (SS-304) sent in to draw off Japanese antisubmarine warfare efforts so that the beaches of Saipan can be surveyed before spring 1944 invasion, pp. 142-143, 159, 531; Japanese submarine sunk in harbor in April 1944, pp. 271-275; Eighth Air Force mistakenly reports having bombed Saipan, p. 286; prior knowledge of 1943 invasion plans prompts Cutter to be directed not to allow himself to be taken prisoner, pp. 288-290

Sanders, Henry R.
  Innovative football coach at UCLA introduces four-man line on defense, p. 119

Saturday Evening Post
  Clay Blair's role in downfall of this publishing institution, p. 370

Schacht, Captain Kenneth G., USN (USNA, 1935)
  Assesses Cutter's discretion, pp. 183-184; involvement in decision to fire Naval Academy football coach Erdelatz in the late 1950s, pp. 327-328; no animosity towards the Japanese despite World War II internment, pp. 520-521; examples of kind nature, pp. 521-522, 616; as Japanese POW and after-effects, pp. 522-523, 568-570; first wife and divorce while interned, pp. 570-572; example of curious nature, pp. 571-572, 588; goes over athletic association books, p. 588

Schneider, Lieutenant (junior grade) Earle C., USN (USNA, 1933)
  Sub qualification held up by USS Pompano (SS-181) skipper to keep experienced officers aboard as war approached, p. 123; misses target during sub qualifications in the early 1940s, pp. 125-128; sub sunk by American patrol plane in October 1943, pp. 166-167

Sculpin, USS (SS-191)
  Embarked submarine division commander elects to go down with the boat when sunk in November 1943 rather than be captured and possibly reveal information, pp. 289-290

Seahorse, USS (SS-304)
  82-1/2-hour action off Palau islands during which three Japanese ships sunk in January-February 1944, pp. 53-54, 191-192; commanding officer Cutter given drugs by pharmacist's

mate, pp. 54-55; Cutter relieved by RADM Babe Brown for rest, pp. 55-56; confusion with ship placement during first patrol off Saipan, p. 57; some crew superstitious about sailing with Cutter after so many successful patrols, p. 60; Cutter handpicks crewmembers detaching from *Seahorse* (SS-304) for his new command in 1944, p. 66; commanding officer McGregor relieved by Cutter in late 1942, pp. 68-69, 152; morale aboard when Cutter assumed command, pp. 70, 74; attacks Japanese trawlers as per directive, but Cutter chooses to leave area rather than continue slaughter, pp. 72-73; patrols off Saipan in spring 1944, sinking five Japanese vessels, pp. 142-143; sinks two Japanese ships near Tsushima Strait in November 1943, pp. 148-149, 189-191; skipper McGregor's hesitation causes submarine to get no hits during initial patrol in mid-1943, pp. 149-151; sinks Japanese tanker in June 1944, pp. 162-164; quality of construction, pp. 209-211; World War II operations, pp. 211-213, 215-219, 236-237, 260-261, 271-275, 286-288, 290-292, 296, 530-534; pursued by U.S. planes, pp. 216-218, 550-551; haste to get R&R results in restraints being applied, pp. 217-219; crew gets R&R in Australia, pp. 219-225; participation in preliminaries to June 1944 Marianas Turkey Shoot, pp. 226, 234-235; officers aboard in 1943, pp. 262-263; enlisted crewmembers receive commissions, pp. 234-237; sinks Japanese submarine off Saipan Harbor in April 1944, pp. 271-275; quality of readiness and training prior to first patrol, pp. 259-260; reunions, pp. 471, 493; detailed discussion of several of the subs' sinkings, pp. 523-526, 529-534; administrative details, pp.539-542; supplies, pp. 542-543; disciplinary problems, pp. 543-545; discussion of enlisted crew in early 1940s, pp. 551-552; engineering plant, p. 553; *See* CDR Donald McGregor

Seaton, Fred
 As assistant for public affairs in the Defense Department in the mid-1950s, responsible for leaks to *Time*'s Pentagon correspondent, pp. 378-379

Second Fleet
 Contact between individual ship commanders and fleet commander, pp. 422-423; Commander Second Fleet works on improving contingency plan for the Caribbean in early 1960s, pp. 606-607; *See* VADM Harold T. Deutermann, USN; VADM Claude V. Ricketts, USN

Selection Boards
 Vagaries of board in possible relation to CAPT Ned Beach's failure to be selected to flag rank, pp. 104-105; circumstances surrounding Admiral Rickover's selection to flag rank, pp. 371-372, 460

Sellers, Rear Admiral David F., USN (USNA, 1894)
   Naval Academy Superintendent in the mid-1930s compared to his predecessor, p. 93

Service Forces
   Questionable quality of personnel assigned to service forces, pp. 407-408, 412-414; steps to raise morale, pp. 417-418

Severn School, Severna Park, Maryland
   A friend attends, and his mother urges Cutter to go in the early 1930s, p. 3; Cutter plays football despite his father's protestations, pp. 4-5, 81; assessed for preparation for Naval Academy, pp. 6, 34

Shaw, Commander James C., USN (USNA, 1936)
   Favorably assessed for his work on the movie "The Caine Mutiny" in the early 1950s, p. 367

Shells
   Japanese use of point-detonating fuzes during World War II, p. 238

Simard, Captain Cyril T., USN
   Commanding officer of Midway Island demoralized after June 1942 battle, pp. 248-249, 251

Sixth Fleet
   Cutter assesses good quality of fleet during deployment in USS Neosho (AO-143) in late 1950s, pp. 409-411; NATO organization not privy to operational details of fleet in early 1960s, p. 440; See Strike Force South

Smedberg, Vice Admiral William R. III, USN (USNA, 1926)
   As Naval Academy Superintendent in the mid-1950s, backs head football coach despite his personality, pp. 323-325; as Chief of Naval Personnel in the early 1960s, frank with Cutter on future billets, pp. 436-437

Smith, Rear Admiral Arthur S.C., Jr., USN (USNA, 1897)
   Disoriented as Commander Battleship Division Three in Idaho (BB-42) in the mid-1930s, pp. 507-508

Smith, Vice Admiral Harold P., USN (USNA, 1924)
   As Chief of Personnel in the late 1950s pushes Cutter out of athletic director billet early and into sea command, pp. 332-333, 406-407

Smith, Captain John V., USN (USNA, 1934)
   As secretary to the academic board at the Naval Academy in the late 1950s, warns Cutter of political pressure brewing to allow an admiral's lackluster-athlete son to compete in a costly meet, p. 463

Smith, Lieutenant Robert H., USN (USNA, 1922)
   As company officer in the early 1930s, puts Cutter on report for perceived trivial offense, pp. 89-91

Sonar
   First USS Seahorse (SS-304) commanding officer, unfamiliar with sonar equipment, is far too cautious in attacking Japanese screens in early 1940s, pp. 69-70, 154-155; poor quality in the late 1930s and throughout World War II, p. 172; allows Seahorse (SS-304) to avoid detection, pp. 284-286; Nautilus (SSN-571) fires practice torpedoes using her advanced sonar equipment in the mid-1950s, p. 395

Sousa, John P.
   Noted bandmaster oversees music competition in Illinois in the late 1920s, p. 27

Special Services
   Director's responsibilities in the early 1950s, pp. 357, 363-364; officers' clubs, pp. 357-360; exchanges, p. 361; liquor sales, pp. 361-362; movies, pp. 362-363

Sperry, USS (AS-12)
   Submarine Force Pacific football team assembled in ship in late 1940s, p. 320; personnel discussed, pp. 339-341

Sprague, Admiral Thomas L., USN (USNA, 1918)
   Effort to keep son from resigning from the Naval Academy, pp. 594-595

Stingray, USS (SS-186)
   Dangerous situation with USS Seahorse (SS-304) during World War II when neither skipper knew that there was a friendly sub in the area, pp. 516, 549-550

Stott, Captain Arthur C., USN (USNA, 1905)
   Leadership qualities assessed as commanding officer of the USS Idaho (BB-42) in the mid-1930s, pp. 105-107

Street, Lieutenant George L. III, USN (USNA, 1937)
   As Medal of Honor winner, pp. 306, 308; relieves Cutter as commanding officer of USS Requin (SS-481) in mid-1946, p. 314

Strike Force South
   Sixth Fleet staff handled all important functions of this NATO assignment in the early 1960s, pp. 432-433; social aspects, pp. 433-434

Submarine Division 32
   Cutter's duties as commander in the early 1950s, pp. 346, 354-355

Submarine Duty
   During World War II, submarine skippers relieved at age 35 to keep leaders young and aggressive, pp. 48, 154, 207-208; correlation between sub duty and contact sports, pp. 46-48, 50-52, 503; importance of teamwork, pp. 50-51; psychological aspect of wartime command, pp. 52-57, 170-171; former Naval Academy athletes as World War II skippers, pp. 65, 502-503; Cutter assesses skilled approach officers from wartime subs, pp. 76-77, 502; value of experience and aggression to wartime patrols, pp. 87, 132; lack of billets in the mid-1930s causes some former sub skippers to be assigned to menial tasks aboard surface ships, pp. 108-110; Cutter influenced to join sub service despite initial aversion as a child, pp. 108-112; indoctrination of Naval Academy midshipmen in late 1930s, p. 113; BuNav demands new submariners be qualified within a year or get an explanation from skipper, p. 123; emotional reaction of Cutter and *Seahorse* (SS-304) crew to attack situations, pp. 143, 524-526; double job assignments for enlisted crewmembers, pp. 158-159; screening and removal from duty for psychological adjustment, p. 159; emphasis on engineering skill in choosing skippers, pp. 167-168; executive officer usually fleets up from crew, not assigned cold, p. 184; handling of trim manifold under depth charge attack, pp. 187-188; crew recruited at Pearl Harbor after Japanese attack, pp. 185-187, 197; relief crews, pp. 244-245; duties of division and squadron commanders, pp. 252-254, 346, 349, 354-355, 401-406; sharing of helpful information among wartime skippers and high esprit de corps, pp. 255-256, 279; job of diving officer, pp. 257-258; routine during patrols in enemy waters, pp. 280-281; health of sub officers, pp. 281-284; food and meals, pp. 284, 286, 295-297; Medal of Honor winners, p. 305; relaxed and pampered pace of shipyard duty, pp. 308-310; shore duty during war, pp. 313-314; demobilization at end of World War II, pp. 315-317; post-World War II morale problems, pp. 347-348, 352; recruiting personnel after war, pp. 352-354; pay and bonuses, pp. 353-354, 566-567; competition for post-war commands, p. 517; administrative duties, pp. 539-542

Submarine Force
    Transitional period between World War II and the nuclear age, pp. 346-347, 351-352

Submarine Force Atlantic Fleet
    Comparison between commanders in the mid-1950s, pp. 389-390; submarine inspection team, pp. 391-393

Submarine Force Pacific Fleet
    Dispatches USS *Seahorse* (SS-304) to Toagel Mlungui after unsuccessful tracking of Japanese convoy in mid-1943, p. 151; message traffic to subs, p. 146; starts rumor of feud between Dusty Dornin and Cutter, pp. 146-147; preliminaries to wartime patrols, pp. 270-271

Submarine Handling
    Intricacies of keeping a submarine in diving trim, pp. 257-258

Submarine Inspections
    Difference between wartime and peacetime attitude towards problems, pp. 213-215, 342-343, 504; inspection team from Submarine Force Pacific Fleet staff in mid-1950s, pp. 391-393, 396

Submarine Operations, World War II
    Submarines used for bombardment duty towards end of war, p. 67; Cutter follows directive to destroy all enemy ships, including civilian, but chooses to leave area rather than continue slaughter, pp. 72-73; role of luck in successful patrols, pp. 77-78; USS *Pompano* (SS-181) picks up Japanese prisoner at Midway shortly after June 1942 action, pp. 128-130; USS *Seahorse* (SS-304) patrols off Saipan around time of invasion in the spring of 1943, pp. 142-143; U.S. subs preyed on Japanese vessels off Kobe entering East China Sea in early November 1943, p. 145; Cutter's strategy for finding Japanese targets, pp. 148-149; *Seahorse* (SS-304) sinks two ships in Japanese convoy near Tsushima Strait in November 1943, pp. 149, 189-191; practice of staying submerged all day and running on the surface at night stopped, pp. 160-161; Cutter describes approach on convoy without instruments, taught him by Lew Parks, p. 162; *Seahorse* (SS-304) sinks tanker in June 1944, pp. 162-164; *Seahorse* subjected to depth charge attack after use of pillen werfers, pp. 169-171; precariousness of torpedoes, pp. 168-169, 174-177; confusion caused by identical handles for different functions on subs brings about changes, pp. 201-202; off Wake, pp. 199-202; off Wotje, pp. 202-203; distribution of patrol areas and preliminaries to patrols, pp. 269-271; Japanese sub sunk off

Saipan harbor in April 1944, pp. 271-275; difficulty with recognition of enemy ships and estimating tonnage sunk, pp. 275-277; patrol reports, pp. 277-279; use of guns on subs, pp. 547-548; communications kept to a minimum, p. 550

Submarine Readiness
In mid-1950s as evidenced by inspections, p. 393

Submarine School, New London, Connecticut
Assignment based on class standing, p. 156; discussion of Cutter's classmates in 1938, pp. 155-157, 512-515; instructors in 1938, p. 158; nature of instruction, p. 158; escape training, p. 161; criteria for selection, pp. 513-514

Submarine Squadron Three
Competition with Submarine Squadron Five in the late 1940s, p. 342

Submarine Squadron Five
Competition with Submarine Squadron Three in the late 1940s, p. 342

Submarine Training
Poor quality of training exercises during World War II, p. 212; transit time spent drilling during the war, p. 547; training of U.S. crews compared to German Navy, p. 553

Sullivan, John L.
Secretary of the Navy from 1947 to 1949 plays golf with Babe Brown, pp. 57-58

Supplies
Mix-up of food stores for USS *Seahorse* (SS-304) at Pearl Harbor during World War II, p. 296

Swartz, Raymond H.
Cutter lets Naval Academy wrestling coach go in the late 1950s, p. 578

Swimming
Cutter pressured to allow admiral's plebe son, a lackluster athlete, to attend a costly swim meet in the late 1950s, pp. 462-464; assessment of Naval Academy's swimming program in the late 1950s, p. 585

Tang, USS (SS-306)
Nine survivors of this submarine's sinking in October 1944 escaped with Momsen lungs, p. 161; difficulties off Saipan in 1944, pp. 530-531

Taylor, Midshipman David W., Jr., USN (USNA, 1935)
   Cutter's brilliant roommate at the Naval Academy was both a help and a hindrance to getting good grades, pp. 43-44

Taylor, Captain Edmund B., USN (USNA, 1925)
   Former Navy football player recommends Cutter for sports position with BuPers in 1946, pp. 317, 355-356

Tenders
   Duties of executive officer, pp. 339, 343-345; quality of personnel, pp. 339-341, 343, 407-408, 561; competition between tenders, p. 342; tender command as preparation for submarine division command, pp. 345-346; See Sperry (AS-12)

Thomas, Charles S.
   Secretary of the Navy praised for his handling of catapult fire disaster in USS Bennington (CVS-20) in May 1954, pp. 575-576; example of attitude towards desegregation, pp. 386-388

Thomas, Commander Willis M., USN (USNA, 1931)
   Lost in USS Pompano (SS-181) in September 1943, pp. 98-99, 258; given command of Pompano even though a relief skipper had already been assigned in mid-1943, pp. 239-241, 246; involved in wild ride through Honolulu in June 1942, pp. 132-137; assigned to destroyer given to British under Lend-Lease in 1940, pp. 239-240; despairs during depth charge attack in August 1942, pp. 302-303

Thresher, USS (SSN-593)
   Artifacts from submarine lost in April 1963 on display at Navy Museum in Washington, D.C., p. 454

Time Magazine
   Publishes story on Navy's supposed dislike of Rear Admiral Rickover in January 1954, p. 369

Tisdale, Commander Mahlon S., USN (USNA, 1912)
   Cutter's battalion officer scolds him after he receives demerits for a trivial offense in the early 1930s, pp. 91-92; assessed as a great influence on Midshipman Cutter, p. 93

"Tobruk (Libya), Rats of"
   Australian soldiers who holed up in underground shelters against the Germans during World War II, pp. 224-225

Topper, Lieutenant James R., USN (USNA, 1924)
   Former submariner relegated to lesser job in Idaho (BB-42) because of lack of billets between the world wars, pp. 109-110

Torpedo Data Computer (TDC)
   Cutter mans the TDC in USS Pompano (SS-181) in unsuccessful firing at beginning of World War II, p. 205; value to World War II submarines, pp. 526-529

Torpedo Launching
   USS Pompano (SS-181) commanding officer Lew Parks insisted that his officers do preliminaries to torpedo firings in their heads, pp. 141-145; equipment available in the early 1940s, pp. 124-125; poppet valves, pp. 273-274

Torpedoes
   Poor quality available during World War II, pp. 168-169, 174, 207; lack of torpedoes given as reason magnetic exploder couldn't be adequately tested, p. 174; electric torpedoes, pp. 174-175; Mark 10s, p. 175; difficulties caused by vertical firing pins, pp. 175-176; steel versus copper warheads, p. 176; unfamiliarity with actual hits leads USS Pompano (SS-181) to mistakenly claim kills in early days of World War II, p. 204; Nautilus (SSN-571) fires practice torpedoes using sonar in mid-1950s exercise, p. 395; test of circular torpedo in 1950s, p. 560

Triebel, Commander Charles O., USN (USNA, 1929)
   Writes letter demanding that RADM Blandy be court-martialed for negligence pertaining to faulty torpedoes during World War II, p. 174

Trigger, USS (SS-237)
   Presence off Kobe in early November 1943 with other submarines, pp. 145-146; luau with USS Seahorse (SS-304) crew leads to brawl, pp. 536-539

Turkey
   Participation in Strike Force South in early 1960s, p. 433; Greek-Turkish relations, pp. 433-434

Ultra
   Broken Japanese code provides valuable intelligence to USS Seahorse (SS-304) in the Pacific, pp. 288, 529; prior knowledge of planned Saipan invasion in mid-1943 prompts warning to Cutter not to be taken prisoner, pp. 288-290; USS Pompano (SS-181) receives message in August 1942 that

Japanese are approaching her position near entrance to Tokyo Harbor, p. 298

Unionization
Strongly discouraged in rural Illinois in 1920s, pp. 20-22

V-J Day (14 August 1945)
USS Requin (SS-481) kept off Pearl Harbor while celebration going on in town, p. 311

Vitucci, Commander Vito L., USN (USNA, 1943)
As commanding officer of the USS Hardhead (SS-365) in the mid-1950s, has his after torpedo hatch creased during periscope approach practice, pp. 389-390

Voge, Lieutenant Commander Richard G., USN (USNA, 1925)
After Cutter's first USS Seahorse (SS-304) patrol in 1943, questions Cutter on successful hits and allows him to choose next patrol area, pp. 189-191, 265, 529

Wadhams, Lieutenant Fay W., USN
Former enlisted man from USS Pompano (SS-181) serves as repair officer in USS Sperry (AS-12) in the late 1940s, p. 341

Wake Island
USS Pompano (SS-181) surfaces by mistake 400 yards from shore in December 1941, pp. 200-202

Walker, Rear Admiral Edward K., USN (USNA, 1925)
Saluted for his work on the torpedo data computer (TDC), pp. 527-529

Ward, Commander Norvell G., USN (USNA, 1935)
Friend pays call of fellow sub skipper Cutter to ascertain reaction to a poor inspection at Key West in 1946, pp. 214-215

Watkins, Rear Admiral Frank T., USN (USNA, 1922)
As Commander Submarine Force Atlantic Fleet in the mid-1950s, impresses assistant chief of staff Cutter with his competency and good judgment, pp. 390-391; questions destroyer commander after an antisubmarine warfare exercise, pp. 402-404; coordinates news conference by Nautilus (SSN-571) commander, p. 563

Webb, Hamilton W. "Spike"
Naval Academy boxing coach enlists Cutter in the early 1930s, pp. 6, 31-32, 34; testimonial dinner in 1961, p. 608

Whelchel, Captain David L., USN (USNA, 1930)
   Assessed as commanding officer of the tender USS Sperry (AS-12) in the late 1940s, pp. 340, 423

Whelchel, Lieutenant Commander John E., USN (USNA, 1920)
   Communications officer in Idaho (BB-42) in the mid-1950s praises commanding officer, Captain Stott, p. 106

White, Commander David C., USN (USNA, 1927)
   Cutter learns from White that a mutual acquaintance is unhappy in his billet, which leads to a request for his reassignment to USS Seahorse (SS-304) in 1943, p. 70

Wilkins, Commander Charles W., USN (USNA, 1924)
   Relieves Cutter as commanding officer of the USS Seahorse (SS-304) after fourth patrol in August 1944, pp. 56, 536

Wilkinson, Commander Eugene P., USN
   First commanding officer of the Nautilus (SSN-571) sends message asking to make speed by diving that is misinterpreted as requesting a cushier ride, p. 394; skilled handling of sub's capabilities during fleet exercise, p. 395; respected by crew, p. 396; skilled poker player, p. 397; potential as wartime skipper, p. 399; contact with media, p. 563

Wilson, Charles E.
   As Secretary of Defense in the mid-1950s, criticized by President Eisenhower for asking Mrs. Eisenhower to sponsor nuclear test platform Nautilus (SSN-571) in January 1954, pp. 374, 377-379

Wolf Packs
   Pros and cons of this method of wartime sub operation, pp. 534-535

Wotje
   USS Pompano (SS-181) reconnoiters island in early 1942 before first U.S. offensive against Japan, pp. 202-203

Wrestling
   Cutter selects a new wrestling coach for the Naval Academy in the late 1950s, pp. 578-579; See Edwin C. Peery; Raymond H. Swartz

Wyoming, USS (BB-32)
   Used for football players during midshipmen summer cruises in early 1930s, p. 491

Yeager, Rear Admiral Howard A., USN (USNA, 1927)
   Energetic as Commandant Ninth Naval District in the mid-1960s, pp. 445-449; control over reserves, p. 453

www.ingramcontent.com/pod-product-compliance
Lightning Source LLC
Chambersburg PA
CBHW080622170426
43209CB00007B/1493